International Dimensions of
FINANCIAL MANAGEMENT

D0217431

THE KENT INTERNATIONAL DIMENSIONS OF BUSINESS SERIES

International Dimensions of Organizational Behavior
Adler

International Dimensions of Accounting, Second Edition
Arpan/AlHashim

International Dimensions of Financial Management
Folks/Aggarwal

International Dimensions of Business Policy and Strategy
Garland/Farmer

International Dimensions of the Legal Environment of Business
Litka

International Dimensions of Management
Phatak

International Dimensions of Marketing, Second Edition
Terpstra

International Dimensions of
FINANCIAL MANAGEMENT

William R. Folks, Jr.
University of South Carolina

Raj Aggarwal
John Carroll University

THE KENT INTERNATIONAL DIMENSIONS OF BUSINESS SERIES
David A. Ricks
Series Consulting Editor

PWS-KENT Publishing Company
Boston, Massachusetts

To Kathy and Karen

Editor: Rolf Janke
Assistant Editor: Kathleen M. Tibbetts
Production Editor: Susan Krikorian
Text Designer: Elise Kaiser
Cover Designer: Julie Gecha
Manufacturing Manager: Linda Siegrist

 PWS–KENT
Publishing Company

PWS-KENT Publishing Company is a division of Wadsworth, Inc.

Printed in the United States of America
1   2   3   4   5   6   7   8   9   —   92   91   90   89   88

Library of Congress Cataloging-in-Publication Data

Folks, William R.
    International dimensions of financial management.

    (The Kent international business series)
    Includes index.
    1. International business enterprises — Finance.
I. Aggarwal, Raj.   II. Title.   III. Series.
HG4027.5.F65   1988   658.1'599   87-29132
ISBN 0-534-87194-1

Series Foreword

Prior to World War II, the number of firms involved in foreign direct investment was relatively small. Although several U.S. companies were obtaining raw materials from other countries, most firms were only interested in the U.S. market. This changed, however, during the 1950s—especially after the creation of the European Economic Community. Since that time, there has been a rapid expansion in international business activity.

The majority of the world's large corporations now perform an increasing proportion of their business activities outside of their home countries. For many of these companies, international business returns over one-half of their profits, and it is becoming more and more common for a typical corporation to earn at least one-fourth of its profits through international business involvement. In fact, it is now rather rare for any large firm not to be a participant in the world of international business.

International business is of great importance in most countries and that importance continues to grow. To meet the demand for increased knowledge in this area, business schools are attempting to add international dimensions to their curricula. Faculty members are becoming more interested in teaching a greater variety of international business courses and are striving to add international dimensions to other courses. Students, aware of the increasing probability that they will be employed by firms engaged in international business activities, are seeking knowledge of the problem-solving techniques unique to international business. As the American Assembly of Collegiate Schools of Business has observed, however, there is a shortage of information available. Most business textbooks do not adequately consider the international dimensions of business and much of the supplemental material is disjointed, overly narrow, or otherwise inadequate in the classroom.

This series has been developed to overcome such problems. The books are written by some of the most respected authors in the various areas of international business. Each author is extremely well known in the Academy of International Business and in his or her other professional academies. They possess an outstanding knowledge of their own subject matter and a talent for explaining it.

These books, in which the authors have identified the most important international aspects of their fields, have been written in a format that facilitates their use as supplemental material in business school courses. For the most part, the material is presented by topic in approximately the same order and manner as it is covered in basic business textbooks. Therefore, as each topic is covered in the course, material is easily supplemented with the corresponding chapter in the series book.

The Kent International Dimensions of Business Series offers a unique and much needed opportunity to bring international dimensions of business into the classroom. The series has been developed by leaders in the field after years of discussion and careful consideration, and the timely encouragement and support provided by the PWS-KENT staff on this project. I am proud to be associated with this series and highly recommend it to you.

David A. Ricks

Consulting Editor to the
 Kent International Dimensions of Business Series
Professor of International Business,
 University of South Carolina

Preface

It is no longer possible to ignore the international dimensions of financial management. In recent decades, both financial and product markets have become increasingly globalized. External, non-domestic financial markets have grown so large and important that they, as well as changing exchange rates, must now be considered in virtually any corporate financing decision. Weekly trading on foreign exchange markets now far exceeds annual trading on all of the world's stock exchanges combined. And while the relative standings of the various countries in the global financial markets fluctuate, the United States has once again emerged as the largest debtor nation in the world. Global trade has become a significant portion of most national economies as companies from an ever-increasing number of industries now compete in global markets. Financial management has become more complex and has acquired strong international dimensions.

This book offers a first introduction to the international dimensions of corporate finance. It is designed for use by the educator who is concerned with preparing financial managers for a world of economic and financial interdependence, and for students who will confront the challenges of such a world directly. It can be used as a supplement in the basic corporate or business finance course at the undergraduate or graduate level. It can also be used as the core text in an international business finance course with the instructor assigning supplementary readings if necessary. In addition, we hope that the practicing financial manager will also find this book useful as it has been written to be understandable by the nontechnical nonspecialist.

The approach to international finance that this book follows is the final responsibility of the authors, as are any remaining errors. The authors acknowledge with deep gratitude the patience and insight of the series editor, Dr. David A. Ricks, whose overall vision for the series, and this component of it, has not wavered. We express our appreciation to Mr. Rolf A. Janke, Associate Editor at PWS-KENT responsible for this series, and the PWS-KENT staff for their work on this project. We are also grateful for the continued support of the following administrators: Dean Frank J. Navratil at John Carroll University; Vice President William N. Free at the University of Toledo; and Dean James F. Kane, Associate Dean James G. Hilton, and Professor Jeffrey S. Arpan at the University of South Carolina; and of our colleagues in international finance, Chun-yau Kwok, Christopher M. Korth, and Ramesh P. Rao. Raj Aggarwal would also like to thank the Mellen Foundation for supporting his research and writing. We extend our sincere thanks to Ruth Closson, Christa Hatting, and Delores Williams who prepared the manuscript with skill, precision, and understanding.

Finally, we thank our colleagues who teach, practice, and write in international finance for providing the source of the ideas reflected in this book and the many students who tested the preliminary versions of this material under combat conditions. Their reactions convinced us that this project was worth the effort.

William R. Folks, Jr.
Raj Aggarwal

About the Authors

WILLIAM RANDOLPH FOLKS, JR. is Professor of International Business at the University of South Carolina. He is the author of over sixty scholarly papers, some appearing in such journals as *Management Science*, the *Journal of International Business Studies, Financial Management*, and the *Journal of Financial and Quantitative Analysis*. Prof. Folks teaches international finance in the University of South Carolina's unique Masters in International Studies program and served as the first program director of international business. His professional affiliations include membership in the Financial Management Association and the Academy of International Business. He has received grants from public and private foundations and businesses, including the Financial Accounting Standards Board and Arthur Andersen & Company, to conduct research in such areas as offshore bonds and foreign exchange risk management. He has served as a visiting professor at the Université Catholique de Louvain (Belgium), the Helsinki School of Economics and Business Administration (Finland), and Xiamen University (People's Republic of China).

RAJ AGGARWAL is the Edward J. and Louise E. Mellen chairholder and Professor of Finance at John Carroll University, where he teaches undergraduate and graduate courses and does research in the areas of financial management, international business, and international finance and accounting. Professor Aggarwal is the author of a number of books, including an international business textbook, and over fifty scholarly papers, some of which have appeared in the *Journal of Banking and Finance*, *Journal of Portfolio Management*, *Journal of Accounting, Auditing, and Finance*, the *Columbia Journal of World Business*, *Management International Review*, and the *Journal of International Business Studies*. Also, he is co-editor of *Advances in Financial Planning and Forecasting: International Dimensions*. He is a member of the editorial boards of *The Journal of International Business Studies, Issues in International Business*, and *Managerial Finance*. He is also an editorial reviewer for a number of scholarly journals, such as the *Journal of Financial and Quantitative Analysis, Financial Management*, and the *Journal of Financial Research*. Professor Aggarwal has held a number of elected and appointed positions in scholarly organizations, including Vice President, Academy of International Business, and has received research grants from private foundations and government agencies such as the National Science Foundation. In 1984, he served as the Senior Fulbright Research Scholar in Southeast Asia.

Contents

CHAPTER 1

▼

The International Dimensions of Financial Management

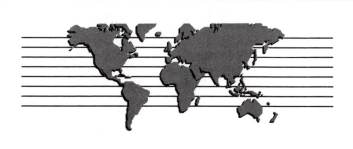

▲

INTRODUCTION

This book provides a broad introduction to corporate financial management in a multinational setting. But why study multinational financial management? What makes financial management in the multinational environment different from financial management in a purely domestic environment?

The study of the international dimensions of financial management has grown in importance as major multinational corporations have, over the past thirty years, created a complex global web of integrated operations that require access to global funding sources. Since 1960, a wholly new set of global external financial markets, commonly known as the Eurocurrency markets, have been created and have become larger than any domestic financial market. New financial products, such as currency options and liability swaps, now enable almost any major corporation to access funds on a global basis without any great increase in risk. The economies of the world have now become much more integrated. More than a quarter of the world's production now moves across national boundaries. And international movement of capital, once limited by significant national restrictions, has expanded substantially as deregulation of national financial markets has lifted barriers.

Consequently, there are now very few companies that can claim to be purely domestic. Today, almost every business is affected by events in the international economy. Either a business imports or exports directly, or it competes in product and raw material markets with foreign firms that import or export. As the global economy becomes much more internationally integrated, influences external to the nation in which a business operates have become much more important for that business. To understand the nature of a firm's business activities and its competition, managers must now understand the general nature of cross-border business operations.

Even firms that acquire resources domestically and sell domestically, with no foreign competition for raw materials or for customers, still must compete for funds in an ever-internationalizing, ever-integrating set of globally oriented financial markets. Interest rates, to a far greater extent than ever before, are the product of complicated interactions in domestic, external, and foreign money and capital markets.

What are the particular dimensions of financial management that we consider uniquely international? Four major factors can be identified. First, multinational business and financial activities are subject to the risks of changes in exchange rates, the prices at which international currencies are traded. Second, multinational corporations have the opportunity to finance their operations on a global basis, requiring that their financial managers determine the strategies most advantageous to their firms. Third, in operating across national boundaries, a firm is faced with costs and restrictions that are specifically related to cross-border activity and that affect both trade in real goods and financial flows between countries. These costs and restrictions also include the need to overcome the barriers of political, cultural, institutional, and legal differences in the business environments and financial markets of foreign countries. But, while cross-border business activities face additional costs and restrictions, they also provide opportunities for extraordinary profits that are not available in the domestic setting. And fourth, multinational corporations have the opportunity to engage in foreign direct investment, offering investors the benefit of international diversification.

CHANGING INTERNATIONAL CURRENCY EXCHANGE RATES

The risk of changing exchange rates is one of the fundamental char acteristics of cross-border business and financial transactions, and these risks can greatly impact the value of a firm. Consequently, the international financial manager must understand the nature of these risks and the techniques that may be useful in minimizing their impact.

Exchange risk arises from the fact that various national currencies change in relative value over time. As an example, suppose that a U.S. firm expects to receive payment of £100,000 three months hence for goods just shipped to a customer in the United Kingdom. At the current spot exchange rate of £1.00 = US$1.50, the £100,000 are worth $150,000. However, unless the firm takes action to eliminate the risk, the actual U.S. dollar amount received in three months, when the U.K. customer pays, will depend on the actual exchange rate in effect at that time. In three months, the U.S. company could actually receive an amount that is less than or more than the $150,000.

Because the value of foreign currency payments is dependent on the rate of exchange, it is vital that the financial manager be aware of how exchange rates are determined by the financial market place. Chapter 2 of this book first provides an introduction to the mechanics of the foreign exchange market. Chapter 3 then outlines in some detail the economic relationships that help determine exchange rates. As we will learn, the intergovernmental agreements and international agencies that constitute the international financial system play a major role in determining how global economic forces produce exchange rates.

Based on this broad understanding of the foreign exchange markets, Chapter 4 looks at how uncertainty in the rate of exchange can affect the outcome of both operating and financing decisions. In particular, this chapter provides a logical framework of analysis for choosing the currency or currencies in which a company finances. Chapter 5 illustrates the essentials of how a company can then assess and manage its exposure to foreign exchange losses.

The process of exchange risk management is highly complex. There is wide diversity in the types of foreign currency transactions in which a firm engages. There are limited but highly complicated financial and operating responses that a firm can take to manage the resulting exchange risk. This management task becomes even more complicated because of the need to respond not only to economic considerations but also to changes in accounting earnings and equity accounts caused by exchange rate movements.

GLOBAL FINANCIAL MARKETS AND FUNDING STRATEGIES

The corporate financial executive of this modern era faces a wide range of potential funding sources, as well as the need to supply funds in support of corporate operations in the global arena. Each new investment project, each subsidiary's operating plan, calls forth a demand for funds in numerous different currencies, which must be met promptly and at minimum cost. The financial manager must remain constantly alert to new funding opportunities and financial products that may offer the manager's firm a competitive edge.

In this book, Chapter 6 provides a comprehensive look at the global funding opportunities available to the financial manager. Central to this review are the relatively recent but enormous external financial markets, the Euromarkets. Both direct (Euronote and Eurobond) and intermediated (Eurocredit) external markets and their accompanying global financial institutions provide broad, innovative funding alternatives in a largely unregulated environment.

The development of a global funding strategy for the firm in response to global funding opportunities is the subject of Chapter 7. The very fact of a firm's multinationality allows it to invest in a number of national environments; the cost of equity to the multinational firm may be lower than that of an equivalent domestic company, if it offers investors an opportunity to diversify across national boundaries. Further, multinational firms have the opportunity to source debt in a wide variety of local financial markets and have at their disposal a wide range of new financial instruments (interest rate futures and options; foreign currency forwards, futures, and options; and liability swaps) that allow the firm to access funds on a global basis and then select the desired maturity, interest rate basis, and currency of its debt obligations. Multinationals engaged in international trade may access well-developed sources of finance in support of this activity, often with a government subsidy.

CROSS-BORDER RESTRICTIONS
ON OPERATIONS AND FUNDING

The costs of doing business across national borders are higher, in part, because of numerous restrictions on cross-border business transactions imposed by national governments. These restrictions are applied in markets for real goods, as well as in financial markets. There are two kinds of restrictions, the first of which is the quota-type restriction, involving a quantitative restriction on the amount of a commercial or financial transaction that is allowed. Examples include quotas on exports, imports, and foreign investments; regulation and licensing requirements, and other barriers to market entry by a new business; ceilings on interest rates and other price controls; mandatory credit allocations; and other restrictions on factor mobility. The second type of restriction has the effect of imposing a fixed or per unit charge on a commercial or financial transaction. Examples of this type of restriction include tariffs and other taxes on cross-border flows of products and funds; information costs of market and financial research and analysis; and transaction costs, such as high brokerage fees and high costs of enforcing contracts internationally. Of particular importance in finance are the withholding taxes frequently charged on interest and dividend payments from a subsidiary to its parent company.

These various costs of going and operating overseas, including the costs of overcoming linguistic, cultural, political, institutional, and other barriers, can be considered to be the costs of operating at an economic distance. To minimalize these costs, firms tend to serve overseas markets that have a large profit potential but that are at a low economic distance. Thus, United Kingdom and French multinationals tend to invest in former colonies (low economic distance), while United States multinationals tend to invest mostly in Western Europe and Latin America for the same reasons. In a similar fashion, firms pay close attention to restrictions on intersubsidiary and parent-subsidiary flows and tend to source funds where the economic distance from their ultimate use is low.

Managers of multinational firms know that whenever they see restrictions on foreign investment and funds transfer, they can typically find the opportunity for highly profitable operations if they can legally overcome the restrictions. Thus, government and other restrictions on foreign investment and funds transfer, and the multinational firm's profit potential from foreign investment and funds transfer, are two sides of the same coin in most cases. Chapter 8 covers the multinational firm's structure of its cross-border funding operations, with an emphasis on techniques, such as multilateral netting, that reduce the cost of such movements.

FOREIGN DIRECT INVESTMENT

Foreign direct investment involves the ownership and control of productive assets in a foreign country. Legally, these assets are typically held by a subsidiary or branch of the investing parent. Theoretically, foreign direct investment is undertaken because of its ability to generate high rates of return by successfully overcoming market imperfections and barriers to cross-border business transactions. If product and financial markets were perfect and internationally integrated, competitive forces would eliminate extraordinary profit opportunities. Thus, in order for foreign direct investment to take place, there must be extraordinary profit opportunities, from which the multinational can benefit by acquiring control of assets located in a foreign country.

Chapter 9 provides a detailed study of the financial aspects of foreign direct investment. One particularly important issue is how multinational firms respond to political risk; the risk that changes in the political structure of the host country of the investment will impact the cash flow that the foreign direct investment generates. Because many of the methods by which a firm protects itself from political risk are financial, financial managers of multinationals must be aware of how political risk is measured and managed.

ABOUT THIS BOOK

This book has been written for three major categories of readers. First, it is designed to be used as a supplement in undergraduate and graduate courses in financial management or corporate finance. It provides the international dimension for a normally domestically oriented course.

Second, it is designed to be used as the basic text in a graduate or undergraduate course in international or multinational financial management. In case of such a use, the text may readily be supplemented by a set of readings selected by the instructor to meet the specific needs of students in the class. Third, this book should make the fascinating subject of the international dimensions of financial management available to a wider audience of people who work in the international finance area or would otherwise like a better overall understanding of the topic.

It is our hope that many readers of this book will seek a career in the fields that it covers. Indeed, although they are avidly sought, both entry-level and higher managerial positions are available in the financial institutions and industrial and service firms that have developed a multinational strategic response.

Success in the field of international finance requires, first, strong analytic skills grounded in a thorough understanding of the fundamental concepts of the field. Global financial operations are complex and sophisticated. New financial products emerge rapidly in these markets and require detailed, accurate analysis. Faulty analysis quickly draws its inevitable consequence: financial loss and financial distress.

Further, while analytic skills are essential, only detailed institutional knowledge and a wide network of personal contacts can bring new financial opportunities to managerial attention. Practitioners in the field must constantly make every effort to keep abreast of recent developments. Windows for astute financing or for desired interunit funds movement open and close continuously; the advantage of new ideas rapidly falls away as market knowledge of them becomes widespread.

Finally, perhaps more than in any other market, personal integrity is necessary for success. In global financial markets, large sums are traded or lent on the word of individuals (although, of course, the legal aspects are clearly spelled out). Market participants depend on their ability to trust that other participants will meet their obligations. Although unethical practices may gain a brief advantage, the market, by exclusion or otherwise, can cut off the unethical practitioner from further business. Relationships in these markets typically involve a constant stream of transactions, and no participant can afford to be cut off from market access over the longer run because of this deficiency. And in these volatile, large-volume markets, the long run may only be an hour or a day.

SUGGESTED READINGS

This book provides an introduction to the international dimensions of corporate finance. A more complete discussion, and discussion of international financial markets and management, can be found in the suggested readings at the end of each chapter.

1. Aggarwal, Raj. *The Literature of International Business Finance*. New York, New York: Praeger Publishers, 1984. (Bibliograpy of readings.)
2. Eiteman, David K., and Arthur I. Stonehill. *Multinational Business Finance*, 4th Edition. Reading, Massachusetts: Addison-Wesley Publishing Co., 1986.
3. George, Abraham M., and Ian H. Giddy (editors). *International Finance Handbook*, Vols. I and II. New York, New York: John Wiley & Sons, 1983.
4. Madura, Jeff. *International Financial Management*. St. Louis, Missouri: West Publishing Co., 1986.
5. Shapiro, Alan C. *Multinational Financial Management*, 2nd Edition. Boston, Massachusetts: Allyn and Bacon, 1987.

CHAPTER 2

▼

The Foreign Exchange Market

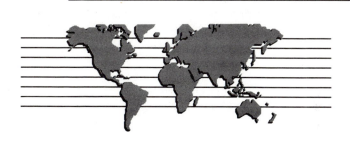

▲

INTRODUCTION

Instability in currency values is both an inescapable fact of life for the multinational corporation and a source of much of the uncertainty that demands the attention of those responsible for financial management. The German mark (DM), which was worth US$0.25[1] in 1969, increased in value to over $0.56 in 1978, fell back to less than $0.30 in 1985, and then strengthened again to more than $0.50 by the end of 1986. On the other hand, the Brazilian cruzeiro (Cr$), which was worth $0.1608 (Cr$6.22 to the dollar) in December 1973, was worth only $0.00007627 (or Cr$13,112 to the dollar) by March 1986, when Brazil introduced a new currency, the cruzado.

The structure of the foreign exchange market and the system of international monetary and economic relationships that generate these dramatic shifts in currency value are the subject of this chapter and Chapter 3. In order to manage the inevitable uncertainty generated by

---

[1]We will assume that the symbol $ or the word *dollars* refers to U.S. dollars unless otherwise specified.

movements of exchange rates, the international financial executive must understand not only the fundamentals of the foreign exchange market and trading practices but also the economic and political factors that determine the direction of foreign exchange rates. These exchange rate changes markedly affect the level of interest rates in each currency market and vice versa. First, this chapter discusses the mechanics of the foreign exchange market. Then, Chapter 3 discusses the economic relationships that determine the present exchange rate, future directions of its movement, and interest rate levels in various currencies. Chapter 3 reviews exchange rate forecasting techniques and how they may be evaluated.

THE FOREIGN EXCHANGE MARKET

The market for foreign exchange is a large one. A 1984 estimate placed daily volume in the global foreign exchange market at $150 billion per day, or well over $37.5 trillion per year. In March 1986, the Federal Reserve Bank of New York estimated volume in the U.S. foreign exchange market at $50 billion daily; the London market is substantially larger; and the Tokyo market volume passed that of New York in 1987. Foreign exchange is actively traded around the world and around the clock: from Tokyo and Singapore to Frankfurt, Zurich, London, and Paris, to New York, Chicago, and San Francisco, the market for foreign exchange never closes.

Despite the volume of transactions, the foreign exchange market is not organized around a physical trading facility such as the New York Stock Exchange or the Chicago Mercantile Exchange. Instead, the foreign exchange market is found in the foreign exchange trading rooms of large commercial banks and brokers that facilitate their transactions. Banks are linked to other banks and to foreign exchange brokers by a massive telecommunications system; traders, backed by highly sophisticated computerized equipment, deal with the bank's corporate and individual customers and with other banks, both in the local market and in other financial centers. Bank transactions with customers are sometimes classified as retail foreign exchange transactions, and this market is called the *retail foreign exchange market*. Bank transactions with each other form the *wholesale* or *interbank foreign exchange market*. A 1986 Federal Reserve analysis showed that 86.6 percent of all bank foreign exchange transactions were interbank, or wholesale, transactions.

In order to participate in the foreign exchange market, a commercial bank needs to have the ability to receive and make payments in foreign currency. The bank has this ability because it maintains foreign currency accounts at banks in foreign countries. When a bank sells foreign exchange, it in essence makes a payment out of this foreign currency bank account and receives payment from the purchaser. When a bank buys foreign exchange, the seller arranges to have the foreign currency paid into this foreign currency bank account.

Thus, to participate actively in the foreign exchange market, a commercial bank must have access to foreign currency balances at banks in the foreign country. Traditionally, these balances were initiated when banks established *correspondent banking relationships.* Among banks considered relative equals, each correspondent bank usually has an account with the others. A U.S. bank would have a German mark account at a German bank, and the German bank would have a U.S. dollar account at its U.S. correspondent bank. Because banks by prearrangement often will be allowed to overdraw their correspondent accounts, an element of credit extension is incorporated in the establishment of correspondent relationships. Banks seek correspondents who provide timely, accurate service in handling foreign exchange transactions and good standing in the local banking community. When a commercial bank has established a branch or subsidiary in the foreign country, the foreign exchange transaction is usually routed through the branch, but the essentials remain the same.

As an example of a typical retail transaction, suppose that a U.S. importing firm has the need to pay DM 2,000,000 to a German exporter. When the U.S. importer calls its bank's foreign exchange trading desk, it asks for the price at which the bank will sell German marks. The bank quotes a price of DM 1.9775 per dollar. If the importer decides to do the deal at this rate, it agrees to pay the bank the dollar value of DM 2,000,000 at this rate, which is $1,011,378.

The commercial bank foreign exchange department then arranges to pay the German exporter the DM 2,000,000. To do so, it needs to know the exact location of the bank account of the German exporter. The U.S. bank then telexes its correspondent bank in Germany, instructing the German bank to transfer DM 2,000,000 from the U.S. bank's correspondent account to the bank of the German exporter. Most likely, the German exporter holds its bank account at a different German bank than the U.S. bank's correspondent, so that the transfer must take place through the domestic German banking system. Typically, it is assumed that the transaction is initiated by the U.S. importer, and the actual payment in Germany is made two days after the transaction date. If prompter transfer is needed, banks can arrange for transactions to take place on the next business day (value tomorrow) or, if the German banks are still open, on the same day (value today). The date on which the foreign currency transfer takes place is known as the *value date* of the foreign exchange transaction.

At the end of the foreign exchange transaction, the U.S. bank would have received $1,011,378 and reduced its correspondent account balance by DM 2,000,000.

The foreign exchange market is thus built on the exchange of correspondent bank balances. Banks sell foreign currency from these balances, and they also may buy foreign exchange by paying domestic currency and having funds transferred into their foreign currency bank account. An exporter that is scheduled to receive a foreign currency payment would arrange to have that payment made into its bank's foreign currency account at the correspondent bank. In turn, the exporter's bank would credit the exporter's account with the dollar equivalent of the foreign currency.

The Telegraphic Transfer and Other Means of Payment

This method of making payments by telexing payment instructions is known as the *telegraphic* or *bank transfer*. It is the fundamental instrument for transfer of funds in the foreign exchange market and is most commonly used whenever large-scale payments are to be made. Foreign exchange rates quoted in the financial press (see Exhibit 2-1) are generally rates for bank transfers in which the foreign currency payments are made two business days later.

Because even telegraphic transfers require significant manual handling by banks, an automated transfer system has been developed that has generally replaced the use of the telex. The Society for Worldwide Interbank Financial Telecommunications, commonly known as SWIFT, operates an automated international funds transfer system, which substantially reduces errors and delays.

Smaller payments may be accomplished by a number of alternate mechanisms. A *mail transfer* works in exactly the same manner as the telegraphic transfer, except that the instructions to pay are mailed rather than telexed. Payments also can be made by *check*, although the recipient of the payment must either sell the check to its bank at a discount or wait until the local bank has collected funds from the bank on which the check is drawn. Payment also can be effected by purchasing a *foreign currency bank draft*; a bank draft is essentially an order drawn by one bank and addressed to a second bank, ordering that bank to pay a specified amount to a particular beneficiary.

Banks that are active in the foreign exchange market stand ready to sell foreign exchange to their customers. The selling rate depends primarily on market conditions and the bank's position in the currency. But, it also depends on factors such as the amount of the payment and the existence of other relationships with the customer. Because banks find foreign exchange transactions with their customers to be an excellent source of profits, banks actively solicit corporate clients' foreign exchange business. Corporations carefully monitor the banks with which they transact foreign exchange and view the foreign exchange business as part of how they structure their bank relationships.

The Interbank Market

The major volume of foreign exchange trading takes place in the *interbank* or *wholesale market*. In this market, banks attempt to adjust the amount of foreign currency that they hold in their correspondent accounts to desired and appropriate levels. Banks are continually managing their foreign currency positions through trading efforts in the interbank markets. Foreign exchange trading units in banks generally are operated as profit centers and are expected by bank management to earn profits commensurate with the capital required for operations.

Bank trading centers around the foreign exchange trading desk. The bank's foreign exchange dealers (or traders) are in constant communication with other banks and with foreign exchange brokers to buy and sell currencies. Most large banks have traders who specialize in one or more foreign currencies and a chief trader who is responsible for establishing trading policy and the general direction of trading.

Only very large amounts of currency are traded in the interbank markets. Typically, the minimum amount traded is 1 million units of

FOREIGN EXCHANGE

Tuesday, May 19, 1987

The New York foreign exchange selling rates below apply to trading among banks in amounts of $1 million and more, as quoted at 3 p.m. Eastern time by Bankers Trust Co. Retail transactions provide fewer units of foreign currency per dollar.

Country	U.S. $ equiv. Tues.	Mon.	Currency per U.S. $ Tues.	Mon.
Argentina (Austral)	.6317	.6317	1.583	1.5830
Australia (Dollar)	.7220	.7225	1.3850	1.3841
Austria (Schilling)	.08006	.0800	12.49	12.50
Belgium (Franc)				
Commercial rate	.02712	.02714	36.87	36.84
Financial rate	.02700	.02702	37.04	37.01
Brazil (Cruzado)	.03182	.03210	31.43	31.15
Britain (Pound)	1.6855	1.6820	.5933	.5945
30-Day Forward	1.6839	1.6804	.5938	.5951
90-Day Forward	1.6810	1.6778	.5949	.5960
180-Day Forward	1.6758	1.6746	.5958	.5972
Canada (Dollar)	.7458	.7455	1.3409	1.3413
30-Day Forward	.7454	.7452	1.3416	1.3419
90-Day Forward	.7442	.7439	1.3430	1.3442
180-Day Forward	.7419	.7418	1.3479	1.3481
Chile (Official rate)	.004669	.004669	214.16	214.16
China (Yuan)	.2687	.2687	3.722	3.722
Colombia (Peso)	.004227	.004227	236.55	236.55
Denmark (Krone)	.1494	.1497	6.6965	6.6800
Ecuador (Sucre)				
Official rate	.005602	.005602	178.50	178.50
Floating rate	.006472	.006472	154.50	154.50
Finland (Markka)	.2309	.2312	4.3320	4.3250
France (Franc)	.1685	.1680	5.9380	5.9530
30-Day Forward	.1684	.1678	.5370	5.9585
90-Day Forward	.1682	.1676	5.9495	5.9675
180-Day Forward	.1680	.1673	5.9530	5.9770
Greece (Drachma)	.007547	.007553	132.50	132.40
Hong Kong (Dollar)	.1282	.1282	7.8022	7.7980
India (Rupee)	.07911	.07918	12.64	12.63
Indonesia (Rupiah)	.0006098	.0006098	1640.00	1640.00
Ireland (Punt)	1.5040	1.5065	.6649	.6638
Israel (Shekel)	.6299	.6299	1.5875	1.5875
Italy (Lira)	.0007782	.0007752	1285.00	1290.00
Japan (Yen)	.007166	.007135	139.73	140.15
30-Day Forward	.007179	.007158	139.28	139.70
90-Day Forward	.007226	.007204	138.38	138.81
180-Day Forward	.007303	.007277	136.93	137.41

FUTURES PRICES

Tuesday, May 19, 1987

Open Interest Reflects Previous Trading Day.

	Open	High	Low	Settle	Change	Lifetime High	Low	Open Interest

— FINANCIAL —

BRITISH POUND (IMM)—25,000 pounds; $ per pound

June	1.6775	1.6855	1.6775	1.6840	+ .0040	1.6860	1.3600	40,311
Sept	1.6765	1.6825	1.6740	1.6805	+ .0040	1.6840	1.3420	4,722
Dec	1.6735	1.6800	1.6715	1.6775	+ .0040	1.6825	1.3675	445

Est vol 7,021; vol Mon 6,211; open int 45,502, +386.

CANADIAN DOLLAR (IMM)—100,000 dlrs.; $ per Can $

June	.7461	.7461	.7448	.7454	− .0006	.7681	.6995	17,189
Sept	.7441	.7441	.7430	.7435	− .0006	.7673	.6950	5,308
Dec	.7422	.7423	.7415	.7416	− .0006	.7667	.6980	1,721
Mr88	.7404	.7405	.7400	.7400	− .0006	.7655	.7052	374

Est vol 1,675; vol Mon 1,655; open int 24,668, +5.

JAPANESE YEN (IMM) 12.5 million yen; $ per yen (.00)

June	.7150	.7180	.7142	.7173	+ .0015	.7283	.6121	43,665
Sept	.7222	.7251	.7216	.7242	+ .0016	.7347	.6160	2,586
Dec	.7310	.7322	.7296	.7220	+ .0017	.7430	.7110	331

Est vol 17,636; vol Mon 19,837; open int 46,617, +2,008.

SWISS FRANC (IMM)—125,000 francs-s per franc

June	.6856	.6895	.6855	.6891	+ .0033	.6953	.5870	31,928
Sept	.6917	.6960	.6915	.6953	+ .0035	.7010	.5960	1,973
Dec	.6981	.7025	.6981	.7025	+ .0039	.7075	.5970	628

Est vol 16,082; vol Mon 15,837; open int 34,534, + 402.

W. GERMAN MARK (IMM)—125,000 marks; $ per mark

June	.5625	.5658	.5625	.5655	+ .0023	.5692	.4850	48,760
Sept	.5683	.5714	.5680	.5712	+ .0025	.5740	.4868	4,795
Dec	.5741	.5777	.5741	.5773	+ .0027	.5790	.5604	643

Est vol 17,542; vol Mon 20,270; open int 54,202, − 894.

EURODOLLAR (LIFFE)—$1 million; pts of 100%

June	92.44	92.48	92.43	92.47		94.15	90.85	13,643
Sept	91.81	91.86	91.78	91.84	+ .04	94.03	91.65	9,162
Dec	91.42	91.48	91.41	91.45	+ .03	93.88	91.35	4,629
Mr88	91.21	91.26	91.20	91.21		93.67	91.18	2,442
June	91.05	91.09	91.05	91.03		93.39	91.05	916
Sept				90.88		93.13	91.33	339

FUTURES OPTIONS

Tuesday, May 19, 1987

— FINANCIAL —

BRITISH POUND (IMM) 25,000 pounds; cents per pound

Strike Price	Calls—Settle Jun-c	Jul-c	Aug-c	Puts—Settle Jun-p	Jly-p	Aug-p
1625	5.95	5.95	...	0.15	0.50	...
1650	3.70	4.05	4.85	0.30	0.95	1.80
1675	1.80	2.50	3.25	0.85	1.95	...
1700	0.75	2.40	2.50	2.30	3.35	...
1725	0.30	1.00	...	...	...	...
1750	0.10	0.35	...	...	...	...

Est. vol. 1,512, Mon vol. 761 calls, 479 puts
Open interest Mon: 22,828 calls, 23,064 puts

W. GERMAN MARK (IMM) 125,000 marks; cents per mark

Strike Price	Calls—Settle Jun-c	Jly-c	Aug-c	Puts—Settle Jun-p	Jly-p	Aug-p
55	1.63	2.29	...	0.08	0.20	0.40
56	0.83	1.50	1.77	0.28	0.40	0.67
57	0.34	0.89	1.19	0.79	0.77	1.07
58	0.11	0.50	...	1.56	...	...
59	0.03	0.28	0.47	2.46	...	...
60	0.01	0.13	0.29	3.45	...	...

Est. vol. 10,252, Mon Mon: 2,608 calls, 4,138 puts
Open interest Mon: 73,237 calls, 65,596 puts

SWISS FRANC (IMM) 125,000 francs; cents per franc

Strike Price	Calls—Settle Jun-c	Jly-c	Aug-c	Puts—Settle Jun-p	Jly-p	Aug-p
67	2.01	2.77	...	0.12	0.30	0.48
68	1.20	2.00	...	0.30	0.71	0.83
69	0.61	1.35	1.75	0.71	1.37	...
70	0.27	0.87	1.27	1.37	2.20	...
71	0.11	0.53	0.91	2.20	...	...
72	0.04	0.32	0.63	3.14	...	...

Est. vol. 2,760, Mon vol. 1,511 calls, 824 puts
Open interest Mon: 34,810 calls, 28,037 puts

JAPANESE YEN (IMM) 12,500,000 yen; cents per 100 yen

Strike Price	Calls—Settle Jun-c	Jly-c	Aug-c	Puts—Settle Jun-p	Jly-p	Aug-p
70	1.91	1.70	...	0.19	0.32	0.60
71	1.18	1.95	...	0.44	0.54	0.87
72	0.58	0.85	1.20	0.84	0.91	1.27
73	0.29	0.48	...	1.56	1.43	...
74	0.13	0.54	...	2.40	...	...
75	0.04	0.33	...	3.35	...	...

Est. vol. 8,938, Mon vol. 1,596 calls, 14,953 puts
Open interest Mon: 49,541 calls, 109,499 puts

FOREIGN CURRENCY OPTIONS

Philadelphia Exchange

Tuesday, May 19, 1987

Option & Underlying	Strike Price	Calls—Last			Puts—Last		
		Jun	Jul	Sep	Jun	Jul	Sep
50,000 Australian Dollars-cents per unit.							
ADollr	70	r	r	r	0.15	r	r
72.14	71	1.01	r	r	0.33	r	r
72.14	72	r	r	1.10	r	r	r
72.14	73	r	r	r	r	r	1.32
72.14	74	0.29	r	r	0.54	r	r
12,500 British Pounds-cents per unit.							
BPound	150	18.00	s	r	s	s	r
168.53	160	r	r	8.80	r	r	r
168.53	162½	6.20	r	r	r	r	1.20
168.53	165	3.80	4.20	r	0.55	r	r
168.53	167½	2.05	2.65	5.25	1.40	r	r
168.53	170	0.40	0.55	4.00	2.90	r	r
168.53	172½	r	r	2.90	3.00	r	2.40
50,000 Canadian Dollars-cents per unit.							
CDollr	73	r	r	r	r	r	r
74.57	74½	0.73	r	r	r	r	0.42
74.57	75	0.17	r	r	r	r	0.98
62,500 West German Marks-cents per unit.							
DMark	52	r	r	r	r	r	r
56.38							

Option & Underlying	Strike Price	Calls—Last			Puts—Last		
		Jun	Jul	Sep	Jun	Jul	Sep
6,250,000 Japanese Yen-100ths of a cent per unit.							
JYen	53	r	r	4.06	r	r	r
56.38	54	r	r	r	r	r	0.27
56.38	55	1.50	r	r	0.17	0.06	0.42
56.38	56	0.90	r	1.90	0.40	0.17	0.71
56.38	57	0.41	0.67	1.39	r	0.33	1.08
56.38	59	r	r	0.65	r	r	r
62,500 Swiss Francs-cents per unit.							
SFranc	64	4.90	r	r	0.01	s	r
68.49	66	2.98	r	r	0.12	r	0.31
68.49	67	1.96	3.04	r	0.50	r	0.64
68.49	68	r	r	r	r	r	r
68.49	70	0.38	r	r	0.16	r	r
71.56	65	r	r	r	r	r	0.30
71.56	67	r	3.82	r	0.10	r	r
71.56	68	r	r	r	0.19	r	0.63
71.56	69	2.06	1.60	2.45	0.34	0.31	0.88
71.56	70	1.15	1.10	2.00	0.56	0.91	1.30
71.56	71	0.79	0.74	1.53	1.18	r	r
71.56	72	0.35	r	r	r	r	r
71.56	73	0.23	r	r	r	r	r
71.56	75	0.11	r	r	r	r	r
Total call vol. 26,472		Call open int. 509,515					
Total put vol. 18,952		Put open int. 474,438					

CANADIAN DOLLAR (IMM) 100,000 Can.$, cents per Can.$

Strike Price	Calls—Settle			Puts—Settle		
	Jun-c	Jly-c	Aug-c	Jun-p	Jly-p	Aug-p
73	1.54			0.02		
74	0.67		0.49	0.15		0.44
75	0.17	0.33	0.23	0.61		
76	0.03	0.03		1.47		
77	0.00	0.01		2.46		
78	0.00					

Est. vol. 280, Mon vol. 12 calls, 32 puts
Open interest Mon: 4,943 calls, 3,394 puts

STERLING (LIFFE) £500,000; pts of 100%

June	91.38	91.40	91.33	91.38	+	91.52	88.97	88.97	10,169
Sept	91.41	91.44	91.35	91.42	−.02	91.82	89.02	89.02	8,091
Dec	91.20	91.22	91.18	91.22	−.05	91.69	88.82	88.82	5,692
Mr88	91.00	91.02	90.98	91.03	−.06	91.47	88.60	88.60	1,038
June	90.85	90.85	90.83	90.84	−.07	91.33	89.65	89.65	458
Sept			90.68			90.98	90.95	90.95	143

Est vol 3,672; vol Mon 5,372; open int 25,689, −894.

(90.73 ... open int 31,035, −58. ... 92.90 91.23 164)
Dec 90.73
Est vol 8,408; vol Mon 8,633; open int 31,035, −58.

Foreign Exchange Rate Quotations (partial listing)

Jordan (Dinar)	3.0120	3.01205	.332	.332
Kuwait (Dinar)	3.6955	3.6955	.2706	.2706
Lebanon (Pound)	.008547	.008547	117.00	117.00
Malaysia (Ringgit)	.4043	.4053	2.4735	2.4675
Malta (Lira)	2.9283	2.9542	.3415	.3385
Mexico (Peso)				
Floating rate	.0008130	.0008197	1230.00	1220.00
Netherland (Guilder)	.4999	.4979	2.0004	2.0085
New Zealand (Dollar)	.5805	.5820	1.7227	1.7182
Norway (Krone)	.1513	.1513	6.6100	6.6075
Pakistan (Rupee)	.05780	.05780	17.30	17.30
Peru (Inti)	.06570	.06570	15.22	15.22
Philippines (Peso)	.04883	.04883	20.48	20.48
Portugal (Escudo)	.007231	.007252	138.30	137.90
Saudi Arabia (Riyal)	.2666	.2666	3.751	3.751
Singapore (Dollar)	.4724	.4724	2.1170	2.1170
South Africa (Rand)				
Commercial rate	.5025	.5025	1.9900	1.9900
Financial rate	.3113	.3100	3.2123	3.3258
South Korea (Won)	.001203	.001203	831.10	831.10
Spain (Peseta)	.008032	.008039	124.50	124.40
Sweden (Krona)	.1604	.1606	6.2325	6.2275
Switzerland (Franc)	.6875	.6838	1.4545	1.4625
30-Day Forward	.6901	.6863	1.4490	1.4570
90-Day Forward	.6940	.6899	1.4410	1.4494
180-Day Forward	.70155	.6973	1.4254	1.4341
Taiwan (Dollar)	.03111	.03105	32.14	32.21
Thailand (Baht)	.03908	.03908	25.59	25.59
Turkey (Lira)	.001246	.001246	802.85	802.85
United Arab (Dirham)	.2723	.2723	3.673	3.673
Uruguay (New Peso)				
Financial	.004728	.004728	211.50	211.50
Venezuela (Bolivar)				
Official rate	.1333	.1333	7.50	7.50
Floating rate	.03774	.03774	26.85	26.85
W. Germany (Mark)	.5643	.5611	1.7720	1.7823
30-Day Forward	.5662	.5629	1.7662	1.7766
90-Day Forward	.5699	.5664	1.7547	1.7655
180-Day Forward	.5752	.5723	1.7385	1.7473
SDR	1.30720	1.31042	0.764994	0.763114
ECU	1.16514	1.16607		

Special Drawing Rights are based on exchange rates for the U.S., West German, British, French and Japanese currencies. Source: International Monetary Fund.
ECU is based on a basket of community currencies.
Source: European Community Commission.
z-Not quoted.

EXHIBIT 2-1 Foreign Exchange Rate Quotations

a specific foreign currency. Banks that are in the market on a regular basis quote both a bid and an offer rate to other banks in the market. The *bid rate* is the rate at which the bank is willing to pay for the foreign currency; the *offer rate* is the rate at which it is willing to sell the foreign currency. The difference between the bid and offer rates is known as the *spread*.

How Banks Earn Profits in Foreign Exchange

A bank that simultaneously buys and resells foreign currency earns the spread as its trading profit. For example, a New York bank might quote bid and offer rates for the British pound sterling at $1.3582/86. The bid rate is thus $1.3582 per pound. The bank stands ready to buy at least £1,000,000 for $1,385,200. The offer rate is $1.3586 per pound. The bank thus evidences its willingness to sell £1,000,000 for $1,385,600. Should it be able to buy and then sell 1 million pounds simultaneously at these rates, it would net a profit of $400 on the transaction. This profit is equal to the spread ($0.0004) times the amount of the transaction.

Usually, however, foreign exchange traders also seek to benefit from anticipating correctly the direction in which a currency will move. Let us suppose that a foreign exchange trader anticipates that sterling will appreciate against the U.S. dollar. The trader will tend to increase both bid and offer rates, seeking to encourage others to sell sterling to the trader's bank and discourage other banks from buying sterling from the trader's bank. In this manner, the trader buys more sterling than is sold, creating a *long position*. If the currency moves as the trader predicts, the trader can then sell the sterling at the higher exchange rate for a substantial profit. On the other hand, should the trader take the view that sterling is about to depreciate, the proper response would be to lower the bid and offer rates. This action would encourage sales and discourage purchases. The trader anticipating a price decrease thus sells more currency than it has purchased, creating a *short position*. If sterling falls as anticipated, the trader can buy the currency back at a lower rate.

Should the trader believe that the general tendency of the market is uncertain and not be able to predict the appropriate direction of movement, the trader may tend to widen the spread between the bid and offer rates to reduce the volume of trading and to increase profits on those trades that do take place. Traders thus earn profits from two sources: (1) the spread and (2) gains made on the correct anticipation of price movements.

Although the opportunity for a profit is large if rates move in the direction anticipated, the foreign exchange trader also risks large losses if rates move in the opposite, unanticipated direction. For this reason, banks have established extensive controls on foreign exchange trading by bank traders. Traders are subject to *position limits*, which indicate the maximum amount by which the trader can be long or short in a specific currency. Even with sophisticated controls, banks have occasionally experienced large losses from unauthorized trading beyond position limits. Because exchange departments of major money center banks are viewed as profit centers to the banks, traders are under great pressure to show a meaningful return on the capital invested in this function.

Interbank Market Practices

The New York and London foreign exchange markets use foreign exchange brokers in interbank dealing. For a small commission, the broker attempts to find a match for a specific bank's bid or offer. Banks may also deal directly with each other. Direct dealing is generally the practice between banks in different countries, although brokers now offer international links, as well.

A bank contacted directly by another bank and asked for a quotation normally gives both its bid and offer rates. Because participants in the foreign exchange market know the general level of rates, the trader usually quotes only the last two digits. For example, if a bank's bid rate for sterling is $1.3582 and its offer rate is $1.3586, the bank would normally quote 82/86. By making this quotation, the bank is obligated to deal in either direction at the minimum lot size (usually 1 million dollars or foreign currency units). The quotes, however, are valid for only a few seconds. The contacting bank must deal immediately; otherwise, the quote may be withdrawn.

The highly liquid and efficient interbank market for foreign exchange is a vital element in the international financial system. When banks deal with customers in the retail market, positions created by transactions with those customers can be adjusted almost instantaneously to meet the bank's desired long or short position. This allows banks to give customers rates that are very close to the rates available in the interbank market. Banks and major corporations can subscribe to financial information services, such as Reuters, that provide current bid and offer rates from a number of banks.

Direct and Indirect Exchange Rates

Foreign exchange quotations are made in two different ways. The *direct exchange rate* is the home currency price of one unit of foreign currency. In the U.S. foreign exchange market, some currencies are quoted in the direct fashion. Sterling, for example, is quoted directly; that is, the rate for sterling represents the price of one pound sterling measured in dollars. Direct quotations in the U.S. market are also referred to as "quotations in U.S. terms."

The *indirect exchange rate* is the foreign currency price of one unit of the home currency. The indirect rate is the reciprocal of the direct rate. Most European currencies are quoted indirectly. For example, an indirect quote for the German mark may be DM 2.0055. This price represents the number of German marks equivalent to one U.S. dollar. Prior to 1978, these currencies were quoted directly, but U.S. banks switched to indirect quotation to facilitate their trading with European banks.

Indirect quotations can be somewhat confusing. Let us suppose that a bank quotes the German mark at DM 2.0052/68. Viewed from the German perspective, this quote can be readily understood. The bank is willing to buy dollars at a price of DM 2.0052 per dollar and is willing to sell dollars at the rate of DM 2.0068 per dollar. But confusion may occur if one attempts to view the transaction from a U.S. perspective. The key is to remember that a bank that is buying dollars is also selling marks and a bank that is selling dollars is also buying marks. Thus the rate for buying marks is DM 2.0068, and the rate for selling marks is DM 2.0052. When rates are quoted indirectly, traders follow the unusual maxim, "Buy high, sell low."

The direct equivalents of the deutsche mark rates DM 2.0052/68 per dollar are $0.4983/87 per mark, the reciprocals of the indirect quote.

Arbitrage

Although foreign currency is traded continuously around the world, the rate of exchange between two currencies in any given market may, for some reason, begin to deviate from rates in other markets. A process known as *arbitrage*, however, tends to eliminate any discrepancies in exchange rates among the different foreign exchange markets. Suppose, for example, that the exchange rate for the French franc in Paris is Ffr 6.6525 and the exchange rate for the French franc in New York is Ffr 6.6475. Traders can obtain more French francs per dollar by buying in Paris than they could in New York. Consequently, traders buying French francs would tend to buy in Paris where they could get more French francs per dollar. Traders wanting to sell French francs would sell in New York, where they would get more dollars per French franc. An astute trader, spotting this discrepancy in rates, would simultaneously buy French francs in Paris and sell them in New York. The buying pressure in Paris and the selling pressure in New York would eventually eliminate the discrepancy between the two rates. In practice, such opportunities do exist, but the arbitrage mechanism removes them efficiently within a matter of minutes if not seconds.

More complicated forms of arbitrage, involving more than two currencies, are also possible. Suppose, for example, that a trader in West Germany wants to buy French francs and finds that he can purchase them in Frankfurt at a rate of 3.0900 francs per deutsche mark. But, when he looks at the New York market, the trader finds that the mark is quoted there at DM 2.1336 and the French franc at Ffr 6.6525. In New York, francs could be exchanged for marks at an effective rate of 3.1180 francs per deutsche mark. This cross-rate is found by dividing the French franc per dollar rate (6.6525) by the deutsche mark per dollar rate (2.1336), which yields the New York French franc per deutsche mark cross-rate of 3.1180. Rather than buy French francs in Frankfurt and get 3.0900 French francs per mark, the trader could first buy dollars in New York at 2.1336, and then exchange these dollars for French francs at a rate of 6.6525, which results in the trader's obtaining 3.1180 French francs per mark. Of course, arbitrage of this type quickly brings the direct price in Frankfurt and the cross-rate in New York into alignment.

In many countries, a two-step mechanism is used to purchase currencies other than the dollar. Usually, the local currency is exchanged for dollars, and then the dollars are exchanged for the desired third currency. Thus the exchange rate between the dollar and the local currency is watched very closely.

Measuring Exchange Rate Movements

When a foreign currency becomes more valuable in terms of the home currency, it is said to *appreciate*. When the foreign currency becomes less valuable in terms of the home currency, it is said to *depreciate*. For example, suppose that the German mark moves from a rate of DM 2.5 per dollar to a new rate of DM 2.0 per dollar. In this case, the mark has appreciated against the dollar, and the dollar has depreciated against the mark.

How do we measure the extent of a currency appreciation or depreciation? By convention, it is measured in terms of the direct exchange rate of the currency being used as a reference currency:

$$\text{Percentage of appreciation} = \frac{\text{New rate} - \text{Old rate}}{\text{Old rate}} \times 100$$

The mark has moved from an old rate of $0.40 to a new rate of $0.50. Consequently, the mark has appreciated ($0.50 − 0.40) ÷ $ 0.40 = .25, or 25 percent, against the dollar. In this example, the dollar is the reference currency against which the movement of the mark is being measured. If the new rate is lower than the old rate, the result of applying this formula is a negative percentage of appreciation, or a depreciation.

If we assume the German perspective and use the mark as the reference currency, we find that the dollar has depreciated against the mark. Applying the same formula, we find that the dollar has depreciated (DM 2.0 − 2.5) ÷ DM 2.5 = −.20, or 20 percent.

Notice that from a U.S. perspective (U.S. dollars as reference currency) the mark has appreciated 25 percent against the dollar but from a German perspective (German mark as reference currency) the dollar has depreciated 20 percent against the mark. It is confusing and somewhat paradoxical that the same exchange rate movement leads to different rates of currency appreciation or depreciation, depending on which currency is chosen as the reference currency.

THE FORWARD EXCHANGE MARKET

In addition to buying and selling foreign currencies for spot, or immediate, delivery, the foreign exchange market also offers the opportunity to buy and sell for future delivery through the mechanism of a forward exchange contract. Unlike most financial futures contracts, which have been developed relatively recently, forward exchange contracts have existed (in one form or another) for centuries.

A *forward exchange contract* is an agreement (usually with a bank) to buy or sell a specific amount of foreign currency on a determined future date at an exchange rate that is fixed now and not changed, regardless of how the market exchange rate may have changed when the contract matures. As an example of a forward contract, a company might agree with its bank to buy DM 10 million at $0.51 per mark for a maturity of one year. If the company's credit with the bank is established, no funds are exchanged when the contract is arranged. However, in one year the company would pay its bank $5.1 million and in return receive DM 10 million. The transfer would take place at the $0.51 rate, even if the mark is worth $0.40, $0.50, $0.60, or any other value at maturity date.

Components of a Forward Contract

A forward exchange contract has five basic components: the type (purchase or sale), the currency, the amount, the forward exchange rate, and the maturity date. In the forward exchange contract described in the previous paragraph, the contract is a forward purchase; the currency is the mark; the amount is DM 10 million; the forward rate is $0.51; and the maturity date is one year.

Forward sales contracts are also available. For example, a firm might sell DM 5 million at $0.51 for one year; at the end of the year, the firm would be required to transfer DM 5 million to its bank and would receive in return $2.55 million (DM 5,000,000 × $0.51).

Forward contracts are available in most major currencies for maturities of one year or less. Banks routinely quote prices for forward contract maturities of one, two, three, six, and twelve months. Prices for intermediate, or broken, dates are readily available, although rates are adjusted slightly because banks cannot readily adjust the forward position that they have created by transactions in the interbank market for the odd date.

Over the past five years, long forwards (contracts with a maturity of more than one year) have emerged. Maturities as far out as ten years, although not readily quoted, are available, particularly to major clients. Most long forwards are tied to the covering of a series of contractual payments (such as interest payments) or large individual future payments, such as the repayment of principal of a major bond issue.

Using Forward Contracts for Covering

Many forward transactions are concluded with bank customers who may be attempting to insure the value of export proceeds or a future debt repayment. Suppose, for example, that a customer needs to make a payment of DM 300,000 in six months. Although the current spot rate is DM 2.4 per dollar, by the time payment is made the rate could move up as far as DM 2.0 per dollar (meaning a dollar payment of $150,000) or down as far as DM 3.0 per dollar (meaning a dollar payment of $100,000); rates might move even further. If the company buys the marks forward at the present six months forward rate of DM 2.32 per dollar, it fixes its repayment obligation at $129,310, regardless of where the exchange rate moves. The company substitutes a known obligation in dollars for an obligation whose value is known in marks but unknown in dollars.

The use of forward contracts to eliminate or reduce the uncertainty in the reference currency value of a foreign currency transaction is called *covering*. When a firm has a foreign currency inflow, it covers by selling that inflow in the forward market. When a firm has a foreign currency outflow, it covers that outflow by a purchase in the forward market.

How Forward Rates Are Quoted

Banks usually quote forward rates to customers exactly as they quote spot prices. A forward transaction not linked to any other transaction is called an *outright forward transaction*, and the rate quoted for it is called an *outright forward rate*.

Most forward contracts in the forward exchange markets are usually coupled with a spot transaction. These simultaneous transactions are known as *foreign exchange swaps*. In a swap transaction, one participant agrees to buy a given amount of foreign exchange on the spot market and simultaneously to sell the same amount of foreign currency in the forward market at some future date. Alternatively, foreign currency might be sold spot and purchased forward. In March 1986, the Federal Reserve Bank of New York found that 63.2 percent of all transactions in the interbank foreign exchange market are spot transactions, 29.8 percent are swap transactions, and only 4.7 percent are outright forward transactions. Bank dealers can combine a swap and a spot transaction to create a forward position. Suppose that the bank wishes to sell the pound sterling ninety days forward. The bank trader first swaps into sterling (buys sterling spot and sells forward) and then eliminates the spot position by selling the same amount in the spot market. The net effect is that the bank has a forward contract to sell sterling in ninety days.

Because the vast majority of forward exchange contracts involve swaps, banks use a relatively simple system of shorthand to quote forward rates in the interbank market. For example, suppose that the spot rate for sterling is quoted at $1.4378/82 and the bank is asked to quote the bid and offer rates for swaps of varying maturity. It might quote as follows:

1 month, 42/44;

3 months, 124/132;

6 months, 245/263.

Interpretation of this shorthand requires some effort, but we can apply the following rules to find the outright forward bid and offer rates:

1. If the first number of the swap rate is lower than the second number, the forward rate is higher than the spot; we add the first number to the spot rate to get the forward bid rate and the second to the spot rate to get the forward offer rate.

2. If the first number of the swap rate is higher than the second number, the forward rate is lower than the spot; we subtract these numbers from the spot rate, instead.

Suppose that we wanted to determine the forward rate for one-month sterling. From the quotation above, we find that 42, the first number, is less than 44, the second number, and therefore that forward sterling is higher than the rate for spot. To find the bid rate for forward sterling, we add $1.4378 (the spot bid rate) to $.0042 (the swap bid rate) to find the outright bid rate of $1.4420. To find the offer rate for one-month forward sterling, we add the spot offer rate of $1.4382 to the swap offer rate of $.0044 and find that the one-month forward outright offer rate is $1.4426. In a similar fashion, we find that the bid and offer rates for three-month forward sterling are $1.4502/14 and for six months $1.4623/45.

Suppose that a customer of the bank wishes to swap into sterling for a three-month period. The customer is able to buy sterling from the bank at $1.4382 and sell it forward to the bank at $1.4502. The total differential between the spot and forward rate ($.0120) equals the bid quote on the swap ($.0124) *less* the spread in the spot market ($.0004).

For a customer swapping out of sterling for three months, the bank buys the sterling at $1.4378 and sells it forward at $1.4514. The total differential between the spot and forward rate ($.0136) equals the offer quote on the swap ($.0132) *plus* the spread in the spot market ($.0004).

Measuring the Forward Premium and Discount

When a foreign currency is worth more in the forward market than it is in the spot market, we say that the forward is at a *premium*. Conversely, when the currency is worth less for forward delivery than for spot delivery, the forward is at a *discount*.

Often, it is useful to measure the forward premium or discount because it can prove particularly valuable in calculating the return on cross-border investment of funds, in which the principal amount is exchanged and then covered by a forward contract in the same amount at maturity. By definition, the forward premium (using direct exchange rates) is

$$\Delta = \frac{(\text{Forward rate} - \text{Spot rate})}{\text{Spot rate}} \times \frac{12}{\text{Maturity (months)}}$$

The factor on the right essentially annualizes the forward premium. The forward premium is frequently expressed as a percentage, which is found by multiplying the forward premium by 100. A negative premium simply means that the currency is at a forward discount.

Using the middle rates (halfway between the bid and offer rates) we can calculate the forward premium for one-, three-, and six-month sterling. For one-month sterling:

$$\Delta_1 = \frac{(\$1.4423 - 1.4380)}{1.4380} \times \frac{12}{1} = .0359$$

One-month sterling is at a 3.59 percent premium. Likewise, for three-month sterling:

$$\Delta_3 = \frac{(\$1.4508 - 1.4380)}{1.4380} \times \frac{12}{3} = .0356$$

For six-month sterling:

$$\Delta_6 = \frac{(\$1.4634 - 1.4380)}{1.4380} \times \frac{12}{6} = .0353$$

Having the exchange rates quoted in swap terms actually facilitates the calculation because the midpoint of the two swap quotes actually is the numerator of the first term in the formula for Δ. For example, in calculating Δ_1, we found that $\$1.4423 - 1.4380$, the first term in the formula, is equal to $\$.0043$. This value is precisely the midpoint between the two swap quotes 42/44. The swap method of quoting forward rates makes calculation of Δ easier.

FUTURES AND OPTIONS IN FOREIGN EXCHANGE

In recent years, an alternative to the bank forward exchange contract has developed. Pioneered in 1972 by the International Monetary Market (IMM) division of the Chicago Mercantile Exchange, foreign currency *futures* contracts are now traded on a number of commodities and financial futures exchanges.

Like forward contracts, futures contracts call for the delivery of a specified amount of foreign currency on a specified future date. To facilitate trading, however, the size of the contract and the delivery date are standardized. For example, the IMM offers futures contracts that call for delivery on the third Wednesday of March, June, September, and December, in currencies and amounts as shown in Exhibit 2-2.

Futures contracts use a standard maturity date, and it is therefore relatively easy to offset the transaction if views about the direction of currency movement change. On the other hand, the standardized size and maturity date of the contract make it difficult to match the size and payment date of a commercial transaction exactly. Because futures contracts are traded on an organized exchange, a brokerage commission is charged and a margin requirement is imposed. Banks in the forward market make money on the spread and usually do not ask for a margin for prime corporate customers. Some firms have been reluctant to use futures because of low market volumes, but recent significant market growth has eased fears of poor market pricing due to low volume.

U.S.-style put and call options on foreign currencies are actively traded on the Philadelphia Stock Exchange, and European-style options on currencies are available on the Chicago Board Options Exchange. Options on foreign currency futures were introduced by the Chicago Mercantile Exchange in 1985. Banks also offer options on foreign cur-

EXHIBIT 2-2 Chicago Mercantile Exchange IMM Futures and Options Contracts

Currency	Contract Size	Number Traded 1985	Number Traded 1986*
British pound futures	25,000	2,799,024	2,406,124
British pound options	—	329,071	423,917
Canadian dollar futures	100,000	468,999	639,698
Canadian dollar options	—	—	209,307
Deutsche mark futures	125,000	6,449,384	5,658,023
Deutsche mark options	—	1,562,438	1,877,222
French franc futures	250,000	9,335	2,445
Japanese yen futures	12,500,000	2,415,094	3,445,457
Japanese yen options	—	—	709,544
Mexican peso futures	1,000,000	12,737	—
Swiss franc futures	125,000	4,758,159	4,178,681
Swiss franc options	—	324,806	677,512
European Currency Unit (ECU) futures	125,000	—	41,582

*January 1 through October 31, 1986.

NOTE: The Mexican peso ceased trading November 1985. European Currency Unit futures began trading June 15, 1986. Canadian dollar options began June 18, 1986. Japanese yen options began March 15, 1986.

SOURCE: Chicago Mercantile Exchange.

rencies tailored to client specifications. Introduction and use of options offer a wide variety of choices to companies attempting to manage their foreign exchange exposure.

SUMMARY

The foreign exchange market makes possible payments from one country to another. Banks service their customers' needs to make or receive foreign payments in the retail foreign exchange market and actively trade foreign currencies with other banks in the interbank market. Banks also operate foreign exchange departments as profit centers with earnings derived both from bid/offer spreads and from taking positions in anticipation of rate movements. In this global foreign exchange market, discrepancies in exchange rates in different financial centers are removed by arbitrage transactions.

Banks also buy and sell exchange for forward delivery, in which the rate is set for currency transactions to take place in the future. Forward contracts can be used to guarantee the dollar value of foreign currency payments to be made at a future date. Foreign currencies may be worth more in the forward market (trade at a premium) or may be worth less (trade at a discount). Financial future contracts in major foreign currencies are also available, as are put and call options on foreign currency.

DISCUSSION QUESTIONS

1. What is the difference between the spot exchange rate and the forward exchange rate? What are the five components of a forward exchange contract? How can forward contracts be used to cover a future payment in a foreign currency?

2. How does the direct method of quoting foreign exchange rates differ from the indirect method? In New York, the German mark is quoted at DM 1.7500 per dollar. From a U.S. perspective, is this quotation direct or indirect? How can an indirect quotation be converted into a direct quotation? How can a direct quotation be converted into an indirect quotation? Illustrate this relationship by converting the DM 1.7500 per dollar quotation mentioned earlier in this problem.

3. Suppose that the deutsche mark per dollar exchange rate in New York is DM 1.7450 per dollar, and at the same time is DM 1.7425 per dollar in Frankfurt. In which market would a buyer of marks purchase them? In which market would a seller of marks sell them? How would these operations affect the discrepancy of market rates?

4. What is the difference between currency appreciation and currency depreciation? Over the next year, a foreign exchange forecaster predicts that the Brazilian cruzado will move from Cz$ 15 per dollar to Cz$ 30 per dollar. What is the forecasted rate of appreciation (or depreciation) of the dollar against the cruzado? What is the forecasted rate of depreciation (or appreciation) of the cruzado against the dollar?

5. How does the swap method of quoting foreign exchange rates differ from the outright method? A foreign exchange dealer quotes a Swiss franc per

dollar spot rate of Sfr 1.5750/60 and a three-month forward swap rate of 100/90.

a. What is the dealer's three-month outright bid rate for dollars?

b. What is the dealer's three-month outright offer rate for dollars?

c. If you wish to buy Sfr 10 million three months forward, how many dollars will you have to pay in three months?

6. In New York, spot sterling is quoted at $1.6000, and forward outright quotes are as follows:

Maturity	Forward Rate
1 month	1.5950
3 months	1.5840
6 months	1.5670
12 months	1.5350

What are the annualized premiums (discounts) for forward sterling for each maturity?

7. How do commercial banks make money in the foreign exchange market? What are the risks of foreign exchange dealing?

SUGGESTED READINGS

1. Kubarych, Roger. *Foreign Exchange Markets in the United States*, Revised Edition. New York, New York: Federal Reserve Bank of New York, 1983. (An excellent introduction to trading practices in the United States.)

2. Tygier, Claude. *Basic Handbook of Foreign Exchange.* London: Euromoney Publications, 1983. (Provides description of bank dealing practices and evaluation of bank positions.)

3. Walmsley, Julian. *The Foreign Exchange Handbook.* New York, New York: John Wiley & Sons, 1983. (A comprehensive treatment of all aspects of foreign exchange market practices.)

CHAPTER 3

▼

The International Monetary System and Exchange Rate Forecasting

▲

DETERMINANTS OF THE EXCHANGE RATE

The foreign exchange market is characterized by a high volume of transactions and rapid sensitivity to new information. In most developed countries, the market for foreign exchange is a relatively free market, with supply and demand from commercial and investment transactions determining the exchange rate.

The demand for foreign exchange (foreign means of payment) arises because residents of one country need to make payments to residents of other countries. The primary need for foreign currency is to pay for imports or to pay for services (such as insurance, transportation, and fees for licensing trademarks or technology). Another need for foreign currency is to acquire foreign funds to make investments: either *portfolio investments*, where the investor is concerned with the investment's financial return, or *direct investments*, where the investor seeks operating control. The demand for foreign exchange arises essentially because residents purchase goods, services, or assets from nonresidents. Likewise, the supply of foreign exchange arises because nonresidents need to make payment to residents for the sale of goods, services, or assets to nonresidents.

In theory, at least, the foreign exchange rate is the price that equates supply and demand in the foreign exchange market. The high volume of interbank transactions and the arbitrage process eliminate large rate discrepancies between markets and foster market efficiency.

A system where exchange rates are determined completely by normal market forces is known as a system of *freely floating exchange rates*. Although such a system has been advocated in theory by many economists for many years, foreign exchange rates typically have not been allowed to float freely, as governments have sought to influence the level of economic activity and the terms of trade by fixing the exchange rate.

FIXED RATES AND GOVERNMENT INTERVENTION

Governments are primary participants in many foreign exchange markets and they enter the foreign exchange markets as buyers and/or sellers of foreign exchange. Governments frequently need foreign exchange to make overseas payments or they are the recipients of such payments. But the primary reason that governments participate in the foreign exchange market is to influence the foreign exchange rate—the price at which currencies are traded. Governments may seek to determine exactly (or within a very narrow range) the price at which foreign exchange is traded. Such a *fixed-rate system* was characteristic of the immediate post-World War II international economic order up to 1973. Alternatively, governments may seek to set or change the direction in which rates are moving by intermittent purchases or sales of foreign exchange. This so-called *managed floating system* (also more pessimistically described as *dirty floating*) has characterized world monetary relations since 1973.

Government activity in the foreign exchange market is known as *intervention*. Foreign exchange traders and corporate treasurers must be alert to government intervention in the market because it may signal changes in government policy that will affect foreign exchange, money, and capital markets significantly. Typically, the central bank of a country carries out interventions in the market; in the United States, the Federal Reserve Bank of New York is charged with trading foreign exchange for the Federal Reserve System and the U.S. Treasury. Government policy in this area is primarily conducted by the U.S. Treasury Department.

DEVELOPMENT OF EXCHANGE RATE POLICY

Post-World War II governments generally attempted to maintain relatively fixed exchange rates with each other. Under an international agreement known as the *Bretton Woods Agreement* (from the New Hampshire location of the 1944 conference that established it), countries set a parity exchange rate usually expressed in relationship to the U.S. dollar. For example, for many years Great Britain set a parity rate of US $2.80 per pound, and the West Germans established a rate of DM 4 per dollar. Countries obligated themselves to intervene in the foreign exchange market to maintain market rates within a narrow band on either side of the parity rate. Until 1971, this band was 1 percent in either direction of the official parity rate. For example, Germany, with a parity rate of DM 4 per dollar, was obligated to keep the DM per dollar exchange rate within the range DM 3.96 to 4.04. When the mark approached the lower limit of DM 3.96, indicating that there was an oversupply of dollars in the market, the German government instructed the Deutsche Bundesbank (the German Central Bank) to buy the excess dollars offered. On the other hand, if the exchange rate approached the upper limit of DM 4.04, indicating excess demand for dollars, the Bundesbank would intervene in the market and sell dollars to meet the excess demand.

When market pressures indicated that a parity exchange rate was inappropriate, countries could *devalue* or *revalue* their currency by changing the official parity rate. For example, in 1967 the pound sterling was devalued from $2.80 to $2.40.

Under the Bretton Woods system, the International Monetary Fund (IMF) was established to administer the fixed exchange rate system and to provide temporary financing to countries that were in need of foreign exchange to finance foreign exchange market interventions. Despite significant market pressures against the U.S. dollar in the later years of the Bretton Woods system, fixed exchange rates provided a stable environment for the expansion of global trade and investment. In particular, the major multinationalization of U.S.-based corporations occurred under Bretton Woods.

Transition to Floating Exchange Rates

By 1971, traumatic market pressures against the U.S. dollar led to a two-stage breakup of the Bretton Woods system. The December 18, 1971 *Smithsonian Agreement* formalized a major realignment of exchange rate parities and authorized wider permissible bands (2¼ percent each way) of market fluctuations before intervention was required. Then, in February 1973, governments generally suspended intervention to maintain fixed exchange rates altogether. Since 1973, most major currencies have not been formally fixed in value but have floated, responding to market supply and demand.

Still, governments are active in the foreign exchange market for a number of reasons. First, governments intervene in the foreign exchange markets to push rates in a direction that is helpful to national economic policies. To encourage exports, a government may keep its exchange rates artificially low. To maintain confidence in a currency, a government may maintain the currency's value at a rate higher than the market would set.

Even in countries that are willing to let their currencies appreciate or depreciate in response to market forces, a government may intervene in order to smooth out the rate at which these movements take place or to slow down the rate of depreciation or appreciation. Thus, if the currency starts to depreciate in response to excess demand for foreign exchange, the government may intervene to sell foreign currency to slow down the rate at which the depreciation is taking place. If the currency is appreciating too rapidly, the country may buy foreign currency.

Governments may also intervene to stabilize the market during disorderly periods. The foreign exchange markets are extremely sensitive to international events. When an important military or political incident takes place, market conditions become disorderly as traders attempt to assess how this information affects the exchange rate. For example, when President Reagan was wounded in the 1981 assassination attempt, the foreign exchange markets could have become disorderly as the markets attempted to assess the seriousness of the situation. But, at that time, the Federal Reserve Bank of New York entered the foreign exchange markets as sellers of foreign currency to maintain temporarily the value of the dollar.

U.S. policy under the Reagan administration initially concentrated on maintaining orderly market conditions and intervened in situations where world conditions tended to lead to disorderly markets. This policy received strong criticism from a number of other governments, which saw the U.S. dollar as significantly overvalued. A number of European countries and Japan intervened to prevent further appreciation of the U.S. dollar, but in most cases, this intervention was primarily directed at smoothing out exchange rate movements rather than reversing the market-generated strengthening of the dollar.

Present Exchange Rate Policy

A key shift in U.S. policy regarding intervention to change the value of the dollar — the key policy variable in the global financial system — was signaled when, over the weekend of September 21–22, 1985, the Group of Five (the United States, West Germany, Japan, the United Kingdom, and France) announced a coordinated effort to intervene in foreign exchange markets to lower the value of the dollar. These steps were motivated primarily by the growing excess of U.S. imports over U.S. exports and the decline of U.S. competitiveness in world markets, both due to the high cost of dollars. The high level of coordination and secrecy needed for the development of this program illustrates the complexity of the issues confronting the international monetary system and the inability of any major country to operate an independent exchange rate policy. Government intervention must be coordinated to be effective.

The market responded dramatically on the Monday following the announcement of the intervention package; late trading in New York showed a decline in the value of the dollar of 5.3 percent against the German mark and 5.4 percent against the Japanese yen. After several weeks of trader testing of governmental resolve to keep the dollar at reduced levels, the coordinated intervention proved its short-run effectiveness in setting rates.

Currently, the key exchange rates that foreign exchange traders and corporate treasurers tend to track most closely to assess the strength of the dollar are those of the Japanese yen and the West German mark. Japan and West Germany are, after the United States, the two largest economic powers in the world.

The European Monetary System

The deutsche mark per dollar exchange rate is also important as an indicator of the value of the currencies of continental Europe. Since the breakup of the Bretton Woods Agreement, beginning in 1972, members of the European Economic Community (EEC) and other European countries have attempted to maintain relatively fixed exchange rates between each other. The latest agreement formalizing a system of inter-European fixed rates is the European Monetary System (EMS), which was initiated in March 1979 after months of intensive negotiations. Through a rather complicated formula, a grid of exchange rate parities between each pair of currencies is created. Exhibit 3-1 shows the set of parities established January 12, 1987 (the most recent as of the writing of this text). Actual market exchange rates may differ from the parity grid rate by up to 2¼ percent each way; as upper or lower limits are approached, the local monetary authorities must intervene to maintain the rate within these limits. For historical reasons, rates between other currencies and the Italian lira are allowed to deviate up to 6 percent from the parity rate.

The currencies of members of the European Monetary System thus are linked together by relatively fixed rates. However, these currencies float as a group against other currencies, such as the U.S. dollar. When graphed against the dollar, the up and down motion of the intervention points looks very much like a tunnel, and the actual market rates appear as a snake within the tunnel. For this reason, the European Monetary System is frequently referred to as the *snake.*

From time to time, exchange market pressures will lead to a realignment of the exchange rate parities in the snake. Through early 1987, some eleven readjustments of intra-European parities have occurred; over time, the West German mark has become stronger and the French franc and Italian lira weaker.

Other major industrial countries, such as Japan, the United Kingdom, and Canada, operate their exchange rate policies outside of formal arrangements such as the European Monetary System. Most developing countries relate the value of their currency to a main trading partner or to a trade-weighted average of major currencies, and try to maintain the level of their exchange rate or adjust it as economic circumstances require. Exhibit 3-2 summarizes the types of exchange rate systems currently in effect.

Both corporate financial executives and international financial

EXHIBIT 3-1 European Monetary System Central Rates (effective January 12, 1987)

Currency	1 ECU	100 Belgian/ Luxem- bourgian Franc	1 German Mark	1 Dutch Guilder	1 Danish Krone	1 French Franc	1,000 Italian Lira	1 Irish Pound
Belgian/ Luxem- bourgian franc	43.1139	—	20.42509	18.12780	5.51540	6.27279	29.19117	56.35981
Deutsche mark	2.11083	4.89594	—	0.88753	0.27003	0.30711	1.42918	2.75934
Netherlands guilder	2.37833	5.51639	1.12673	—	0.30425	0.34603	1.61030	3.10903
Danish krone	7.81701	18.13107	3.70329	3.28676	—	1.13732	5.29267	10.21863
French franc	6.87316	15.94187	3.25614	2.88991	0.87926	—	4.65362	8.98480
Italian lira	1476.95	3425.69	699.70	621.00	188.94	214.89	—	1930.71
Irish pound	0.764976	1.77431	0.36241	0.32164	0.09786	0.11130	0.51794	—

Currency Units per:

NOTE: EMS central rates are expressed in terms of the European Currency Unit (ECU), a composite unit of account. For example, 1 ECU = DM 2.11083. The table shows the number of units of the currency in each row equal to the given number of currency units in each column, at the central rate. For example, at the central rate DM 4.89594 is equal to 100 Belgian/Luxembourgian francs, lira 621.00 equals 1 Netherlands guilder, etc.

EXHIBIT 3-2 Exchange Rate Systems of IMF Member Countries, 1986

---

1. *Pegged to U.S. dollar (32 countries)*

Antigua & Barbuda	Honduras	St. Lucia
Bahamas	Iraq	St. Vincent &
Barbados	Lao P.D.R.	Grenadines
Belize	Liberia	Suriname
Djibouti	Libyan A.J.	Syrian A.R.
Dominica	Netherlands Antilles	Trinidad and
Egypt	Nicaragua	Tobago
Ethiopia	Oman	Venezuela
Ghana	Panama	Yeman A.R.
Grenada	Paraguay	P.D.R. of Yemen
Guatemala	Peru	
Haiti	St. Christopher & Nevis	

2. *Pegged to the British pound sterling (1 country)*
   Gambia

3. *Pegged to the French franc (14 countries)*

Benin	Chad	Ivory Coast
Burkina Faso	Comoros	Mali
Cameroon	Congo	Niger
Central African	Equatorial Guinea	Senegal
Republic	Gabon	Togo

4. *Pegged to other currencies (4 countries)*

Bhutan (Indian rupee)	Swaziland (South African rand)	Tonga (Australian dollar)
Lesotho (South African rand)		

5. *Pegged to the special drawing right (12 countries)*

Burma	Jordan	Seychelles
Burundi	Kenya	Sierra Leone
Guinea	Rwanda	Vanuatu
I.R. of Iran	Sao Tone & Principe	Viet Nam

6. *Pegged each to its own basket of currencies (32 countries)*

Algeria	Finland	Malta
Austria	Guyana	Mauritania
Bangladesh	Hungary	Mauritius
Botswana	Kuwait	Mozambique
Cape Verde	Madagascar	Nepal
P.R. of China	Malawi	Norway
Cyprus	Malaysia	Papua New
Fiji	Maldives	Guinea

EXHIBIT 3-2 continued

Romania	Sudan	Thailand
Singapore	Sweden	Tunisia
Solomon Islands	Tanzania	Zimbabwe

7. *Limited in flexibility with respect to a single currency (5 countries)*

Afghanistan	Qatar	United Arab
Bahrain	Saudi Arabia	Emirates

8. *Members of the European Monetary System (7 countries)*

Belgium &	France	Italy
Luxembourg	Germany	Netherlands
Denmark	Ireland	

9. *Floated according to set of indicators (5 countries)*

Brazil	Colombia	Somalia
Chile	Portugal	

10. *Managed float (22 countries)*

Argentina	India	Pakistan
Costa Rica	Indonesia	Spain
Ecuador	Israel	Sri Lanka
El Salvador	Korea	Turkey
Greece	Mexico	Uganda
Guinea-Bissau	Morocco	Western Samoa
Hong Kong	Nigeria	Yugoslavia
Iceland		

11. *Independent float (15 countries)*

Australia	Japan	United Kingdom
Bolivia	Lebanon	United States
Canada	New Zealand	Uruguay
Dominican Republic	Philippines	Zaire
Jamaica	South Africa	Zambia

SOURCE: International Monetary Fund, *"Exchange Arrangement and Exchange Restrictions,"* Annual Report 1986 (Washington, D.C.: International Monetary Fund, 1986).

managers need to develop a clear understanding of the exchange rate relationships in effect in the major countries of the world where they do business. The values of these currencies determine the profitability of local operations and conditions that prevail in local financial markets. Particularly in developing countries, where currency values are adjusted frequently for economic purposes, the exchange rate is a key indicator of the efficacy of government economic policies.

Exchange Controls

Most countries do not restrict greatly the use of their currencies for over-seas payments. A U.S. resident, for example, can use U.S. dollars to purchase foreign exchange to make almost any kind of legal payment overseas. Currencies whose uses are basically unrestricted are referred to as *convertible currencies* because they can be converted freely into other currencies to make payments.

Currency convertibility has been the norm for the currencies for most industrialized nations since 1958, when the currencies of the European Economic Community were made convertible for trade trans-actions. But currency convertibility is rare in the developing world. Most developing nations manage their currencies very tightly. Foreign ex-change, which is earned primarily as a result of exports, is carefully allocated to uses that purportedly have a high value for economic de-velopment. Access to the foreign exchange market is tightly restricted. Foreign exchange may be a monopoly of the central bank, or authority to deal in foreign exchange may be granted only to a limited number of banks and their foreign exchange operations closely monitored.

The objective of most foreign exchange control systems is to max-imize the amount of foreign exchange generated from export transac-tions and to allocate this scarce resource to certain uses in accordance with government economic policies. To this end, exporters from these countries are usually required to sell the foreign currency proceeds of all export transactions to the central bank or to authorized banks. For-eign exchange is made available to pay for imports only if they meet certain national needs. Stringent restrictions are placed on the amount of money that may be taken out of the country for travel and educa-tional expenditures. With the emergence of the debt problems of de-veloping countries, foreign exchange has become even more scarce be-cause large portions of export earnings are required to repay the interest and principal on foreign debts.

Exchange controls can severely limit the long-term dollar profit-ability of foreign investments by U.S. corporations. Corporate subsid-iaries may encounter burdensome restrictions on their ability to make payments to the parent firm. For example, dividends from subsidiary to parent are usually heavily restricted, sometimes on the theory that large dividends are indicative of exploitation of the local economy.

In most countries that operate an exchange control system, a *par-allel*, or *black*, foreign exchange market develops. In this market, local currency is exchanged for the dollar and other foreign currencies at rates far different from the official exchange rate. In some countries, black market transactions may be carried out with government sanction or with such a low level of prosecution for violations as to be relatively common. In other countries, black market trading can lead to severe judicial penalties. In judging whether it is appropriate to participate in such trades, the corporate financial executive must be guided both by corporate ethical practices and by a clear understanding of what is and what is not allowable by the local countries. In any case, the financial manager must understand foreign government exchange control policies and their economic purposes in assessing how they affect corporate operations.

MAJOR RELATIONSHIPS IN THE FOREIGN EXCHANGE MARKET

The exchange rate system in which the market operates is determined by the economic policies of major industrial countries and, to a lesser extent, by the international agencies involved in the international financial system, such as the International Monetary Fund (IMF). However, certain economic relationships do exist that summarize the forces that are at work in the foreign exchange market. Five key relationships form a framework for understanding the economic processes and help determine the rate of exchange between two currencies at any point in time:

1. Purchasing power parity In its strongest form, purchasing power parity means that exchange rates move to make equivalent values in each currency equal in purchasing power. As an alternative to this strong assertion, a weaker formulation of purchasing power parity states that relative rates of inflation in different countries are related to the rate of appreciation or depreciation between two currencies.

2. The Fisher effect The level of nominal interest rates in a given economy is related both to the real return on assets that investors demand and to the rate of inflation. The real return on assets is equalized across national boundaries.

3. The international Fisher effect Differences in nominal interest rates between currencies are related to the rate of appreciation or depreciation between currencies.

4. Interest-rate parity Differences in nominal interest rates between currencies are related to the premiums or discounts on currencies in the forward market.

5. *Forward-spot relationship*   The premiums or discounts on currencies in the forward market are related to the rate of currency appreciation or depreciation anticipated over the life of a forward contract.

Although scholars disagree as to the extent to which these relationships actually hold empirically, their underlying theoretical validity certainly provides a basic analytic framework for anyone attempting to predict the direction of future exchange rate movements. Interest rate and currency rate forecasts other than those predicted by these relationships certainly would require careful examination before acceptance by a financial manager. Deviations from these economic relationships caused by market imperfections or other sources provide a broad range of opportunity for the multinational corporation, particularly in its finance function. Let us examine separately each of these relationships and how they are connected with one another.

Purchasing Power Parity

The purchasing power parity relationship, in its strong form, states that exchange rates move with changes in the prices of goods and services in the national economics of any two countries to equalize the purchasing power of equivalent amounts of their two currencies.

For example, suppose that the price of one loaf of bread in the United States is $0.50 and the price of one apple is $0.50. In Germany, the price of one loaf of bread is DM 1, and the price of one apple is DM 1. A consumer in the United States would pay $1.00 to buy a loaf of bread and an apple. A consumer in Germany would pay DM 2 to buy the same basket of goods. According to purchasing power parity, the rate of exchange should be DM 2 = US $1.00, or DM 1 = US $0.50, because that rate of exchange equalizes the cost of the basket of goods containing one loaf of bread and one apple in the two currencies.

Suppose now that the rate of exchange was something other than that implied by purchasing power parity. For example, suppose that the rate of exchange was DM 1 = US $1.00. Consumers in Germany could then buy $1.00 for DM 1 and then use the dollar to buy a loaf of bread and an apple in the United States, instead of paying DM 2 for one loaf of bread and one apple in Germany. (Of course, we are ignoring transaction costs and shipping charges on the basket of goods.) On the other hand, consumers in the United States would have no incentive to buy DM (or sell dollars) because they could buy only one-half of a basket of goods with the DM 1 that their dollar would buy. German demand for dollars would eventually drive the price of the dollar up to DM 2 = US $1, at which point Germans would be indifferent to dollars versus deutsche marks, and so would U.S. consumers.

Such is the economic logic of purchasing power parity in its strong form. Despite the difficulty of developing realistic empirical tests of the theory, its general usefulness in assessing pressures on a currency cannot be questioned. When a currency is generally overvalued against a second currency, wherever possible, consumers will attempt to purchase goods in the undervalued currency. Such activity leads to an increase in demand for the undervalued currency, which in turn tends to raise its price to restore purchasing power parity between the two currencies.

What would happen if there were a sudden increase in prices in one country? Let us suppose that the price of a loaf of bread in Germany rose to DM 1.25 and the price of an apple also rose to DM 1.25. The total price of the basket of goods in Germany would be DM 2.5. Because we assume no price change in the United States, the price of the basket of goods remains unchanged at $1. According to purchasing power parity, the rate of exchange should be DM 2.5 = US $1, or DM 1 = US $0.40.

A 25-percent increase in prices in Germany has led to a 25-percent appreciation of the U.S. dollar against the German mark. From the perspective of the United States, the deutsche mark has depreciated 20 percent against the dollar. This relationship between the relative rates of inflation in countries and the rate of currency appreciation or depreciation is the *relative* formulation of the purchasing power parity relationship. For a variety of reasons, but primarily because relative rates of inflation are readily observed, the relative form of purchasing power parity is the one that holds the interest of currency forecasters.

To understand the relative form of purchasing power parity more completely, let us provide a symbolic formulation of the concept. Let X_0 represent the *direct* spot exchange rate at the beginning of a particular time period and X_1 represent the anticipated direct rate at the end of that period. We let P_d and P_f represent the anticipated domestic and foreign rates of inflation over the time period. The relative formulation of purchasing power parity indicates that the period ending exchange rate is

$$X_1 = X_0 \frac{(1 + P_d)}{(1 + P_f)}$$

or

$$\frac{X_1}{X_0} = \frac{(1 + P_d)}{(1 + P_f)}$$

Let us define as δ the anticipated rate of currency appreciation over a particular time period, $(X_1 - X_0) \div X_0$. Mathematical manipulation of the relative formulation of purchasing power parity shows that the rate of currency appreciation is

$$\delta = \frac{P_d - P_f}{(1 + P_f)}$$

When inflation rates were low, it was customary to ignore the $(1 + P_f)$ term in the denominator and to say that δ was simply equal to the differential in inflation rates, $P_d - P_f$. In an era of double- or even triple-digit inflation in some countries, ignoring this term is inappropriate.

Suppose that the German inflation rate is 5 percent and the U.S. inflation rate is 10 percent. From a United States perspective, one expects the rate of appreciation of the German mark to be $(.10 - .05) \div 1.05 = .0476$, or a 4.76-percent appreciation. If the exchange rate at the beginning of the period is DM 1 = \$0.50, the rate implied by purchasing power parity can be found from the first equation,

$$X_1 = (0.50) \frac{1.10}{1.05} = .5238$$

Whether purchasing power parity holds in its relative form has been a question of substantial academic debate. Relative inflation rates seem to provide a relatively good guide to the long-term direction in which exchange rates move, but the capacity of government action to manage exchange rates, lags in adjustment of prices to exchange rate changes, anticipated or actual changes in the political environment, capital movements, and a host of other factors may lead to substantial differences between actual exchange rates and those predicted by relative inflation rates. Technical factors, such as selection of the appropriate price indexes and base year, may also cause problems in applying the technique. Thus, purchasing power parity may prove of limited use in generating realistic forecasts of exchange rate movements for periods shorter than several years. However, deviations of actual exchange rates from purchasing power parities are used in some forecasting models as one predictor of the direction and magnitude of exchange rate movements.

The Fisher Effect

When investors buy financial assets, such as government bonds or certificates of deposit, they forgo current consumption in favor of future consumption. When the financial asset matures, investors hope that they will be rewarded for their sacrifice of past consumption by being able to now consume more. The increment in consumption that investors receive is the real return on their investment.

Of course, the nominal financial return that investors receive must not only provide for the real return, which is the investor's reward for saving, but also make up for the erosion of purchasing power caused by inflation. An investor who has received a cash return of 20 percent on a financial investment has not been rewarded for saving if the rate of inflation has also been 20 percent; the increase in financial wealth has been completely offset by the reduction of the currency's purchasing power.

Thus, the nominal interest rate in a country, which we will designate as i, is the product of the real rate of return on assets, r, and the rate of inflation, P. Symbolically,

$$(1 + i) = (1 + r)(1 + P)$$

If, continuing our example, the real rate of return demanded by German investors, r_G, is 5 percent, and the German rate of inflation, P_G, is 5 percent, the nominal rate of return on German assets, i_G, is found by solving the equation

$$(1 + i_G) = (1.05)(1.05)$$

Here, i_G equals .1025, or 10.25 percent. If nominal assets pay 10.25 percent, they will exactly compensate investors for the 5-percent inflation and provide a 5-percent return.

For each country, we can consider nominal interest rates and inflation rates to find the real rate of return for the particular country. The general presumption contained in the Fisher effect is that real rates of return are the same in each country or that there is one global real rate of return, r_W. Symbolically, the Fisher effect means that $r_W =$

$r_G = r_{US}$; the economic argument in support of this assertion is that, if one country had a better real rate of return than another, that country would suddenly become a very popular place for investment. Investors naturally would seek to put their funds out in the country with the superior real rate of return, driving down the real return until it matched all other countries.

Thus, if in our example, the real rate of return in Germany, r_G, is 5 percent, the real rate of return in the United States, r_{US}, also would be 5 percent, according to the Fisher effect.

A direct corollary of the Fisher effect is the relationship that should exist between nominal returns on financial assets and relative inflation rates. Through mathematical manipulation we find that

$$\frac{(1 + i_{US})}{(1 + i_G)} = \frac{(1 + P_{US})}{(1 + P_G)}$$

Relative changes in price levels between countries are reflected in relative differences in interest rates and vice versa.

If the U.S. inflation rate, P_{US}, is 10 percent, and the required real return globally, r, is 5 percent, the nominal interest rate in the United States should be 15.50 percent. Assuming the same data for Germany as before, we find that

$$\frac{(1 + i_{US})}{(1 + i_G)} = \frac{1.1550}{1.1025} = 1.0476$$

Similarly,

$$\frac{(1 + P_{US})}{(1 + P_G)} = \frac{1.10}{1.05} = 1.0476$$

and the relationship between nominal interest rates and inflation rates is seen to hold.

The relationship between nominal interest rates and inflation rates implied by the Fisher effect is sometimes approximated as

$$i_G - i_{US} = P_G - P_{US}$$

Verbally, the approximation states that the difference in nominal interest rates equals the difference in anticipated relative inflation rates. As can be seen from our example, this formulation is only approximate. For our example, $(P_G - P_{US}) = .05 - .10 = -.05$ and $(i_G - i_{US}) = (.1025 - .1550) = -.0525$. Despite the minor discrepancy, this approximation is the most commonly encountered formulation of the Fisher effect.

The International Fisher Effect

The Fisher effect provides an economic relationship between nominal interest rates and anticipated inflation rates; purchasing power parity provides a relationship between exchange rates and anticipated inflation rates. We can put the two relationships together to develop a third:

$$\frac{X_1}{X_0} = \frac{(1 + P_d)}{(1 + P_f)} = \frac{(1 + i_d)}{(1 + i_f)}$$

Eliminating the middle term in this expression, we find that

$$\frac{X_1}{X_0} = \frac{(1 + i_d)}{(1 + i_f)}$$

This relationship between anticipated exchange rate movements and the nominal level of interest rates is called the international Fisher effect.

The international Fisher effect relationship states that anticipated exchange rate changes can be derived from inspecting differences in nominal interest rates. Because nominal interest rates can be readily observed in the marketplace, they provide the currency forecaster with one clear indication of the anticipated movement of exchange rates.

In our example, the U.S. interest rate is 15.50 percent ($i_{US} = .1550$) and the German interest rate is 10.25 percent ($i_G = .1025$). The current spot rate for the German mark is $0.50. The spot rate anticipated at the end of one year is

$$X_1 = (0.50)\frac{1.1550}{1.1025} = 0.5238$$

Just as we rewrote the purchasing power parity relationship to express the relationship in terms of the rate of currency appreciation δ, we similarly find that

$$\delta = \frac{(i_d - i_f)}{(1 + i_f)}$$

That is, the rate of foreign currency appreciation is equal to the interest rate differential between countries, adjusted by the level of foreign interest rates. The denominator $(1 + i_f)$ is again sometimes neglected, although with significant problems of accuracy when interest rates are large.

In our example,

$$\delta = \frac{.1550 - .1025}{1.1025} = \frac{.0525}{1.1025} = 0.0476$$

The German mark is anticipated to appreciate by 4.76 percent against the dollar.

The empirical and theoretical validity of the international Fisher effect is a topic of vigorous academic debate. Relatively high interest rates, according to this theory, would reflect market expectations of inflation in the country with high rates and, consequently, would be a major indicator of impending depreciation of that country's currency. Alternatively, if the real return to financial assets were not the same in each country, a relatively high interest rate might signal higher real rates of return, which would attract capital and strengthen the exchange rate. Because of the success of the United States in reducing inflation, high real returns during the period 1981 through 1985 attracted substantial capital inflows into the United States, which caused a substantial appreciation of the dollar beyond levels considered desirable by U.S. monetary authorities. Capital flows have played an increasingly important role in determining currency values in recent years, as barriers to funds flows have been removed.

Interest Rate Parity

Nominal interest rates have a much more empirically valid relationship with the level of forward exchange rates. Letting Y_0 represent the direct forward rate for the foreign currency, the interest rate parity relationship indicates that

$$\frac{Y_0}{X_0} = \frac{(1 + i_d)}{(1 + i_f)}$$

This interest rate parity relationship provides that the forward rate is at a discount whenever domestic interest rates are lower than foreign rates and that the forward rate is at a premium whenever the foreign interest rate is lower. We can rewrite this relationship to show that the forward premium is

$$\Delta = \frac{(i_d - i_f)}{(1 + i_f)}$$

That is, the forward premium on a foreign currency is equal to the difference in domestic and foreign interest rates, adjusted by $(1 + i_f)$. On occasion, the denominator is neglected as an approximation.

The interest rate parity relationship is based on the assumption that investment funds will flow across national boundaries in search of higher guaranteed nominal yield. Domestic investors, for example, have two choices to obtain a guaranteed yield. First, they can invest their funds domestically and receive the domestic nominal rate i_d. Alternatively, they can convert their funds to foreign currency at the current direct spot rate X_0, invest them at the foreign nominal rate i_f, and sell both principal and interest forward at the current one-year rate Y_0. The proceeds from the domestic investment are $(1 + i_d)$ and the per unit proceeds from the foreign investment are

$$\frac{1}{X_0} (1 + i_f) (Y_0)$$

We note that all the values in the expression for the proceeds of foreign investment — the spot rate, the forward rate, and the nominal foreign interest rate — are known to investors prior to the time that they must make their decision. Thus, the proceeds of their investment are known completely and can be compared directly to the proceeds from a domestic investment. The forward sale of the proceeds essentially guarantees or insures their domestic value.

Investors make their investment decisions by comparing the proceeds of foreign investment with those of domestic investment. If proceeds from foreign investment are larger, they will choose to move their money abroad to take advantage of the higher yields available. The process of moving funds into foreign currencies to take advantage of higher yields is called *interest arbitrage*. Because the proceeds are protected from currency fluctuations by being sold forward (covered), the process is known as *covered interest arbitrage*.

If foreign currency yields on a covered basis are higher, funds will flow out of the domestic currency and into the foreign currency, with four effects:

1. Demand for domestic financial assets will fall, raising domestic nominal rates, i_d.

2. Demand for spot foreign currency will increase, causing the direct spot rate, X_0, to increase.
3. Demand for foreign financial assets will fall, reducing foreign nominal rates, i_f.
4. Supply of forward foreign currency will increase as investment proceeds are sold, causing the direct forward rate, Y_0, to fall.

Because the forward market tends to be generally thinner, most of the effect of covered interest arbitrage operations tends to occur in the forward market.

If domestic currency yields are higher, funds will flow into domestic currrency financial assets as foreign investors engage in covered interest arbitrage.

The interest rate parity relationship is based on the assumption that fund flows from covered interest arbitrage will equalize the proceeds from investment in two currencies; that is,

$$\frac{1}{X_0} (1 + i_f) Y_0 = (1 + i_d)$$

Dividing both sides by $(1 + i_f)$ provides the interest rate parity relationship.

Forward exchange tends to trade at prices close to interest rate parity, although having a number of different financial instruments available in each currency tends to lead to slight deviations from interest rate parity when looking at specific transactions. Nonetheless, the interest rate parity relationship certainly is supported most strongly by the empirical evidence.

In our example, the nominal interest rate in Germany, i_G, is 10.25 percent, the nominal rate in the United States is 15.50 percent, and the current spot rate $X_0 = 0.50$. The forward rate is

$$Y_0 = (0.50) \frac{1.1550}{1.1025} = 0.5238$$

and $\Delta = .0476$. The forward mark should sell at a 4.76-percent premium. If it does, the covered yield of investing in German marks at a nominal 10.25 percent exactly equals the yield of investing in dollars at 15 percent.

The Forward Rate as Predictor of the Spot Rate

The international Fisher effect provides a relationship between current nominal interest rates and the anticipated period-end spot rate. Interest rate parity provides a relationship between current nominal interest rates and the current one-period forward rate. The two relationships can be combined to provide a relationship between the anticipated period-end spot rate and the current one-period forward rate:

$$\frac{Y_0}{X_0} = \frac{(1 + i_d)}{(1 + i_f)} = \frac{X_1}{X_0}$$

After simplification, we find that $X_1 = Y_0$; that is, the current one-period forward rate should be equal to the anticipated rate at the end of the period.

We found this relationship to hold in our example. From the international Fisher effect we found $X_1 = 0.5238$; from interest rate parity we found $Y_0 = 0.5238$.

Another way of expressing this relationship is to say that the premium or discount on forward exchange, Δ, equals the anticipated rate of appreciation of a currency over period, δ. Our example confirms that $\Delta = .0476 = \delta$.

One interpretation of this derived relationship is that the forward rate predicts what the spot rate will be at maturity of the forward contract. Indeed, some would consider the forward exchange rate as the best available forecast of what the spot rate will be because the forward rate is based on nominal interest rates, which in turn are based on inflation rates, which according to purchasing power parity, are the final determinants of the magnitude of exchange rate appreciation or depreciation.

The ultimate test of any method of forecasting exchange rates is whether it provides forecasts that consistently are better than the forward rate. The forward rate is a (virtually) free prediction of what spot rates would be. The purchase of exchange forecasts can be justified only if they outperform the forward rate.

Although we have developed this relationship between the forward rate and the anticipated spot rate by reference to two other relationships, it has a certain logic of its own. For example, if the forward rate were higher than the anticipated future spot rate ($Y_0 > X_1$), speculators could profit by selling the currency forward and buying it back at maturity at the anticipated lower spot rate. If $X_1 > Y_0$, speculators could buy the currency forward and then sell it at the anticipated higher spot price. Theoretically, the forward rate would be moved by these speculative operations until the incentive for speculation in the higher direction had been removed; that is, until $Y_0 = X_1$.

Review of Exchange and Interest Rate Relationships

The five relationships that we have now introduced are closely linked. Using them, one can begin with a very limited set of assumptions about inflation rates and the global real return on assets and determine a number of useful economic values. Let us review briefly how we use these relationships, using the limited information of our basic example. If we know that U.S. inflation, P_{US}, is anticipated to be 10 percent, that German inflation, P_G, is anticipated to be 5 percent, that the real world return on assets, r, is anticipated to be 5 percent, and that the current spot rate for the German mark is $X_0 = \$0.50$, we find from purchasing power parity that the anticipated spot rate is

$$X_1 = (0.50)\,\frac{1.10}{1.05} = 0.5238$$

From the Fisher effect we find that the nominal U.S. interest rate is

$$i_{US} = (1 + .10)(1 + .05) - 1 = 0.1550$$

and that the nominal German interest rate is

$$i_G = (1 + .05)(1 + .05) - 1 = 0.1025$$

From the interest rate parity relationship, we find that the forward rate is

$$Y_0 = (0.50)\,\frac{1.1550}{1.1025} = 0.5238$$

which is equal to the anticipated spot rate.

The currency forecaster uses these relationships in a slightly different fashion. Nominal interest rates and the current spot exchange rate are readily observable. From these values, we can find the forecast for the spot rate at the end of the forecasting period using the international Fisher effect.

Where forward markets are available, the forecaster may alternately use the forward rate to predict the period ending spot rate. Of course, if interest rate parity holds, this forecast should equal the one developed using the international Fisher effect.

The forecaster may also have access to activity of anticipated rates of inflation over the forecasting period. These can be incorporated into a currency forecast using the purchasing power parity relationship. If the Fisher effect holds, of course, the forecast can be generated by looking at nominal interest rates because these nominal rates would incorporate fully the anticipated inflation rates.

Free Markets, Market Imperfections, and the Equilibrium Relationships

The five relationships that we have studied have one major common idea: they all rely on market forces to produce an equilibrium relationship. Purchasing power parity, for example, assumes that exchange rates will adjust so that the consumer will have no incentive to prefer one market to another. The Fisher effect assumes that investors will invest in such a way as to provide equal real returns on their investments, regardless of the country of investment. Interest rate parity assumes that investors will move funds to equalize the guaranteed certain returns on financial investment among countries. The forward rate/ expected spot rate relationship requires that speculators buy or sell currency forward to the point that the incentive for further speculation is removed. Although we did not review the market assumption of the international Fisher effect, it also assumes action on the part of investors to equalize nominal returns after exchange adjustments between currencies.

The question of just how free transactors are to engage in the economic activities needed to secure that these equilibrium relationships hold has a different answer depending on the particular market and country under consideration. For example, speculation in the forward exchange market is generally viewed with distrust by most governments, particularly when it contributes to a weakening of the home currency. In the United States, banks have been reluctant to assist individual speculators in taking currency positions. Most corporations have adopted explicit or implicit policies against forward market speculation. Even banks, the forward market makers, generally have self- or government-imposed limits on their ability to take positions to reflect their expectations. Governments have been known to intervene in the forward market to move the forward rate to a particular premium or discount. These restrictions on activity may make it difficult for the market to reach the equilibrium position.

Of course, the spot market is also subject to government intervention, which may temporarily or permanently counter the economic activities that push exchange and interest rates to equilibrium. One might view the fixed exchange rate system as the ultimate attempt to resist market forces, the ultimate market imperfection.

These market imperfections—or more precisely, the legal, political, and cultural environments in which the market must function—are very important factors to review when attempting to develop an exchange rate forecast. The five equilibrium relationships provide a fundamentally sound picture of the basic economic forces at work in the exchange market, but they serve only as a point of departure for the development of an exchange rate forecast for use in financial decisions. Logically, there exists the possibility that a currency forecast that consistently outperforms the forward market can be developed; any forecast that successfully incorporates an analysis of how market imperfections affect these equilibrium relationships would prove useful. One unanswered question is whether the cost of generating or purchasing the forecast is less than its value to the purchaser. Empirical studies demonstrate that forecasting models have been developed that, if followed, lead to positive returns from currency speculation. These returns appear to be extraordinary, even when adjusted for risk.

CURRENCY FORECASTING
IN MULTINATIONAL CORPORATIONS

Most multinational corporations prepare currency forecasts for internal management. Generally, the responsibility for preparing currency forecasts is assigned to international finance personnel.

Corporations need exchange rate forecasts for a variety of reasons. The most important or at least most visible reason is that multinational companies need exchange rate forecasts to develop an operational plan and budget during the planning cycle. These forecasts are particularly sensitive because many companies use performance against plan as a major criterion in overall performance evaluation. An exchange forecast that differs significantly from the actual may make fair evaluation difficult and provide a highly visible potential embarrassment for the forecaster.

Short-term forecasts are also needed for the myriad of short-term financial decisions that must be made continuously. Any financial transaction that requires the movement of funds from one currency to another at a future point in time or that involves the comparison of alternate currencies for funding and investment can be analyzed only with some idea of what the exchange rate will do.

Long-term strategic planning, particularly for foreign investment decisions, requires explicit assumptions about where exchange rates will move in the long term. The directions of exchange rates, price levels, and interest rates are key factors that companies must consider in deciding which future markets should be served and where facilities should be located to serve them. How one structures the financing of new international ventures is heavily dependent on where exchange rates are expected to move.

The exchange rate forecasting effort of a particular company should be determined by the types of decisions for which they will be used. Those charged with designing the system must decide

1. which currencies to forecast
2. how far into the future forecasts should be made (forecast horizon)
3. how many intermediate points should be forecast (weekly, monthly, quarterly, annually)
4. how frequently regular revisions of the forecasts should be made
5. what form of forecast (expected direction of movement, point estimate of rate, interval estimate, probability distribution, or other) should be used
6. who should prepare forecasts and how
7. who should receive the forecasts.

The answers to these issues could easily differ according to the currency under consideration and the needs of the potential users.

Short-term forecasts (with a time horizon of one year or less) are by far more prevalent than long-term forecasts. A survey of corporate forecasting practices at 156 U.S. multinationals conducted by a team of researchers at the University of South Carolina found that 75 to 80 percent of the respondents prepared currency forecasts for major currencies but that no more than 11 percent forecast for more than one year. Most companies did forecast for a year, but some limited their forecasts only to the currencies most significant for their operations. Forecasts were revised at least every quarter at most firms.

The South Carolina survey found that, in general, companies attempt to generate a point estimate of the average or ending spot rate for the forecast period. Surprisingly, more than one-fourth of the companies generating forecasts attempted to forecast the likely direction of rate movement (up or down) only. Less frequently, companies generated a range of possible rates or attached probabilities to possible values. As might be expected, a number of companies generated more than one form of forecast, depending on the anticipated use of the information.

Many companies decide that forecasts purchased from external sources are an economical method of securing useful information about anticipated rate movements. Such forecasts range from video screens or hard copy, accessible, standardized forecasts to "listening-post" interviews with forecast service personnel who not only provide their own estimates of exchange movements but also respond to specific concerns of the client. Such forecasting services have proliferated in recent years, as the volatility of exchange markets and corporate concern with how these changes affect operating results have grown.

The Art of Forecasting Currencies

The economic relationships discussed in the first part of this chapter serve as a point of departure for the construction of any type of exchange rate forecasting system. How one approaches the task depends on whether one is attempting to forecast rates that are fixed or floating.

Forecasting parity changes in fixed exchange rates calls for the determination of the timing, direction of change, and amount of change in formal exchange rate parities. The direction of change is usually the easiest to identify. Persistently higher relative inflation rates, loss of reserves, an excess of imports over exports (a trade deficit), and a rapidly growing money supply mark the devaluation-prone currency. As the government continues to postpone indicated downward parity changes, speculation in the currency begins to lead to highly visible capital outflows and economic actions to stabilize the currency that are politically difficult. Because of the asymmetrical nature of the fixed-rate system, currency revaluations are more readily postponed, but the type of pressure against a fixed rate (whether for revaluation or devaluation) leaves no doubt that a parity change is inevitable.

The more difficult forecasting question for fixed rates is the identification of the timing of the parity change. Because these changes can be postponed through the use of reserves and because a general bias exists in favor of stable exchange rates, parity changes often are deferred well past the economically appropriate time. Yet it is important to identify the timing of a parity change. These changes tend to be large because countries are attempting to release several months or years of accumulated pressure against the currency. Parity changes up to 30 percent are not unusual.

Timing of parity change is essentially a political issue: It is a government decision, and parity changes are sometimes viewed negatively by the uninformed. Careful attention must be paid to the economic policy formulation process in the country under study, as well as the general political environment. Parity changes sometimes tend to cluster about power or personnel transitions in governments because the necessity for the change can be laid at the door of the departing government, and the new government can reap whatever economic benefits the parity change brings.

Although we currently live in an environment of managed floating, certain currencies still set the value of their currency in terms of the U.S. dollar. Changes in the dollar parity of these currencies still follow the general pattern of large-scale devaluation. In 1982, both Mexico and Chile instituted large-scale exchange rate changes resulting from attempts to maintain values of their currencies out of line with the economic realities of purchasing power parity. Although parity changes in the European Monetary System generally are less than 10 percent for each currency involved, the total effect of the changes over time has been substantial.

Types of Forecasting Models

The focus of forecasting parity changes rates is almost entirely on analysis of the political situation, but forecasting floating rates is a far more complex, controversial task. Roughly speaking, three general forecasting methodologies are utilized. In *econometric models*, more or less complicated models of national economies, or at least of certain economic relationships, are developed using statistical regression techniques. These models use as input various observable economic variables and produce as output forecasted exchange rate levels.

A second classification of models is known as *momentum models*. These models look at past values of exchange rates and attempt to discern a pattern that can be extended into the future. Various statistical time series methods or naive filter rules are used to develop these models.

The third class of models can be referred to as *subjective* or *common sense models*, depending on one's bias. Essentially, they involve the collection of a broad range of economic and political data and the interpretation of this data in terms of the direction, timing, and extent of exchange rate changes.

Evaluating Foreign Currency Forecasts

There are many ways of evaluating the relative merits of foreign exchange forecasting services. Companies might want to conduct such an evaluation in order to determine whether to purchase forecasts externally and which forecast service to select. In the discussion that follows, X_1 is the spot rate being forecast, Y_0 the forward rate at the time the forecast is being made, and F_1 the forecast of the spot rate.

The absolute error in a forecast is the absolute value of the difference between the spot rate and the forecast, $|X_1 - F_1|$. Typically, one would express this as an absolute percentage error:

$$\frac{|X_1 - F_1|}{X_1} \times 100$$

Over a period of time, one can track the percentage of errors of various forecast services and see which has the lowest average forecast errors.

In foreign exchange forecasting, however, forecast accuracy does not translate into correct managerial decisions. To see this, consider a situation in which a company is trying to forecast the German mark in order to determine whether or not to sell forward DM 100,000 in export proceeds in six months. The current spot rate for the mark is $0.50 and the forward rate is $0.53. One forecast service predicts the mark will be at $0.49, and a second predicts that the mark will be at $0.54. If the company believes the first forecast, it will sell the DM 100,000 forward, netting $53,000. If the company believes the second forecast, it will not sell the mark forward. Suppose that the actual spot rate in six months is $0.52. If the company sells the DM 100,000 in the spot market, it will realize $52,000.

The first service was off in its forecast by $0.03 ($0.52 − 0.49); the second service was off in its forecast by $0.02 ($0.54 − 0.52) and consequently gave the most accurate forecast. Nonetheless, the company would lose $1,000 by following the advice of the second service because the forecast indicated that the company should not sell forward when it actually should have. The second forecasting service gave a wrong *indication for action.*

Earlier in this chapter, we indicated that the free forward exchange rate would prove a major guide in evaluating the accuracy of a forecast service. The concepts introduced in this example can be used to show how the forward rate can provide such an evaluation.

An exchange rate forecast provides an indication to sell a currency forward if the forecast F_1 is lower than the forward rate Y_0; it provides an indication to buy if the forecast F_1 is higher than the forward rate.

A sale of foreign currency forward is profitable if the spot rate X_1 is lower than the forward rate Y_0; it is unprofitable if the spot rate X_1 is higher than the forward rate Y_0. Likewise, a forward purchase is profitable if the spot rate X_1 is higher than the forward rate Y_0; it is unprofitable if the spot rate is lower than Y_0.

Putting these together, we find that a forecast is profitable, or correct, if both the forecast and the spot are on the same side of the forward rate (X_1 and F_1 both less than Y_0, or X_1 and F_1 both greater than Y_0). A forecast is unprofitable, or incorrect, if the forecast and the spot are on opposite sides of the forward rate ($X_1 < Y_0 < F_1$ or $F_1 < Y_0 < X_1$).

Over time, competing forecast services can be evaluated on the percentage of times that they give correct forecasts, according to the criterion of correctness in the preceding paragraph. The forecast service that provides the higher percentage of correct forecasts is viewed as a better service. Of course, chance provides at least 50 percent correct forecasts over the very long run. Statistical tests can be performed to determine whether forecasting results are reasonably attributed to chance or to superior performance.

More sophisticated evaluation methods can be developed. A hypothetical portfolio of currencies could be managed against each competing forecast service to determine which service provides the highest return. Alternatively, the forecasts could be evaluated in terms of the corporate decisions that would have been changed through use of the forecasts.

All evaluations of forecast services are historical in nature and can evaluate only the historical track record of the service. Whether this track record can be extrapolated into the future is an unanswered question. Nonetheless, many corporations choose to purchase foreign exchange forecasts on the basis of their track record, cost, and other considerations. Should a financial decision prove incorrect because of an erroneous forecast, there is at least some bureaucratic protection if the forecast has been externally purchased from a highly reputable service.

SUMMARY

Governments may influence the exchange rate system by establishing fixed exchange rates, or they may allow the market to set exchange rates through the floating rate system. Foreign exchange controls are often found in developing countries, along with parallel markets that may more accurately reflect the currency's value.

Certain key economic relationships materially affect exchange rate movements. Although purchasing power parity may not hold empirically, it provides a useful point of departure for analysis of exchange rate changes. The Fisher effect points out that relative inflation rates and a global real rate of return determine nominal interest rates. The international Fisher effect shows that the spot rate is anticipated to move to levels indicated by the difference in nominal interest rates between currencies. Interest rate parity indicates that differences in these same nominal interest rates determine the forward rate premium or discount. According to these last two observations, the forward rate is a free estimate of the future spot rate.

Currency forecasts ought to be evaluated in terms of their relationship to the forward rate, and numerous methods of evaluating forecast performance exist. Multinational corporations have many uses for these exchange rate forecasts and usually rely on the international finance group to purchase or generate them.

DISCUSSION QUESTIONS

1. What is the difference between a fixed exchange rate system and a floating rate system? Trace the development of today's exchange rate system from the postwar Bretton Woods system.

2. What is the objective of exchange control? What types of restrictions can a country impose on transactions in its currency? How do these restrictions affect multinational corporations operating in the country? What is the black market?

3. Identify the five key relationships that determine spot and forward rates of exchange. What are the underlying market assumptions of each relationship? How is each relationship affected by the existence of market imperfections?

4. Why do multinational corporations need to forecast foreign exchange rates? What decisions must be made regarding the information to be supplied by a forecasting system? What types of forecasting models are currently used by multinationals?

5. An economist forecasts that U.S. price levels will increase by over 4 percent over the coming year and that French price levels will increase by 6 percent. The economist also estimates that the real (inflation-adjusted) return on assets in the United States and France will be the same, 2 percent per annum.

   a. According to the Fisher effect, what nominal interest rates should prevail in the United States and France?

   b. Suppose that the current direct exchange rate for the French franc is $0.20. According to purchasing power parity, what exchange rate would be expected to prevail in one year?

   c. According to the interest parity theory, what should be the forward premium or discount of the French franc against the U.S. dollar?

6. Interest rates on U.S. treasury bills are 7 percent per annum, and the forward premium of the Swiss franc against the dollar is 4 percent per annum. What is the maximum yield on Swiss treasury bills that the marketplace would show before U.S. investors would begin to shift funds to Switzerland on a covered basis to take advantage of arbitrage opportunities? Ignore transaction costs, but give an exact answer and not an approximation.

7. Nominal per annum rates in the United States are 10 percent and in Germany, 6 percent. What annual forward premium of the German mark against the dollar would provide exactly the same yield in each country for a U.S.-based investor? Give the exact answer, not an approximation.

8. A U.S. arbitrageur can invest dollars for one year at 8 percent and borrow them at 8¼ percent. She can invest in pounds sterling at 10¾ percent and borrow sterling at 11 percent. The current bid/offer rates for the spot pound are $1.4980/$1.5000, and the one-year forward bid/offer rates for the pound are $1.4600/1.4635. Is there any arbitrage opportunity for the arbitrageur in this market? Demonstrate, with numerical calculations, how the arbitrageur should proceed. (Hint: The arbitrageur could either borrow dollars and invest in sterling or borrow sterling and invest in dollars.)

SUGGESTED READINGS

1. Aliber, Robert Z. *Exchange Risk and Corporate International Finance*. New York, New York: Halsted Press, 1978. Chapters 1–7.

2. Giddy, Ian H. "An Integrated Theory of Exchange Rate Equilibrium," *Journal of Financial and Quantitative Analysis* (December 1976). Pp. 863–892.

3. Levich, Richard M. "Analyzing the Accuracy of Foreign Exchange Forecasting Services: Theory and Evidence." In Clas Wihlborg and Richard Levich (editors). *Exchange Risk and Exposure: Current Developments in International Financial Management*. Lexington, Massachusetts: Lexington Books, 1980. Chapter 5, pp. 99–128.

4. Levich, Richard M. *The International Monetary Market: An Assessment of Forecasting Techniques and Market Efficiency*. Greenwich, Connecticut: JAI Press, 1979.

5. Maldonado, Rita, and Anthony Saunders. "Foreign Exchange Restrictions and the Law of One Price," *Financial Management* (Spring 1983). Pp. 19–23.

6. Ungerer, Horst, Owen Evans, Thomas Meyer, and Philip Young. *The European Monetary System: Recent Developments*. Washington, D.C.: The International Monetary Fund, December 1986.

CHAPTER 4

▼

Currency Uncertainty and Financing Decisions

▲

INTRODUCTION

Unfavorable exchange rate changes, if they are large, can influence the operations and financing of a multinational corporation by making profitable markets unprofitable and by changing a firm's revenue and cost structure. In a similar manner, movements in exchange rates can render attractive sources of financing unattractive and can alter the value of foreign currency repayment streams to jeopardize the firm's financial stability. It is important to understand how exchange rate changes affect financing decisions and how anticipated changes can be incorporated into funding decisions.

Financial instruments generally are denominated in a single currency. For example, a borrower might sign a promissory note promising to pay $1 million in thirty days. When the promissory note matures, the holder has every right to expect to be paid $1 million; the holder does not expect to be paid an equivalent amount of Japanese yen, German marks, or Bhutanese ngultrums.

We say that a financial liability is *denominated* in a particular currency if, at maturity, discharge of the obligation is made by payment in that currency. The choice of the *currency of denomination* of a financial liability is one of the major decisions made by international finance executives. The availability of alternative choices is one of the distinguishing characteristics of international corporate finance as an academic discipline.

Almost all corporations have a *home*, or *reference*, *currency* — the currency in which they measure their results and pay dividends to their shareholders. When a corporation acquires a financial asset or issues a financial liability denominated in its reference currency, it can be certain of the reference currency value of that asset or liability at maturity. A German firm that borrows DM 1 million for six months knows that it will repay DM 1 million (plus interest, we hope) in six months. Its payment in its reference currency, the deutsche mark, is absolutely certain.

Suppose, however, that the German firm chose to borrow $400,000 for six months at a time when the exchange rate was DM 2.5 per dollar. As long as the exchange rate remained at DM 2.5 per dollar, the firm would pay back DM 1 million ($400,000 × DM 2.5/$). However, if the exchange rate changed, the German firm might pay back more or less than DM 1 million.

If the deutsche mark became less valuable in terms of the dollar, the German firm would have to pay more than DM 1 million to buy the dollars needed to pay back $400,000. For example, if the rate moved to DM 3.0 per dollar, the firm would need DM 1.2 million ($400,000 × DM 3/$). On the other hand, if the mark became more valuable in terms of the dollar, the German firm would pay less than DM 1 million to buy the dollars to pay back the debt. If the rate moved to DM 2.2 per dollar, the firm would need only DM 880,000 ($400,000 × DM 2.2/$). The German firm is exposed to currency, or exchange, risk on this transaction because the currency of denomination of the debt (the U.S. dollar) is not the same as the reference currency (the German mark) of the German firm.

Multinational corporations typically hold financial assets and issue financial liabilities denominated in currencies other than their reference currency, which exposes them to one kind of exchange risk. Currency changes have other significant effects on the multinational firm, and a comprehensive discussion of exchange risk management is deferred to Chapter 5. The remainder of this chapter presents extended examples that explore how exchange risk arises from a difference between the currency of denomination of a financial instrument and the reference currency of its holder or issuer.

A MOTIVATING EXAMPLE

To see more clearly the distinction between the reference currency and the currency of denomination, consider the situation of Agfolk Industries, a diversified manufacturer that needs a loan of $10 million to fund operations over the coming year. Normally, Agfolk management would approach its friendly U.S. bank and negotiate a one-year loan at the bank's current lending rate for firms like Agfolk, which is now 13 percent per annum. To simplify the analysis, assume that the entire $10 million would be made available to Agfolk at the beginning of the year and that the principal and interest would be paid at the end of the year.

Before Agfolk decides to borrow from its U.S. bank, a German bank offers to lend the firm DM 25 million at 8-percent interest. Because one deutsche mark currently sells for $0.40 on the foreign exchange market, Agfolk could borrow the marks, convert them into dollars, and have the $10 million required. At the end of the year, Agfolk could use the dollars earmarked for repayment of the debt and purchase the DM 25 million needed to repay the principal and the DM 2 million needed to pay the interest. This example problem will be carried out throughout the rest of this chapter to demonstrate the issues discussed.

THE CURRENCY OF DENOMINATION DECISION

Which alternative funding proposal should Agfolk select? The decision that Agfolk faces in this simplified problem recurs continuously in international finance. Companies are constantly required to determine which currency to use to meet specific funds needs. We refer to this decision problem as the *currency of denomination decision* because by choosing whether to fund in marks or dollars Agfolk is deciding in which currency its debt will be denominated.

At 8 percent, the mark loan carries a lower nominal interest rate than the 13 percent carried by the dollar loan. If the mark were guaranteed to remain worth $0.40, no further analysis would be needed because 8-percent money is always preferred to 13-percent money. At an exchange rate of $0.40, Agfolk would require $10.8 million to buy the DM 27 million needed to discharge its obligation. With the dollar loan, it would pay $11.3 million. The net cost of the loan, the amount repaid less the amount borrowed, would be only $800,000 for the mark loan, compared to $1.3 million for the dollar loan.

What If the Exchange Rate Changes?

The price of the mark, however, is not guaranteed to remain at $0.40. The mark might depreciate, or become less valuable, in terms of the dollar. In such a case, it would require fewer dollars to buy DM 27 million. If the mark appreciates, or becomes more valuable, more dollars would be required.

Exhibit 4-1 gives the pertinent information regarding the loan alternatives at four possible levels of exchange rate that might prevail on the date of repayment: $0.35, $0.40, $0.45, and $0.50. Other intermediate rates are quite possible, of course, but these four rates are chosen to illustrate the general tendencies. The first column in Exhibit 4-1 shows the four possible exchange rates. The second column indicates the amount to be repaid in marks; the constant value of DM 27 million illustrates the important point that changes in exchange rate do not affect the foreign currency value of a foreign currency obligation. If Agfolk borrows marks, it must repay marks, regardless of rate movements.

What changes with the exchange rate, as the third column clearly indicates, is the amount of dollars that Agfolk requires to discharge its mark obligation. At the favorable rate of $0.35, Agfolk needs to spend only $9.45 million to purchase the DM 27 million. As the rate increases, though, Agfolk requires more and more dollars to repay its mark obligation; at the rate of $0.45, Agfolk must pay $12.15 million, and at $0.50, $13.5 million.

Thus, Exhibit 4-1 clearly shows that a *depreciation*, or decrease in relative value of a foreign currency, benefits the borrower of that currency; an *appreciation*, or increase in relative value, of the foreign currency penalizes the borrower of that currency.

The fifth column of Exhibit 4-1 calculates the net cost (total amount repaid less the amount borrowed) of the mark loan at the various exchange rate levels. As one would expect, the net cost increases as the exchange rate appreciates; on the other hand, if the mark depreciates

EXHIBIT 4-1 Cost of the DM Loan

(1) Exchange Rate ($/DM)	(2) Repayment Amount (DM millions)	(3) = (1) × (2) Repayment Amount ($ millions)	(4) Amount Borrowed ($ millions)	(5) = (3) − (4) Net Cost ($ millions)
$0.35	DM 27.0	$ 9.45	$10.00	$ −0.55
0.40	27.0	10.80	10.00	0.80
0.45	27.0	12.15	10.00	2.15
0.50	27.0	13.50	10.00	3.50

to $0.35, Agfolk makes a profit of $550,000 from the loan. Borrowing a foreign currency that is anticipated to depreciate is one way of speculating in that currency.

Another Way to Calculate Loan Cost

The net cost of a foreign currency loan cannot be found by multiplying the nominal mark interest cost by the level of the exchange rate. Exhibit 4-2 provides an alternate method of calculating the net cost that illustrates its various components. Column 1 shows the various period-ending exchange rate levels under consideration; Column 2 indicates dollars needed to pay back the DM 2 million in interest at each exchange rate level. The interest payment alone will never exceed $1 million.

The real gain or loss on the foreign currency loan arises because Agfolk must repay the DM 25 million in principal. One method of calculating the loss on the principal is to determine the dollars needed to repay the principal at the ending exchange rate and then subtract the $10 million that the principal was worth originally. For example, if the rate appreciates to $0.50, it would require $12.5 million to repay the principal. A loss of $2.5 million has been incurred.

It is even more useful to develop yet another method of calculation. In the fourth column in Exhibit 4-2, we determine the amount by which the mark has appreciated over the period. The appreciation is simply the difference between the period ending exchange rate and the rate of the beginning of the period, $0.40. If the mark goes to $0.50, the appreciation is $0.10, for example.

The loss arising from a change in value of the principal is found by multiplying the deutsche mark value of the principal by the mark's appreciation, as shown in column five. For example, if the mark appreciates by $0.10 to $0.50, the loss on the principal is

$$(DM\ 25,000,000)(\$0.10) = \$2,500,000$$

On the other hand, if the mark moves to $0.35, the loss is $-\$1.25$ million. Of course, a negative loss means a gain, and this gain arises because the mark is cheaper on repayment date.

The net cost of the mark loan, the sixth column in Exhibit 4-2, is found by adding the dollar equivalent of the interest (the second column) with the loss on the principal (the fifth column). If the mark

EXHIBIT 4-2 Alternate Calculation Cost of the DM Loan

(1) Exchange Rate ($/DM)	(2) Interest Payment ($ millions)	(3) Principal Repayment (DM millions)	(4) = (1) − 0.40 Appreciation of DM ($/DM)	(5) = (3) × (4) Exchange Loss on Principal ($ millions)	(6) = (2) + (5) Net Cost ($ millions)
$0.35	$0.70	DM 25.0	−0.05	$−1.25	$−0.55
0.40	0.80	25.0	0.00	0.00	0.80
0.45	0.90	25.0	0.05	1.25	2.15
0.50	1.00	25.0	0.10	2.50	3.50

appreciates to $0.50, the net cost of the loan is $3.5 million — $1.0 million in interest and a loss of $2.5 million on the principal. On the other hand, as we have seen, when the mark depreciates to $0.35, Agfolk makes a profit of $550,000 on the loan transaction, as the interest cost of $700,000 is more than offset by the $1.25 million reduction in the amount needed to repay the principal.

To summarize, exchange rate changes materially affect the net cost of a foreign currency loan. Currency appreciation or depreciation causes only a slight change in the dollar value of the interest that must be paid. Most of the change in cost arises because of the change in the value of the principal.

Analyzing the Mark and Dollar Loans

If the management of Agfolk knew the exchange rate that would prevail at the date one year in the future when the loan would be paid off, the decision as to which currency to borrow could be made by reference to Exhibit 4-2. If the rate appreciated to $0.50, the dollar would be preferred because this cost of $1.3 million would be significantly lower than the $3.5 million cost of the mark loan. On the other hand, if the mark depreciated to $0.35, Agfolk would prefer the mark loan because it would generate a profit of $550,000 rather than an interest cost of $1.3 million. The last column of Exhibit 4-2 shows the cost advantage (or savings) of the mark loan over the dollar loan.

But Agfolk management has no certain knowledge of where the exchange rate is headed. There is some chance, in its view, that the mark will remain at its present level, or even depreciate, but it feels that there also is a good chance it will appreciate to $0.45 or possibly even $0.50. Consultation with several foreign exchange forecasting services confuses the matter even further because some predict a further depreciation of the mark and others believe that the mark will rise in value.

After a thorough analysis of the information available to it, Agfolk management decides that it is willing to quantify its uncertainty regarding the mark as follows: There is a 20-percent chance (or .2 probability) that the mark will depreciate to $0.35; a 30-percent chance (.3 probability) that it will remain at $0.40; a 40-percent chance (.4 probability) that it will appreciate to $0.45; and only a 10-percent chance that it will go to $0.50.

Agfolk has quantified the uncertainty of the exchange rate in the form of a probability distribution function, a function that assigns to each possible value of the exchange rate the probability that the given value will occur. In a realistic situation, of course, there are many possible values of the exchange rate (as we saw in Chapter 2, rates in many currencies are normally quoted to four decimal places), and the probability of any particular value is quite small; in such a situation a continuous probability model is more appropriate. Using a simple probability distribution function, however, simplifies the problem and improves understanding of the essentials.

A number of methods can be employed to analyze decisions under uncertainty. An approach that has great intuitive appeal is the comparison of mathematical expectation of the consequences of each decision. In Agfolk's problem, the consequences of management's decision are measured in terms of the cost of the alternative selected.

We first calculate the expected cost of the decision to borrow marks. Exhibit 4-3 shows each possible ending exchange rate, the associated probability, and the net cost of the mark loan and dollar loan for each exchange rate. The expected net cost of the mark loan is found by multiplying the net cost at each exchange rate value by the associated probability. The expected cost (in millions) of the mark loan is

$$(.2)(\$-0.55) + (.3)(\$0.08) + (.4)(\$2.15) + (.1)(\$3.50) = \$1.34$$

EXHIBIT 4-3 Determining the Expected Cost of Each Loan

(1)	(2)	(3)	(4)
Exchange Rate ($/DM)	Probability	Cost of DM Loan ($ millions)	Cost of Dollar Loan ($ millions)
$0.35	.20	$-0.55	$1.30
0.40	.30	0.80	1.30
0.45	.40	2.15	1.30
0.50	.10	3.50	1.30

NOTES: Expected exchange rate: $(\overline{X}_1) = (0.35)(.20) + (0.40)(.30) + (0.45)(.40) + (0.50)(.10) = 0.42$.

Expected cost of DM loan: $(0.20)(\$-0.55) + (0.30)(\$0.80) + (0.40)(\$2.15) + (0.10)(\$3.50) = \$1.34$.

Expected cost of $ loan: $(0.20)(\$1.30) + (0.30)(\$1.30) + (0.40)(\$1.30) + (0.10)(\$1.30) = \$1.30$.

The expected cost of the dollar loan is $1.3 million, which is slightly lower than the cost of the mark loan and less expensive on an expected cost basis. If expected cost is the decision criteria that Agfolk's management believes the company should use in evaluating financing decisions, the appropriate decision is to fund the $10 million requirement with a dollar loan; that is, Agfolk should denominate its loan in dollars.

Consideration of the uncertainty in exchange rates led to a different decision than would have been reached if Agfolk's management had looked only at the nominal interest rates of 8 percent for marks and 13 percent for dollars. It is an important axiom of international financial management that uncertainty regarding the exchange rate must be included in the analysis of any financing decision; to ignore it is to risk extremely unfavorable consequences from possibly anticipated exchange rate changes.

A Simpler Method for Analyzing the Loans

We can simplify the process of selecting the currency with the lowest expected net cost by first calculating the expected exchange rate and then evaluating the two funding alternatives at that rate. The expected exchange rate is

$$(.2)(\$0.25) + (.3)(\$0.40) + (.4)(\$0.45) + (.1)(\$0.50) = \$0.42$$

The net cost of a mark loan when the ending exchange rate is $0.42 is DM $2,000,000 \times 0.42 = \$840,000$ in interest and DM $25,000,000 \times \$0.02 = \$500,000$ in loss on the principal, for a total of $1.34 million. The $0.02 represents the difference between the expected exchange rate $0.42 and the initial rate of $0.40 and is multiplied by the mark value of the principal to determine the loss on the principal. Of course, the cost of the dollar loan at any exchange rate is $1.3 million. As was determined previously, the dollar loan has a lower expected cost.

A Formula Approach to Analysis

We can gain further insights into the relationship between the exchange rate and the cost of financing by writing formulas that show the cost of each financing alternative as a function of the ending exchange, which we will designate by the symbol X_1. The cost of the mark loan, in millions, is

$$C_{DM} = (2.0)X_1 + (25.0)(X_1 - 0.40) = 27.0X_1 - 10.0$$

The first half of the formula represents the dollar value of the mark interest paid on the loan, and the second half represents the loss on the principal, found by multiplying the mark value of the principal by the appreciation $(X_1 - 0.40)$. The cost of the dollar loan is constant; in millions,

$$C_\$ = 1.3$$

Although these formulas are labeled C_{DM} and $C_\$$, it is important to remember that the values on the right-hand side are measured in dollars, the reference currency. It is the cost of the mark loan measured in dollars that is needed for comparison with the cost of the dollar loan measured in dollars. The cost of the mark loan measured in marks is always DM 2 million, regardless of the exchange rate.

The expected cost of the mark loan $\overline{C}_{DM}$ can be found by substituting the expected exchange rate $X_1 = \$0.42$ in the formula

$$\overline{C}_{DM} = (27.0)(0.42) - 10.0 = 1.34$$

The expected cost of the dollar loan is

$$\overline{C}_\$ = 1.3$$

Because $\overline{C}_\$$ is less than $\overline{C}_{DM}$, the dollar loan has the lower expected cost and is preferred by Agfolk's management.

Breakeven Analysis

The analysis so far has been based on Agfolk's quantification of the uncertainty in the ending exchange rate, X_1. A type of breakeven analysis may be used to reduce the dependence on the assignment of specific probabilities. The approach is to find the exchange rate, X_b, at which the two financing alternatives have the same cost. In other words, at what *breakeven exchange rate*, X_b, does $C_{DM} = C_\$$?

Equating the formulas developed for C_{DM} and $C_\$$, we find

$$27.0\, X_b - 10.0 = 1.3$$
$$X_b = 11.3 \div 27.0 = 0.4185$$

If the period ending exchange rate X_1 is less than 0.4185, the mark loan would be cheaper; if X_1 is greater than 0.4185, the dollar would be preferred.

Exhibit 4-4 provides a graphical interpretation of the approach. The horizontal axis measures the exchange rate X_1, and the vertical axis

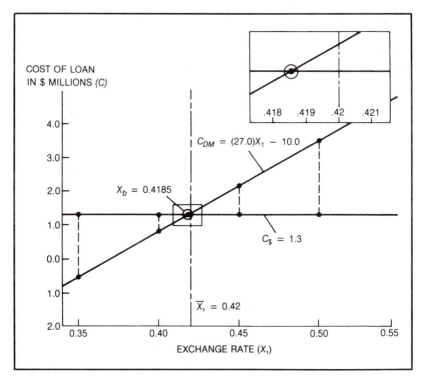

EXHIBIT 4-4 Breakeven Exchange Rate Analysis

measures the cost of the funding alternatives, in millions. The line labeled C_{DM} graphs the function $C_{DM} = 27.0X_1 - 10.0$; the line labeled $C_\$$ graphs the function $C_\$ = 1.3$.

The two lines intersect when $X_1 = X_b = 0.4185$, the breakeven exchange rate. As the graph clearly shows, C_{DM} is higher when $X_1 > 0.4185$ and C_{DM} is lower when $X_1 < 0.4185$.

A simple comparison between the breakeven exchange rate, $X_b = 0.4185$, and the expected exchange rate at the end of the period, $\overline{X}_1 = 0.42$, is the appropriate methodology for using the information generated by calculating the breakeven exchange rate. Because $\overline{X}_1 = 0.42$ is greater than $0.4185 = X_b$, the expected cost of dollar financing is cheaper, and the dollar loan should be chosen.

It is not necessary for management to calculate the expected ending exchange rate X_1 to use the breakeven rate methodology. All that is required is the assessment that $\overline{X}_1 \gtrless 0.4185 = X_b$. Regardless of the actual value of X_1, as long as it exceeds the breakeven rate, dollar financing is preferred. It is important that management assess the expected exchange rate $\overline{X}_1$; it is not appropriate to simply state that it is more likely that X_1 is greater than X_b. In our example, X_1 is just as likely to be below \$0.4185 as it is to be above \$0.4185. The probability that $X_1 = 0.35$ or 0.40 is $0.2 + 0.3 = 0.5$. The probability that $X_1 = 0.45$ or 0.50 is $0.4 + 0.1 = 0.5$. This observation might lead one to conclude that Agfolk would be indifferent as to which funding alternative it selects because it has a .5 probability of being right regardless of the currency selected. However, it is most important to note that the appropriate decision criterion is not the probability of making the correct decision but the economic consequences of the decision as incorporated in the expected net cost of the borrowing.

Including Standard Deviation in the Analysis

Thus far in the analysis, we have looked at only the expected net cost of borrowing and have not taken into account the potential aversion to risk of Agfolk's management. As can be seen by inspection of the C_{DM} and $C_\$$ formulas, it is uncertainty in the exchange rate that causes the variability in the cost of borrowing in marks. Because the exchange rate does not affect the cost of borrowing in dollars, there is no uncertainty (and hence no variability) arising from the decision to borrow dollars. In the example as given, dollar borrowing has both a lower expected cost and lower variability and would be selected by Agfolk's management as long as it was averse to risk.

This conclusion can be confirmed by calculating an explicit measure of variability for each borrowing strategy. The first step is to calculate the standard deviation of the period ending exchange rate, $\sigma(X_1)$; this calculation is done in Exhibit 4-5. We then can proceed to the calculation of the standard deviation of the cost of the two borrowing strategies. The standard deviation of the dollar strategy is $\sigma(C_\$) = 0$. The standard deviation of the mark borrowing strategy is

$$\sigma(C_{DM}) = \sigma(27.0\, X_1 - 10.0) = 27.0\,\sigma(X_1) = (27.0)(0.0458) = \$1{,}237{,}300$$

The complete analysis thus shows that

$$\overline{C}_\$ < \overline{C}_{DM}$$

EXHIBIT 4-5   Calculation of the Variance of the Exchange Rate (X_1)

(1)	(2)	(3) = (1) − (0.42)	(4) = (3)²	(5) = (2) × (4)
X_1	$P(X_1)$	$X_1 - \overline{X}_1$	$(X_1 - \overline{X}_1)^2$	$P(X_1)(X_1 - \overline{X}_1)^2$
0.35	0.2	−0.07	0.0049	0.00098
0.40	0.3	−0.02	0.0004	0.00012
0.45	0.4	0.03	0.0009	0.00036
0.50	0.1	0.08	0.0064	0.00064
				$\sigma^2(X_1) = 0.00210$
				$\sigma(X_1) = 0.045826$

NOTES: $\sigma(C_{DM}) = 27.0\sigma(X_1) = (27.0)(0.045826) = \$1{,}237{,}300.$
$\sigma(C_\$) = 0.0\ \sigma\ (X_1) = (0.0)(0.045826) = \$0{,}000{,}000.$

The expected cost of dollar borrowing is lower than the expected cost of the mark borrowing. Further,

$$\sigma(C_\$) < \sigma\ (C_{DM})$$

The standard deviation of the dollar loan is lower than the standard deviation of the German mark loan. Because it has both a lower cost and a lower standard deviation, the dollar loan is clearly preferable for any risk-averse firm.

Borrowing and Foreign Currency Cash Flows

Thus far, the analysis seems to indicate that borrowing marks would be an inappropriate strategy for Agfolk to pursue. However, under certain circumstances, Agfolk might want to borrow marks, even with the twin disadvantages of higher expected cost and greater variability of cost. An exploration of these circumstances will allow a review of another major issue in the analysis of the currency of denomination problems.

Suppose that on the same date on which Agfolk is to repay its loan, it will be receiving a payment of DM 30 million from an export sale. Because the buyer of the goods was a German company, Agfolk had denominated its sales contract in deutsche marks.

The following analysis requires a switch in perspective. Instead of examining the cost of the financing in isolation, this analysis examines how the financing affects Agfolk's total cash position. Agfolk will receive DM 30 million at the end of the period; the value of this payment in dollars, Agfolk's reference currency, depends on the exchange rate that prevails at the end of the period. If the rate remains the same as it is at the beginning of the period (X_1 = $0.40), Agfolk will receive $12 million when it sells its German marks in the foreign exchange market. If X_1 = 0.50, Agfolk will receive $15 million. In general, the value (in millions) of the payment is $30.0(X_1)$. A U.S. company like Agfolk that has a financial asset or future receipt denominated in a foreign currency clearly benefits (in terms of its reference currency, the dollar) when that currency appreciates against the dollar and just as obviously suffers a loss when the currency depreciates.

The value of Agfolk's position at the end of the period is

$$V_\$ = 30.0(X_1) - 1.3$$

if the dollar loan is selected. The first term represents the dollar value of the DM 30 million inflow, and the second is net cost of the dollar loan.

The value if the mark loan is selected is

$$V_{DM} = 30.0(X_1) - [27.0(X_1) - 10.0] = 3.0(X_1) + 10.0$$

Again, $30.0(X_1)$ is the value of the DM 30 million inflow, and the second term $[27.0(X_1) - 10.0]$ represents the net cost of the mark borrowing, C_{DM}.

The Impact of Cash Flows on Expected Value Analysis

The existence of the large mark denominated cash inflow does not change the fact that the dollar loan is desirable on an expected value basis. The expected value of the DM 30 million is $(30)(0.42)$, or $12.60 million. The expected net cost of the mark loan remains $1.34 million and $\overline{V}_{DM}$ is $12.60 - $1.34 = $11.26 million. The same result can be developed by substituting X_1 = $0.42 in the formula for V_{DM}:

$$\overline{V}_{DM} = 3.0(0.42) + 10.0 = \$11.26$$

On the other hand,

$$\overline{V}_\$ = 30.0(0.42) - 1.3 = \$11.3$$

Because the expected position value of the dollar loan $\overline{V}_\$ = \$11.3$ million is greater than the expected position value of the mark loan $\overline{V}_{DM} = \$11.26$ million, the dollar loan is preferred.

Addition of the large mark cash inflow does not change the relative desirability of the two loan packages when evaluated on an expected value basis; such a result should be intuitively obvious because the expected value of the mark payment measured in dollars is the same whether a mark or dollar loan is selected.

The Impact of Cash Flows on Mean-Variance Analysis

What does change is the relative ranking of each loan's desirability from the standpoint of its standard deviation. We find that

$$\sigma(V_{DM}) = (3.0)(0.04586) = \$137{,}500$$

and that

$$\sigma(V_{\$}) = (30.0)(0.04586) = \$1{,}374{,}800$$

The standard deviation is ten times greater if the dollar is borrowed compared to borrowing the mark. Exhibit 4-6 allows a comparison of the expected value and standard deviation of the cash flows resulting from the two funding options.

The choice of funding currency is now much more difficult. The dollar loan has the higher expected value, but it also has ten times the standard deviation of the mark loan. Although a complete assessment of the attitude toward risk of Agfolk's management would be necessary before a conclusive statement could be made, most risk-averse individuals would accept a 0.3-percent (.040 ÷ 11.3) reduction in expected cash flow for a 90-percent (1.2373 ÷ 1.3748) reduction in standard deviation. Put another way, by selecting the mark loan and accepting a reduction in expected cash flow of \$40,000, Agfolk can eliminate 90 percent of the risk to which it is exposed from currency fluctuations.

EXHIBIT 4-6 Comparison of Mark and Dollar Loan

	Mark Loan	*Dollar Loan*
Expected value	$\overline{V}_{DM} = \$11.26$	$\overline{V}_{\$} = \$11.30$
Standard deviation	$\sigma(V_{DM}) = \$\ 0.1375$	$\sigma(V_{\$}) = \$\ 1.3748$
Expected value -2 (standard deviation)	$\$10.985$	$\$\ 8.55$
Expected value $+2$ (standard deviation)	$\$11.535$	$\$14.05$

Agfolk management may very well select the mark loan to secure this reduction in risk.

The existence of the large mark cash flow on the repayment date may well change the decision that Agfolk makes with regard to its choice of a currency in which to denominate its debt. If the mark appreciates, the loss that Agfolk would have from its mark borrowings is more than offset by the gain that it would have because its anticipated mark cash inflow is worth more in dollar terms. On the other hand, should the mark depreciate, the gain that Agfolk derives from the fact that it needs fewer dollars to buy the marks to pay off its debt is more than offset by the loss that Agfolk has because its mark receipt is worth less in dollars. The risk to the dollar value of the mark receipt balances the risk to the dollar value of the mark payment arising from the debt. If Agfolk borrows dollars, there is no mark payment to balance out the risk to the mark receipt.

Thus, before Agfolk can make a complete analysis of the currency of denomination decision for borrowing, management must identify whether or not there are other cash inflows denominated in the currencies that are under consideration. Unless Agfolk makes its financial decisions on an expected value basis, it must pay attention to the effect of its borrowing operations on the variability of its cash flows caused by exchange rate changes. Borrowing a foreign currency may increase that variability, or if it offsets anticipated receipts in the currency, it may reduce that variability.

In practice, the financial executive of a multinational corporation faces a multitude of planned cash inflows and outflows in a variety of currencies. Selection of the currency in which to borrow often is made to reduce or eliminate the risk to the value of these flows arising from potential exchange rate changes. The multinational corporation's debt strategy is a powerful tool for achieving precisely that balance of risk and return from exchange rate changes that management desires.

Exchange risk management is the task of achieving the managerially desired balance between risk and expected return from potential exchange rate changes. It is arguably the most complicated and most misunderstood task of international financial management. Chapter 5 will discuss both the exchange risk and techniques for its management in more detail. However, we have already discovered one of the principal methods of controlling exchange risk — the balancing of anticipated foreign currency cash inflows with anticipated cash outflows in the same currency. From a balance sheet standpoint, one acquires a foreign currency asset to offset a foreign currency liability or vice versa.

Applying Forward Contracts to Financing Decisions

In the rather complete analysis of the Agfolk problem, one important factor has not yet been considered. Agfolk has the opportunity to remove the uncertainty in the value of the marks that it must repay by entering into a forward exchange, or futures, contract in the mark.

The opportunity to use forward exchange markets to cover future payments in a foreign currency can have a major effect on the funding decisions of the multinational firm. Let us reconsider the decision facing Agfolk in the light of the availability of forward exchange contracts to cover the repayment obligation of the mark borrowing opportunity.

We recall that if Agfolk borrows marks to meet its $10-million funds requirement, it would have a repayment obligation of DM 25 million in principal and DM 2 million in interest, or a total of DM 27 million. It is the uncertainty of the dollar value of the DM 27 million repayment obligation, arising from the uncertainty of the period ending exchange rate, that causes the mark loan to have a significant exchange risk.

Agfolk can eliminate this uncertainty completely with a forward purchase to cover the DM 27 million total repayment obligation, made at the same time the loan is taken out. Suppose that the forward rate for marks for delivery in one year is $0.41; Agfolk buys DM 27 million forward at this rate. When the loan matures, Agfolk is guaranteed to be able to buy the DM 27 million for $11.07 million (DM 27,000,000 × $0.41).

Agfolk has done more than just make the dollar value of the amount repaid certain. It also has fixed the net cost in dollars of the mark loan at $1.07 million, the difference between the amount repaid ($11.07 million) and the amount borrowed ($10.0 million). This net cost amount can be compared directly with the net cost of dollar borrowing, $1.30 million. Agfolk finds that the cost of borrowing marks at 8 percent and buying the repayment obligation forward is cheaper than borrowing dollars at 13 percent.

It is most important to note that the net borrowing cost of $1.07 million obtained by borrowing marks and buying forward is fixed and certain regardless of what happens to the mark per dollar exchange rate. If the mark goes to $0.45, $0.50, or even $0.60 on repayment date, Agfolk still pays only $0.41 for the marks it needs. Of course, if the mark depreciates to $0.35 or $0.30, Agfolk still must pay $0.41 for the marks required. Regardless of where the mark goes, Agfolk exchanges $11.07 million for the DM 27 million that it needs. The exposure of

Agfolk to the uncertainties of exchange rate movements before the maturity date of its loan has been totally eliminated by the forward covering purchase.

To summarize, the act of entering into a forward contract to eliminate the effect of future exchange rate changes on the dollar value of a future foreign currency receipt or payment is called *covering*. Agfolk has covered its payment of DM 27 million one year from now by buying DM 27 million forward for one year. A payment in a foreign currency is covered completely by entering into a forward purchase contract in the exact amount of the foreign currency payment that matures on the same date that the payment is to be made. A future receipt in a foreign currency is covered completely by entering into a forward sales contract for the exact amount maturing on the date that the receipt is due.

A company that has covered its exposure to the effects of exchange rate changes by a forward exchange contract (or, stated more simply, has taken *forward cover*) has acted to eliminate the effect of exchange rate movements on the dollar value of future payments or receipts. Covering is one of the two major uses to which forward exchange contracts are put.

SPECULATION IN FORWARD EXCHANGE

The second major use of forward contracts is for speculation. Although covering may be considered to be the elimination of the exchange risk to reduce uncertainty and possible loss, *speculation* in forward exchange involves the deliberate creation of additional exposure to exchange rate movements in pursuit of a gain.

Speculating on Foreign Currency Appreciation

We can illustrate the speculative use of forward contracts by an example. Because Agfolk's management is very conservative and would not dream of speculating in foreign exchange, we shall consider a more flamboyantly managed outfit, Single C Enterprises. Single C is a purely domestic company, with no export sales or import purchases, only dollar financing, and, in general, no exposure to exchange risk from any of its operations whatsoever. Single C's management, for whatever reason, anticipates that the mark will increase from its current value of

$0.40 to a level of $0.50 in one year. Knowing that the present one-year forward rate of the mark is $0.41, Single C management contrives to buy DM 10 million one year forward at this forward rate. When the forward contract matures in one year, Single C will be obligated to buy DM 10 million at $0.41.

If the mark is worth $0.50 when the forward contract is completed, as Single C management anticipates, the company can sell for $0.50 the marks it just purchased at $0.41, for a $0.09 gain on each mark bought forward. The total profit on Single C's speculative transaction would be $900,000. The speculative profit from a forward contract is equal to

(Amount purchased)(Exchange rate at maturity − Forward rate)
= (DM 10,000,000)($0.50 − $0.41) = $900,000

If, of course, the exchange rate for the mark at maturity is $0.35, Single C would receive

(DM 10,000,000)($0.35 − $0.41) = −$600,000

In other words, Single C would have a speculative loss of $600,000.

Single C purchased exchange forward because its management was speculating that the mark would appreciate from its initial rate of $0.40 to a rate above the $0.41 forward rate before the maturity date of the contract. If the mark did appreciate beyond $0.41, Single C would have a gain from its speculation; if it appreciated by less than $0.01, or depreciated, Single C would have a loss.

Speculating on a Currency Depreciation

Suppose that Single C's management had anticipated that the mark would depreciate, rather than appreciate. A forward purchase of marks would not have been appropriate. However, Single C could still have profited from its assessment that the mark would depreciate by selling the mark forward.

Suppose that Single C sells DM 10 million forward at $0.41 and the mark does indeed depreciate to $0.35. At the maturity date of the forward contract, Single C must deliver DM 10 million and will receive $0.41 per mark; to obtain the marks needed for delivery, Single C buys them for $0.35 each. Single C makes a profit of $0.41 − $0.35 = $0.06 on each mark sold forward, or $600,000 on the total contract. Of course, if the mark appreciates to, say, $0.45, Single C must pay $0.45 for marks that it has contracted to sell at $0.41, and Single C loses $0.04 per mark, or $400,000 in all.

The speculative profit on a forward sales contract can be calculated using the same formula as that for the speculative profit on forward purchases, with sales being treated as negative purchases. For example, if Single C sells DM 10 million forward at $0.41 and the exchange rate at maturity is $0.35, the profit from speculation is

$$(-DM \ 10,000,000)(\$0.35 \ - \ 0.41) \ = \ (-DM \ 10,000,000)(-\$0.06)$$
$$= \ \$600,000$$

If, on the other hand, the mark moves to $0.45, Single C realizes

$$(-DM \ 10,000,000)(\$0.45 \ - \ 0.41) \ = \ (-DM \ 10,000,000)(\$0.04)$$
$$= \ -\$400,000$$

Single C loses $400,000 on its speculation.

For further analysis, it will be convenient to develop a symbolic representation of the gain or loss from speculation in forward exchange. Let P represent speculative purchase of forward exchange, Y represent the forward exchange rate, and X_1, as before, represent the exchange rate prevailing at the end of the period, when the forward contract matures. Then the speculative gain is simply $P(X_1 - Y)$. For example, if Single C sells DM 10 million ($P = -10,000,000$) forward at $0.41 ($Y = 0.41$) and the mark moves to $0.35 ($X_1 = 0.35$), the speculative gain is

$$(-DM \ 10,000,000)(\$0.35 - 0.41) = \$600,000$$

as shown before.

Realistically, the opportunity for a company such as Single C to speculate using forward exchange contracts with a bank is limited because most U.S. banks discourage such blatant speculation on the part of their noninternational customers. However, companies or individuals involved in international business on a large scale have the opportunity to enter into speculative forward contracts, even if most of them have corporate policies that limit or forbid such activities. On the other hand, some offshore banks permit corporate or individual speculative transactions routinely, sometimes with a modest margin requirement or, in more favored cases, with no margins whatsoever. Speculators do not even have to take delivery of the foreign exchange and resell it; rather, the bank computes the speculative profit or loss on the contract and either increases or decreases the client's account by the appropriate amount.

SPECULATION, COVERING, AND THE CURRENCY OF DENOMINATION DECISION

The world, fortunately, is not divided neatly into those who only speculate in the forward markets and those who only cover in the forward markets. Suppose, for example, that Agfolk is willing at least to consider a speculative flyer in the mark. Should the desire to speculate have an impact on which currency is chosen for financing? The answer, which may seem surprising to some, is no.

The first step in demonstrating the reason for this answer is to develop the covering decision. To do this, return to the currency of denomination decision that Agfolk faces. As was discovered earlier, if Agfolk borrows $10 million dollars at 13 percent, the net cost of financing in dollars is $1.3 million. If Agfolk borrows DM 25 million, the net cost of the financing is $27(X_1) - 10$, in millions of dollars, if Agfolk does not cover. Here again X_1 is the period-ending exchange rate.

The Basis for Evaluation

So that development can be consistent, we will evaluate these alternatives not in terms of cost but in terms of their total gain, the negative of cost. Therefore, the gain of borrowing dollars (in millions) is

$$V_\$ = -1.3$$

The gain of an uncovered borrowing of marks (in millions, again) is

$$V_{DM} = 10.0 - 27.0(X_1)$$

V_{DM} is given by a linear equation in the ending exchange rate. Whenever the value of a particular decision is a linear function of the exchange rate, the exchange risk can be eliminated by a covering operation. As was shown earlier, the covering operation that eliminates the exchange risk is a forward purchase in the amount of DM 27.0 million at the forward rate $0.41; the profit on this forward purchase is $27.0 (X_1 - 0.41)$. We add the profit on the covering transaction to V_{DM} to find the value of borrowing on a covered basis,

$$CV_{DM} = (10.0 - 27.0X_1) + 27.0 (X_1 - 0.41)$$
$$= 10.0 - 27.0X_1 + 27.0X_1 - 11.07$$
$$= -1.07$$

This result corresponds to the initial calculation that the cost of a covered borrowing in marks is $1.07 million. Because borrowing marks on a covered basis costs $1.07 million and borrowing dollars costs $1.3 million, it is better to borrow marks.

Adding the Opportunity to Speculate

The next step is to include in this formula the opportunity to engage in speculative forward transactions. The value of borrowing dollars and entering into speculative purchases of marks at the level P is

$$V_\$ = -1.3 + P(X_1 - 0.41)$$

The value of borrowing marks on a covered basis is $CV_{DM} = -1.07$. The value of borrowing marks on a covered basis and entering into speculative purchases of marks at the same level P is

$$CV_{DM} = -1.07 + P(X_1 - 0.41)$$

Regardless of the level of P that Agfolk management selects,

$$CV_{DM} - V_\$ = -1.07 + P(X_1 - 0.41) - [-1.3 + P(X_1 - 0.41)]$$
$$= -1.07 - (-1.3)$$
$$= 0.23$$

Agfolk will always be $230,000 ahead by borrowing marks, regardless of whether it speculates in marks or not. In other words, to decide which currency to borrow in, Agfolk simply needs to determine which currency is cheaper on a covered basis.

The analysis of the Agfolk decision revealed that the mark loan was the optimal financing alternative. From the equation

$$V_{DM} = 10.0 - 27.0 (X_1)$$

we found that the level of covering purchase was equal to DM 27 million. Suppose that Agfolk anticipates that the mark is actually going to appreciate above the forward rate of $0.41. In addition, suppose that after a complex analysis Agfolk management concludes that its optimal level of forward speculative purchases is $P^0 = 4.0$; that is, Agfolk believes that it should buy DM 4 million forward. Rather than buying

DM 27 million forward as cover and simultaneously buying DM 4 million forward as a speculation in two separate transactions, Agfolk should simply combine the two purchases and buy 27,000,000 + 4,000,000 = DM 31,000,000 forward to achieve its optimal position.

Speculation by Uncovered Borrowing

We have discussed at length speculation in the forward market — one of the two methods frequently used to speculate in a currency. The other method of speculation involves borrowing or investing without cover. If a currency is expected to depreciate, the technique is to borrow that currency and leave the repayment uncovered; if the currency is expected to appreciate, the approach is to invest funds in that currency and leave the investment proceeds uncovered. In the first case, currency depreciation reduces the value of the repayment obligation; in the second, the appreciation of the currency increases the value of the investment proceeds.

Suppose that Agfolk did not believe that the mark would appreciate above the forward rate of $0.41 but instead believed that there was little chance that the mark would appreciate and a substantial chance that it would depreciate. By borrowing marks, leaving them uncovered, and not speculating in the forward market, Agfolk creates a position equivalent to a forward speculative position $P = -27,000,000$; the covering purchase of DM 27 million is exactly offset by a speculative sale of DM 27 million. Although this position may be a very good position, there is no *a priori* reason that the optimal level of speculation is exactly -27.0; indeed, P^0 might be greater or less, depending on Agfolk's attitude toward risk. Agfolk has made the right currency of denomination decision (that is, to borrow marks) but has not chosen the optimal level of forward purchase.

If the interest rate on the dollar loan had been only 10 percent, the value of borrowing dollars, $V_\$$, would be $-\$1.0$, which is greater than $-\$1.07 = CV_{DM}$. The correct funding decision would be to borrow dollars. A company that had chosen to speculate by borrowing marks on an uncovered basis here would have made the wrong funding decision because it would have done better to borrow the dollars and sell DM 27 million forward on a speculative basis.

The fundamental thesis of this chapter holds: Regardless of where one believes the exchange rate is going, one denominates debt in the currency that is cheapest on a covered basis and then uses the forward market to select the desired level of exposure to exchange risk.

84

SUMMARY

We have used the simple currency of denomination decision of Agfolk to discuss a number of important principles of international financial management. Because exchange rates change over time, the choices that confront the financial decision maker have consequences that are uncertain at the time the decision must be made. Exchange rate changes make it impossible to compare financing alternatives in different currencies purely on a nominal (stated) interest rate basis.

Techniques exist for evaluating financial alternatives whether or not there exists a futures or forward market for foreign currency. Without a forward market, selection of the appropriate funding currency can be done on an expectations basis by comparing the cost of dollar borrowing with the cost of foreign currency borrowing, adjusted for the effect of expected exchange rate changes on the principal and interest. The foreign currency borrowing may increase or decrease the company's exposure to exchange risk; if the borrower is risk averse, this exposure must be considered in reaching a final decision.

Where a forward market exists, the choice between two funding alternatives should be made on the basis of a comparison of their covered costs. Companies can select the exact position with regard to return and risk by selecting the appropriate level of forward exchange purchases or sale. The opportunity to speculate, as a general rule, does not change the decision as to which currency to select for financing.

DISCUSSION QUESTIONS

1. You work for a U.S.-based company whose reference currency is the U.S. dollar. Your company needs to borrow $10 million for one year. You have assembled the following data:

Currency	Interest Rate (percent per annum)	Forward Premium (percent per annum)
U.S. dollar	10	—
German mark	6	4
British pound sterling	15	−4
French franc	12	−2

Which currency should you borrow? Support your answer with appropriate calculations.

2. In this chapter, the situation of Agfolk was analyzed using the dollar as the reference currency (Agfolk was considered to be a U.S.-based firm). Suppose instead that Agfolk is a German firm using the mark as reference currency. Agfolk needs DM 25 million for one year and can borrow marks at 8 percent and dollars at 13 percent. Agfolk has the same assessment of exchange rate uncertainty as follows:

$/DM Exchange Rate	Probability
.35	.2
.40	.3
.45	.4
.50	.1

Assuming that there is no forward market available to Agfolk, which currency should Agfolk borrow? (Hint: Before doing anything else, convert the $/DM exchange rate quotes to DM/$ exchange rate quotes—for example, $0.40 per deutsche mark is the same as DM 2.5 per dollar). Does the breakeven exchange rate change? If your decision is different from the decision that you would make using the dollar as reference currency, try to identify why.

3. A small Dutch manufacturer of confectionery products, Nederkooken, needs to borrow 10 million Dutch guilders (fl) for 360 days for working capital. Management considers a wide variety of short-term foreign currency borrowing alternatives. The chart below shows the rate at which Nederkooken can borrow various currencies; in calculating actual interest charged on the loan, use this formula:

Interest charged = Principal × Nominal rate × (Number of days ÷ 360)

The number of days here is 360. The chart also shows the spot and 360-day forward U.S. dollar direct exchange rate for each currency.

Currency	360-Day Interest Rate	Spot $ Exchange Rate	360-Day $ Exchange Rate
U.S. dollar ($)	8 1/8%	—	—
German mark (DM)	4 11/16%	0.4185	0.4356
Dutch guilder (fl)	5 13/16%	0.3707	0.3800
British pound sterling (£)	12 7/8%	1.4140	1.3540
Swiss franc (Sfr)	4 3/16%	0.4931	0.5132
French franc (Ffr)	14 %	0.1366	0.1300

Which currency should Nederkooken borrow? (Hint 1: The cross-rate between the guilder and other currencies can be found using the guilder per dollar and dollar per other currency exchange rates. Hint 2: You do not need any estimate of where these currencies will be in one year. Hint 3: Once you figure out how to do this for one currency, you may want to use a computer for the calculations.)

SUGGESTED READINGS

1. Folks, William R. "The Analysis of Short-Term, Cross-Border Financing Decisions," *Financial Management*, Vol. 5, No. 3 (Autumn 1976). Pp. 19–27.

2. Robichek, Alexander, and Mark R. Eaker. "Debt Denomination and Exchange Risk in International Capital Markets," *Financial Management*, Vol. 5, No. 3 (Autumn 1976). Pp. 11–18.

3. Severn, Alan K., and David R. Meinster. "The Use of Multicurrency Financing by the Financial Manager," *Financial Management*, Vol. 7, No. 4 (Winter 1978). Pp. 45–53.

4. Tucker, James V., and Clovis de Faro. "The Selections of International Borrowing Sources," *Journal of Financial and Quantitative Analysis*, Vol. 10, No. 3 (September 1975). Pp. 381–407.

CHAPTER 5

▼

Exchange Risk Management

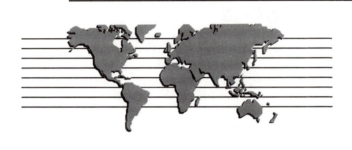

▲

INTRODUCTION

A fundamental characteristic of cross-border business transactions is the risks of changing exchange rates. Because these risks can increase or decrease the value of a firm, it is useful to understand their nature and to examine techniques that can minimize their negative effect.

Exchange risk arises from the change in relative value of various national currencies over time. For example, a U.S. firm expects to receive a payment of £100,000 three months hence for goods just shipped to a customer in the United Kingdom. With a current spot exchange rate of £1.00 = US $1.50, the £100,000 are worth $150,000. However, unless the firm hedges the risk, the actual U.S. dollar amount received three months hence when the U.K. customer pays—if it is a good credit risk; if there is no political or economic risk; and if the U.K. government allows remittance and conversion of the amount—will depend on the actual exchange rate in effect at that time. This means that in three months the U.S. company could actually receive an amount that is less than or more than the $150,000.

But the company, knowing of this uncertainty in the future value of the expected cash flow, examines its forecast of the British pound sterling three months hence. If the British pound is forecasted to decline in value, the company will sell the expected £100,000 in the forward market fixing the amount of U.S. dollars that it will receive three months hence. This seems especially profitable if the company forecast of the exchange rate is lower than the current three-month forward rate.

This simple example illustrates the essentials of how a company can assess and manage its exposure to foreign exchange losses. However, in practice the process of exchange risk management becomes more complex because of the wide diversity in the types of foreign currency transactions and hedging options that a typical multinational corporation (MNC) faces.

A company that operates in more than one nation or currency area and has cash inflows and outflows over time in more than one currency faces currency exposure. As a matter of fact, if the overall cash inflows in terms of a given currency cannot be matched exactly in time and amount to the cash outflow in that same currency, then the company faces currency exposure and possible losses because of changing exchange rates. Because perfect (temporal and quantitative) matching of cash inflows and outflows is rarely possible in practice, most MNCs face at least some exposure to foreign currency losses. In addition, most MNCs have assets and liabilities denominated in various currencies, and unless these assets and liabilities in each currency are completely matched (in amount and term structure), the MNC also is exposed to changes in their values because of changing exchange rates. Therefore, under most normal circumstances, an MNC is likely to have not only short-term operating exposure to exchange losses but also long-term exposure to exchange losses because of mismatches in its projected cash flows and in its asset and liability maturity structure. Further, all companies, domestic or multinational, also face economic exposure as they are exposed to changes in *future* cash flows (and therefore in their values) because of price and other changes, induced by fluctuating exchange rates, in the markets in which they operate.

DEFINING EXPOSURE TO EXCHANGE LOSSES AND THE NATURE OF THESE RISKS

An asset denominated in or valued in terms of foreign currency cash flows will change in value if that foreign currency changes in value over time. Such an asset is exposed to exchange rate risk if that change is a decline rather than an increase in value. But this possible decline in asset value is not the only element involved in assessing a firm's exposure risk. The decline in asset values may be offset by a parallel decline in the value of a liability that also is denominated or valued in terms of that foreign currency. Thus, a firm normally would be interested in its *net exposed position* (exposed assets minus exposed liabilities) for each period in each currency. Three different measures of exposure to foreign currency losses have been developed: transactions exposure, translation exposure, and economic exposure.

Transactions Exposure

Transactions exposure is the net total of foreign currency transactions whose monetary value is fixed at a time different from the time when these transactions are actually completed. Examples of such transactions include receivables, payables, and fixed price sales or purchase contracts. Thus, transactions exposure is net contracted foreign currency transactions for which the settlement amounts are subject to changing exchange rates over a period too short to allow for compensating changes in prices. A company normally must set up an additional reporting system to track transactions exposure because a number of these amounts are not recognized in the accounting books of a firm.

Translation Exposure

Translation exposure is the net total of exposed assets less exposed liabilities. Foreign currency assets and liabilities are considered exposed if their foreign currency value for accounting purposes is to be translated into the parent company currency using the current exchange rate — that is, the exchange rate in effect on the balance sheet date. Other assets and liabilities and equity amounts that are translated at the historic exchange rate — that is, the rate in effect when these items were first recognized in the company's accounts — are not considered to be exposed. The rate (current or historic) used to translate various accounts depends on the translation procedure used.

Translation Procedures

For U.S. companies, Financial Accounting Standards Board (FASB) *Statement No. 52* specifies the translation procedure to be used. Under

FASB *Statement No. 52*, a company must first identify the functional currency for each entity or foreign affiliate. If the foreign affiliate does not face high rates of inflation and conducts most of its business in local currency terms, the local currency is generally considered to be its functional currency. In such a case, all foreign asset and liability (other than equity) accounts are translated using the current exchange rate. Translation losses or gains are not combined with other reported income but are combined with the equity account. If, however, the currency is suffering from hyperinflation (over 100-percent cumulative inflation over a three-year period) or if the foreign affiliate conducts most of its business in U.S. dollars, the functional currency will be considered to be the U.S. dollar. In such a case, foreign currency accounts are translated using the temporal method outlined in a prior account translation standard, FASB *Statement No. 8*, and such translation losses and gains are included in reported income. FASB *Statement No. 52* also requires that foreign currency accounts be restated to conform to U.S. generally accepted accounting principles before translation.

In addition to the all-current and temporal methods used in FASB *Statement No. 52*, other translation procedures commonly used internationally include the monetary/nonmonetary and the current/noncurrent methods. Each of these translation methods prescribes the translation rate (current or historic) that should be used to translate various foreign currency asset and liability accounts. Naturally, the net translation exposure for a foreign affiliate depends on the translation procedure used, and firms based in other countries use the translation procedures prescribed by the accounting rules prevalent in their home countries. Exhibit 5-1 summarizes the four main translation procedures.

Procedural Difficulties

Forecasting and minimization of translation exposure are sometimes made difficult in practice because of the problems encountered in obtaining up-to-date and consistent data from foreign operations. For example, because different dates are used for their fiscal year-ends, the quality, consistency, and timeliness of financial information received by a multinational varies greatly among its different foreign operations. Different overseas operations are likely to be using accounting systems with varying degrees of compatibility compared to those used at the MNC's world headquarters. In addition, each operation also may be at a different stage of the phase-in process, depending on: how long ago it was

EXHIBIT 5-1 The Four Basic Translation Procedures

Balance-Sheet Item	Translation Procedure			
	All Current	*Temporal*	*Monetary/ Nonmonetary*	*Current/ Noncurrent*
Assets				
Cash	C	C	C	C
Marketable securities				
At cost	C	H	C	C
At current price	C	C	C	C
Accounts receivable	C	C	C	C
Inventories				
At cost	C	H	H	C
At replacement	C	C	H	C
At realizable or sale	C	C	H	C
Prepaid expenses	C	H	H	C
Fixed assets	C	H	H	H
Liabilities				
Accounts and notes payable	C	C	C	C
Accrued expenses	C	C	C	C
Other current liabilities	C	C	C	C
Deferred income	C	H	H	C
Long-term debt	C	C	C	H
Owners' equity	H	H	H	H

C = the exchange rate in effect on the balance-sheet date.

H = the exchange rate in effect when the item was first recognized in the company's accounts.

NOTE: FASB *Statement No. 52* is primarily based on the all-current method with some accounts, such as those in a hyperinflationary country, being translated using the temporal method.

SOURCE: Schedule based on various accounting standards and a table in Raj Aggarwal, "The Translation Problem in International Accounting," *Management International Review*, Vol. 15, Nos. 2–3 (1975): 67–79.

acquired by the parent corporation; the progressiveness of its management; and the magnitude of the differences between its local accounting practices and those of the parent.

Although transaction exposure can result in exchange rate–related losses and gains that are realized, and can affect both reported and taxable income, translation exposure usually results in losses and gains that are reflected only in the company's accounting books, are not realized, and may have little or no effect on taxable income in the U.S. (except for the calculation of the Alternative Minimum Tax). Thus, if translation losses or gains do not influence corporate taxes, financial markets are efficient, and managerial goals are consistent with owners' wealth maximization (that is, if agency and signaling costs are negligible), a firm should not waste real resources hedging against possible paper losses caused by translation exposure. If, however, there are significant agency or information costs or if markets are not efficient (that is, if translation losses and gains raise information costs for investors, or if they endanger the firm's ability to satisfy debt or other covenants, or if the evaluation of the firm's managers depends on translated accounting data), a firm might indeed use real resources to hedge against paper translation losses or gains even if such losses or gains do not correspond to real gains and losses.

Economic Exposure

Economic exposure is the extent to which the economic value of a company can decline because of exchange rate changes. This decline in value can be caused by a decline in the level of expected cash flows, induced by the exchange rate, and/or by an increase in the riskiness of these cash flows. Thus, economic exposure refers to the overall effect of exchange rate changes on the value of the firm. It includes not only the strategic effect of changes in competitive relationships between alternative foreign locations that arise from exchange rate changes but also the economic effect of transactions exposure and of translation exposure.

Thus, economic exposure to exchange rate changes depends on the competitive structure of the markets for a firm's inputs and outputs and how these markets are influenced by changes in exchange rates. This influence, in turn, depends on a number of economic factors including price elasticities of the products, the degree of competition from foreign markets, and direct (through prices) and indirect (through incomes) effects of exchange rate changes on these markets. Assessing the economic exposure faced by a particular firm thus depends on the ability to understand and model the structure of at least the markets for its major inputs (purchases) and outputs (sales).

It should be noted here that a company need not engage in any cross-border business activity in order to be exposed to losses due to exchange rate changes. This is because product and financial markets in most countries are related and influenced, to a large extent, by the same global forces. The output of a company engaged in business activity within only one country may be competing with imported products or may be competing for its inputs with other domestic and foreign purchasers. The degree of competition in the markets provided by these firms may change with changes in exchange rates. For example, a Canadian chemical company that did no cross-border business nevertheless found that its profit margins depended directly on the U.S. dollar per Japanese yen exchange rate. The company used coal as an input in its production process, and the Canadian price of coal was influenced heavily by the extent to which the Japanese bought U.S. coal, which in turn depended on the dollar per yen exchange rate.

Although translation exposure normally need not be managed, it might be useful for a firm to manage its transaction and economic exposures because they affect a firm's value directly. In most companies, transaction exposure is generally tracked and managed by the office of the corporate treasurer. On the other hand, economic exposure is difficult to define in operating terms and has a long-term horizon. It is generally best evaluated and managed in the company's long-range or strategic planning process.

MANAGING FOREIGN CURRENCY EXPOSURE

The basic idea in managing a company's net foreign currency exposure (FCE) is to decrease projected levels of foreign currency assets or cash inflows that are denominated in a weakening foreign currency, while increasing the projected levels of foreign currency liabilities or cash outflows that are denominated in a weakening currency. The opposite is true in the case of cash flows, assets, and liabilities denominated in a strengthening currency. Exhibit 5-2 illustrates this decision criteria.

It is argued by some that as long as fundamental economic forces, such as international interest rate and purchasing power parities, drive relative changes in exchange rates, there is no need to manage foreign

EXHIBIT 5-2   Managing Foreign Currency Exposure

	Projected Cash	
	Inflows and/or Assets	*Outflows and/or Liabilities*
Strengthening currency	Increase	Decrease
Weakening currency	Decrease	Increase

NOTE: These recommendations are subject to the operating needs of the company; the completeness and efficiency of financial markets; governmental regulations and tax laws; and the opportunity costs of nonoptimal capital structure and of nonoptimal working capital and fixed asset levels.

currency exposure. However, for most currency markets there are significant deviations from these parity conditions, and a number of factors make these deviations difficult to forecast. First, government intervention in foreign exchange and related financial markets makes it difficult to judge when currency changes will deviate from the trends implied by these fundamental economic forces. Second, even in free and efficient markets the exact timing and amount of exchange rate change is difficult to forecast. In free and efficient markets exchange rates change in a random pattern as they react to new information. It also has been shown that in government-controlled or -influenced currency markets, as well as in black markets or parallel markets, exchange rates also change in an unpredictable manner because government intervention is usually most effective when conducted without prior notice to these markets.

Thus, exchange risk management (ERM) must take into account the uncertainty surrounding the direction and extent of exchange rate changes. Unfortunately, ERM is further complicated by the additional uncertainty a firm must face in assessing the amounts that are exposed to possible loss because of exchange rate changes. The firm's uncertainty about amounts exposed to exchange risk can arise because of its inability to forecast with certainty future foreign currency cash flow amounts or their timing. Naturally, this uncertainty regarding exposed amounts increases as the planning horizon lengthens. The nature and cost of procedures to hedge against unfavorable exchange rate changes must be weighed and the resulting plan for carrying out the management of exchange risk must be implemented.

In short, to manage its exposure to currency exchange losses, a firm must be able to

1. assess the net amounts exposed to exchange risk for each of the periods in its planning horizon
2. develop a forecast of the projected exchange rates for each period
3. evaluate the various options available to it to optimize its exposure
4. identify the organizational unit or units responsible for implementing its exposure management program.

Assessing the Amounts Exposed to Exchange Risk

Real exchange losses depend on three factors: net nominal foreign currency amounts exposed to exchange rate changes, the degree to which foreign currency values of such assets and liabilities change because of exchange rate changes, and the extent and timing of the exchange rate change. Tradeoffs between the three measures of exposure to exchange loss may also need to be considered; certain actions designed to minimize one type of exposure may appear to increase another type of exposure. But this is more likely to be a problem in a firm that is trying to minimize its translation exposure along with its transaction or economic exposure. Conflicts between the minimization of transaction and economic exposures are less likely and, if they do occur, typically involve a tradeoff between short- and long-term objectives.

In defining its net exposure, a firm also must account for the nature and extent of the natural hedges that relate to its foreign assets and liabilities. Because a depreciating currency is often accompanied by higher levels of inflation, the value of a company's assets and liabilities in that country may change because of local inflation and may offset, fully or partially, an apparent loss in value based solely on the original value and the nominal change in exchange rates. Thus, the net amounts exposed to exchange losses depend on the nature of the firm's assets and liabilities—that is, on how they change in value when exchange rates change.

In addition, exposure management policies and strategies must take into account the tax consequences of the expected exposure losses and of the various hedging actions being considered. They also must consider restrictions on such actions that often are imposed by national governments. A number of financial transactions that may be used to hedge against a weakening currency, such as the purchase of hard currencies for remittance, are often restricted by the government to prevent or slow down the fall in the value of its currency.

Developing Exchange Rate Forecasts

The extent and timing of exchange rate changes are an essential input in determining foreign currency exposure. For exposure management purposes, a company must set up procedures that generate forecasts for the currencies and periods required on a regular basis. In addition, in order to evaluate tradeoffs among hedging strategies, it is useful to develop not only point estimates of future exchange rates but also their probability distributions.

The procedures used in developing exchange rate forecasts are described in Chapter 3. In addition to the economic forces discussed in that chapter, exchange rate forecasting must sometimes also account for the timing and extent of government intervention in foreign exchange markets. Forecasting exchange rates is thus a difficult task: it is often impossible to consistently develop a more accurate forecast than a market-based forecast, such as the forward rate. Nevertheless, many companies expend a great deal of money, time, and effort in developing exchange rate forecasts that are then used not only in exposure management but also in other areas such as budgeting and corporate planning. One reason for developing internal exchange rate forecasts is that forecasts based on free markets are often either not available or are available in a form unsuitable for corporate use.

Evaluating the Options to Optimize Exposure

There are many procedures available to hedge against loss due to exchange rate changes. Their natures and costs must be weighed carefully in developing a strategy of exchange risk management. The optimization of foreign currency exposure generally involves activities that can be classified into two major categories: (1) making decisions to possibly engage in financial transactions that are designed to offset expected losses due to currency changes, and (2) making operating decisions to possibly reduce the level of exposure.

Hedging with Financial Instruments

In the case of the simple example of hedging a foreign currency receivable, a U.S. firm could enter into an appropriate forward contract to fix the U.S. dollar value of the foreign currency amount due to be received. It also could hedge its foreign currency exposure using a number of other procedures. It could use some of the financial instruments widely available in the financial markets such as foreign currency options, futures, and interest-bearing securities, or it could rely on hedging actions that depend on internal operating decisions.

Although forward contracts are generally written by banks for the amounts and maturities required by their corporate customers, futures contracts are traded on organized exchanges and are available from brokers only in fixed amounts and for fixed maturities. Further, the purchase of a futures contract requires a margin deposit that must be marked to market each trading day and therefore may result in calls for additional deposits if the initial margin falls below a minimum. Purchase of forward contracts generally does not require such deposits, but only customers with appropriately high credit standards have access to forward contracts.

Another alternative increasingly available through banks and organized exchanges is the foreign currency option that gives the holder the privilege but not the obligation to buy (*call*) or sell (*put*) a given amount of a foreign currency at a set (*strike*) price anytime before the expiration of the option (usually a few months). Because of their flexibility, foreign currency options generally carry a significant premium above the value of the underlying foreign currency. The magnitude of this premium generally depends on the time to maturity, the volatility of the underlying foreign currency, and the difference between the strike price and the value of the underlying currency.

Thus, in view of their characteristics, each of these three financial instruments is useful for reducing foreign exchange exposure in different situations depending on the degree of uncertainty in the amount and timing of foreign exchange exposure. If the timing or existence of a projected foreign currency cash flow is uncertain (as in a bidding contest), an option may be the best hedging alternative because it offers the greatest flexibility even though at a considerable cost. In such a case (that is, if an expected cash flow does not materialize), the use of a forward or a futures contract would itself then give rise to foreign exchange exposure because these contracts must be unwound either by means of delivery (using the expected cash flow) or by paying the difference between the forward or futures price that was fixed initially and the price of the underlying currency at maturity.

The use of financial instruments to manage foreign currency exposure is, in many cases, much simpler to evaluate than the use of operating decisions even though the range of financial transactions that are available to hedge foreign currency exposure has expanded greatly in recent years. They not only include forward and futures foreign currency contracts and foreign currency options, as discussed above, but also cross-currency and interest rate swaps, and lending and borrowing foreign currency. Each of these transactions has a specific cost that is usually easier to assess, especially if there is an active market in these instruments, than the costs of operating decisions undertaken to reduce foreign currency exposure.

It should be noted here, though, that if financial markets are efficient, the costs of each of these procedures increasingly reflect the amount of the expected exchange rate change, especially as the time horizon shortens. For example, the forward rate is an unbiased and an increasingly accurate forecast of the future spot rate as the time horizon shortens. In addition, the firm using any of these financial instruments also must pay some transaction costs such as brokerage fees and the spread between bid and ask prices.

Thus, in order for hedging actions to result in a net economic benefit under conditions of market efficiency, a company either must on average have a forecasting ability better than that of the financial markets or have access to hedging opportunities that do not fully reflect the economic costs of the expected exchange rate change. However, it should be noted that external and internal markets in which an MNC operates often provide significant opportunities for engaging in hedging actions that have positive economic value, especially because of the existence of information costs and government-based barriers to cross-border activity. Considerable evidence indicates that markets are not fully integrated internationally and financial and currency markets in many countries are not free or efficient.

One other reason for undertaking various hedging actions, even if their cost balances their expected benefit, is to change the risk level of the firm so that it is more consistent with that desired by its owners or its managers. This is especially useful and feasible if the markets for hedging instruments are fairly efficient and costs of hedging actions do not reflect any extraordinary costs on a risk-adjusted basis. A company may engage in hedging actions if it finds it uneconomical to maintain the ability to continually monitor and assess foreign exchange markets or to maintain the managerial expertise necessary to make exposure decisions.

Hedging with Operating Decisions

Most foreign affiliate operating decisions have some effect on the level of foreign currency exposure because they lead to changes in projected levels of cash flows, assets, or liabilities. One such strategy that can be used to reduce exposure to exchange losses is sometimes known as *leading and lagging* (further discussed in Chapter 8). Exposure reduction is accomplished by delaying receivables and accelerating payables in a strengthening currency and accelerating receivables and delaying payables in the currency that is weakening. Such leading and lagging may, however, be limited not only by the working capital needs of the local operation but also by current and expected government regulations on foreign-currency transactions. A variation of conventional leading and lagging is accelerating remittances to the parent company from areas with weakening currencies, either directly or through other indirect means such as changing transfer prices if possible.

To reduce net exposure of a foreign subsidiary to exchange losses, sometimes it may be advisable to finance with funds denominated in a weakening currency, especially if it is the local currency. A variation on financing in a weak currency is to arrange a swap if strong-currency funds are needed for a short period. In a swap, a bank will arrange for a temporary exchange of funds between companies that have complementary needs and availability of funds. Thus, in a swap, both companies can avoid exchange risk. However, the economic value of these options in efficient foreign exchange and money markets is subject to the same restrictions as noted in the case of the use of forward contracts.

Other examples of operating decisions that are often considered as a part of the procedures used to manage foreign currency exposure include changing prices and invoicing currencies, developing exports to offset imports and vice versa, and changing the level and currency composition of assets like inventory and liabilities like short-term debt. Of course, each of these procedures has some costs that, in some cases, may be difficult to assess, especially because they may involve both direct and opportunity costs. Examples of opportunity costs incurred include the costs of decreased debt capacity and decreased financing flexibility faced by the foreign affiliate because of the effect of the strategy on the affiliate's balance sheet and capital structure. In order to ensure that the foreign subsidiary's operations do not suffer beyond acceptable levels, some companies require that critical financial ratios (such as the ratio of current assets to current liabilities) for such subsidiaries be maintained within specified limits.

Thus, a foreign affiliate facing a decline in the value of its currency could, in the short run,

1. reduce to a minimum level all local currency cash and marketable securities, converting such items into plant or inventory or preferably into a cash transfer to the parent or a strong currency affiliate by, for example, accelerating remittances for fees and dividends to the parent

2. tighten credit to reduce local receivables and delay collection of receivables denominated in hard currency

3. increase the importation of foreign currency inputs and stockpile inventory sourced or sold in strong currencies and minimize local inventories and fixed plant

4. borrow local currency but minimize the cash retained; a simple offset would be of no help

5. delay the payment of local accounts payable and surrender discounts if necessary and economical

6. accelerate the settlement of intersubsidiary strong currency accounts payable and delay collection of strong currency intersubsidiary accounts receivable.

Over a longer time horizon, such a foreign affiliate also could

1. try to invoice exports in foreign currency and imports in local currency and avoid fixed price contracts; also, provide for price escalation based on currency exposure

2. where currency risks cannot be avoided, try to develop business opportunities with offsetting cash flows

3. use local borrowing to acquire local companies with export potential to hard currency areas

4. emphasize product research and market development that can lead to sales in hard currency areas

5. divest units having continuing and extreme exposure positions, unless large enough countervailing margins are available.

The actual use of any of these strategies may be limited not only by the cost effectiveness of such strategies but also by government or creditor and other restrictions faced by a foreign affiliate.

ORGANIZING FOR FOREIGN CURRENCY EXPOSURE MANAGEMENT

Once a firm has identified its exposure to exchange losses and the hedging procedure that it would like to use, it must be able to implement the hedge efficiently and quickly. In order to do so, it must develop and put in place an organizational structure to coordinate and implement its policy on exchange risk management. In addition to identifying the organizational unit responsible for exchange risk management (generally the treasurer's office), the firm must also develop policies to serve as guidelines for exchange risk management and to resolve the resulting interdepartmental conflicts that are likely to arise occasionally.

Thus, an effective system of exchange rate management generally encompasses the following four major components:

1. a system for forecasting exchange rates
2. a system for projecting and tracking exposure
3. a sytem for tracking hedging options and costs
4. an organization to implement exposure management policies.

Exhibit 5-3 summarizes these four components of an effective system of exchange rate management.

In a large multinational company, there are numerous opportunities for self-hedging because of the existence of offsetting exposures in different parts of the company. Consequently, most large companies tend to centralize the management of foreign exchange exposure. By doing so, the company can avoid the unnecessary expense of hedging transactions or positions that are offset by transactions or positions in another part of the company and take advantage of patterns of highly correlated currency movements. In addition, it can take advantage of possible economies of scale if it has to purchase financial instruments as part of its hedging strategy. It also can integrate currency exposure management with its financing policy. One technique that can facilitate coordination of foreign exchange hedging and working capital management is the use of multilateral netting centers. A multilateral netting center assesses and calculates net interdivisional cash flows with only net amounts transferred periodically (say, twice a month); see discussion of netting in Chapter 8.

In centralizing the currency exposure function, however, a firm

1. *Exchange Rate Forecasting*

   A system for forecasting exchange rates provides forecasts not only of the timing and extent of exchange rate changes for each time-period in the planning horizon but also, when necessary, estimates of some probability distributions of these rate changes.

2. *Measuring Foreign Currency Exposure*

   Information collection and reporting systems estimate the net system-wide exposure for each currency for each period in the planning horizon. A report on the extent of natural hedges that are present should accompany this report.

3. *Covering against Exchange Losses*

   Cost estimates are done of the various operating, financial, and strategic instruments available to cover against currency exposure and of how these costs vary over time and with changes in the exchange rate. These estimates of costs should include an assessment of appropriate opportunity costs and tax implications.

4. *Organization and Policy*

   The organizational units that are responsible for developing and implementing the policy, strategy, and tactics necessary for the optimization of the company's foreign currency exposure should be identified. This part of the policy should also have clear guidelines on how to resolve interdepartmental conflicts that may arise.

EXHIBIT 5-3 Managing Foreign Exchange: System Components

should try to involve foreign affiliate managers as often and as closely as possible so that it includes a local perspective and local information in its currency exposure function. Many hedging opportunities may be available only at a local level, and local managers can provide valuable insight and information concerning exchange rate changes.

In addition to the question of the degree of centralization, corporate policy on foreign exchange exposure should address the overall objective of the policy. Depending on the size and nature of its foreign operations, one of three distinct policies can be followed by a company.

A Conservative Policy

Theoretically, it is possible to make all decisions concerning intercurrency cash flows based on the expected exchange rate (to the extent that it can be forecast) and take no exchange risk. In this extreme case, cashflow decisions are undertaken only if profitable even with adverse exchange rate changes or with the immediate sale or purchase of the foreign currency in the forward market. For example, according to the comptroller of a small U.S. subsidiary of a West German MNC, "Our parent company in Germany holds us responsible for all losses related to exchange-rate changes, and it is up to us to make up these losses by appropriate price increases if necessary."

In practice, however, such an attitude would mean that many, if not most, intercurrency transactions would become unfeasible and unattractive. The opportunity cost of forgone opportunities with such an extremely conservative policy means that such a policy will be considered impractical for most business. Such a policy may be followed only by some exporters and importers (traders) with limited cross-border business.

An Easy-Going Policy

Another approach to the management of exchange risks in an MNC is to ignore them. In such cases, a foreign subsidiary can be treated as an independent business, and any losses because of an occasional, unexpected exchange rate change are considered the normal cost of doing business. This policy can save an MNC the considerable cost and managerial effort that may be required to implement an optimal policy. Such a policy is particularly attractive if the normal intercurrency cash flows are small or unimportant relative to other cash flows, or the expected exchange rate changes during the planning horizon, if expected at all, are forecast to be small. Such a policy can be safely followed by companies whose commitment is of a short-term nature, such as exporters and importers that do business on a cash basis or extend only short-term credit. Such a policy also can be followed by a large MNC if it expects a large volume of offsetting foreign currency transactions so that, at any given time, its net losses because of foreign currency changes are relatively small.

An Intermediate Policy

This policy would fall somewhere between the two previous extremes. When the MNC in question has projected intercurrency flows that are a significant portion of its operations and, in addition, its cash inflows involve currencies not closely tied to the currency in which cash outflows must take place, its optimal course may be to actively manage its foreign currency exposure. If, in addition, the company has long-term commitments internationally, such as investments in foreign subsidiaries, then its exposure policy must optimize the management of foreign exchange over the entire planning horizon and over all of the currency areas involved. According to the financial manager of a major U.S. electrical equipment MNC that has extensive investments overseas,

> We have to take exchange-rate changes into account for many different currency areas for both working capital and long-term investment and financing decisions. The situation is further complicated for us here at headquarters because we treat foreign susidiaries as profit centers.[1]

In other words, the exchange risk management policy that may be optimal is one that involves not only the company's overall financial planning process but also other operating and financial policies including financing, working capital management, capital bugeting, intracorporate borrowing and lending, dividend remittance and transfer pricing, tax planning, and other short- and long-term financial policies.

Furthermore, a corporate policy for the management of foreign exchange risks also should include guidelines clearly specifying the limits and constraints within which exposure management is to be conducted, especially with regard to the level of foreign currency options and forward and futures contracts that can be undertaken. Management also should develop clear procedures to resolve conflicts among the various parts of the company that may be involved in the exposure management process.

In addition to creating policies specifically designed to manage foreign currency exposure, management may consider foreign currency

---

[1]Raj Aggarwal, *Financial Policies for the Multinational Company* (New York, New York: Praeger Publishers, 1976), p. 65.

exposure explicitly within a company's operating and strategic decisions. However, hedging actions should be taken only after considering how currency exposures created by each decision may be offset by exposures created by other decisions.

CONCLUSIONS

Managing foreign currency exposure is an important aspect of international financial management. Corporate policies and strategies for foreign currency exposure management have both an operating short-term aspect and a strategic long-term aspect. In addition to policies explicitly designed to manage foreign currency exposure, the possibility of currency losses should be considered in all of a company's operating and strategic decisions. Hedging actions, however, should be undertaken only after the overall corporatewide exposure is calculated.

Policies for exchange risk management involve a continuing assessment of the company's transaction, translation, and economic exposures. In addition, a company should track the nature and costs of the hedging actions available and consider the efficiency and depth of financial markets available, as well as any government restrictions on their use. Finally, it should have an organization that can implement exposure management actions quickly and efficiently.

DISCUSSION QUESTIONS

1. What are some of the tools for managing foreign exchange exposure? What are the advantages and disadvantages of each?
2. How is exposure netting possible with currencies of two countries that tend to go up and down together in value? Explain.
3. Are translation gains or losses important if they are not realized? Why or why not?
4. Compare and contrast transaction, translation, and economic exposures. How do they interact with each other in affecting the value of the firm?
5. Your firm has an affiliate in Taiwan that recently declared a dividend of NT $5 million and that is to be transferred in six months to the parent company in the United States. Developments in the economic climate are such that you are worried about a sharp depreciation of the Taiwanese dollar within the next six months. You are unable to hedge in the forward market

because forward rates are not available for the Taiwanese dollar at this time. There are two options, however, that appear to be open to you:

a. A U.S. firm operating in Taiwan needs local funds. The company wants to borrow NT $5 million from your affiliate in Taiwan against a payment in six months of US $138,000 in the United States.

b. Invest the money in Taiwan government securities that are yielding 10 percent per annum. You have decided to accept the exchange rate that will prevail in six months even though you are uncertain about it.

An economic forecast appearing in Taiwan's leading business journal has estimated that the Taiwan government may support the current spot rate of NT $35.06 per U.S. dollar and thus they forecast that there will be no change in this spot rate for six months. A business journal in the United States estimates that in six months the Taiwanese dollar will depreciate to NT $38.35 per U.S. dollar. Another journal from Japan has estimated that in six months the spot rate will have depreciated to NT $40.75 per U.S. dollar. Your corporate experts estimate that there is a 30-percent chance that the forecasts by the Taiwan business journal will be correct, a 25-percent chance that the U.S. journal will be correct, and a 45-percent chance that the Japanese journal will be correct. What course of action should you take?

6. A British firm has contracted to buy camera parts worth ¥33 billion from a Japanese manufacturer. The invoice for the parts is payable in three months. The British firm also has receivables for completed cameras sold to another Japanese firm. These receivables are valued at ¥21 billion, also due in three months. The firm's policy is to hedge all residual currency positions. Disregard transaction costs and assume that the current spot exchange rate is £1.00 = ¥225 and the three-month forward rate is £1.00 = ¥223. Interest rates in the United Kingdom and Japan are 12.8 percent per annum and 6.0 percent per annum, respectively.

a. How can the British firm undertake an effective hedge in the forward market?

b. How can the British firm undertake an effective money market hedge?

c. What would be the cost or benefit of an unhedged position vis-à-vis a hedged position if the spot rate in three months was £1.00 = ¥224?

SUGGESTED READINGS

1. Adler, Michael, and Bernard Dumas. "Exposure to Currency Risk: Definition and Measurement," *Financial Management*, Vol. 13, No. 2 (Summer 1984). Pp. 41–50.

2. Aggarwal, Raj. *Financial Policies for the Multinational Company: The*

Management of Foreign Exchange. New York, New York: Praeger Publishers, 1976.

3. Babbel, David F. "Determining the Optimum Strategy for Hedging Currency Exposure," *Journal of International Business Studies*, Vol. 14, No. 1 (Spring/Summer 1983). Pp. 133–139.

4. Baker, James C., and Raj Aggarwal. "Foreign Exchange Risk in Multinational Companies: The Exposure Management Function," *The Business Graduate*, Vol. 14, No. 1 (January 1984). Pp. 25–29.

5. Dufey, Gunter, and S. L. Srinivasulu. "The Case for Corporate Management of Foreign Exchange Risk," *Financial Management*, Vol. 12, No. 4 (Winter 1983). Pp. 54–62.

6. Jacque, Laurent L. "Management of Foreign Exchange Risk: A Review Article," *Journal of International Business Studies*, Vol. 12, No. 1 (Spring/Summer 1981). Pp. 81–101.

7. Lessard, Donald R., and John B. Lightstone. "Volatile Exchange Rates Can Put Operations at Risk," *Harvard Business Review*, Vol. 4, No. 4 (July/August 1986). Pp. 107–114.

8. Soenen, Luc A. "Portfolio Model for Foreign Exchange Exposure Management," *Omega: International Journal of Management Science*, Vol. 7, No. 4 (1979). Pp. 339–334.

9. Wihlborg, Clas. "Economics of Exposure Management of Foreign Subsidiaries of Multinational Companies," *Journal of International Business Studies*, Vol. 11, No. 3 (Winter 1980). Pp. 9–18.

CHAPTER 6

▼

The Global Financial System

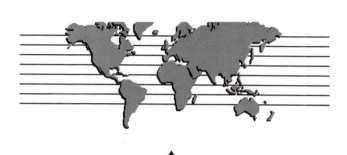

▲

INTRODUCTION

The financial executives of today's multinational corporations face challenges and opportunities unparalleled in history. Their primary challenge is to provide the corporation as a whole and each of its constituent subsidiaries with the appropriate level of financial resources. These resources must be secured at a minimum cost consistent with the maintenance of an appropriate currency and maturity structure of corporate liabilities. Although the ultimate goal of professional financial management remains shareholder wealth maximization, financial executives must develop an overall corporate financing strategy and implement that strategy within both internal organization constraints and external environmental limitations.

Faced with this challenge, unparalleled opportunities are offered by the global financial system, which has three main components:

1. the foreign exchange market
2. the domestic financial markets of the world's major economies
3. the external financial markets (the Eurocurrency and Eurobond markets, described in detail in this chapter).

Over the past decade, four major trends have materially enhanced the opportunities for creative corporate financing. First, many of the major domestic financial markets and their supporting institutions have been deregulated. Second, deregulation and other policy changes favoring international activity have led to a major integration of domestic and of external financial markets. Third, both deregulation and global market integration have led to the development of a multitude of financial innovations, such as foreign currency options, interest rate swaps, and Euronotes, which offer significant new mechanisms for managing the currency and interest rate risks that develop from global financing operations. Finally, the rapid change in environment and market products has led to a blurring of the traditional distinction between commercial banking and investment banking and a heightened competitive environment, resulting in reduced cost of financial services to the user.

THE FOREIGN EXCHANGE MARKET IN THE GLOBAL FINANCIAL SYSTEM

The foreign exchange market is the first building block of the global financial system. (It is described in some detail in Chapter 2.) Its primary function is to create a mechanism by which payments can be made across national boundaries. Historically, that mechanism was developed to allow payment for real goods and services, but the existence of the foreign exchange market makes possible both cross-border investment and cross-border borrowing.

DOMESTIC FINANCIAL MARKETS IN THE GLOBAL FINANCIAL SYSTEM

The domestic financial markets of the world's major economies form the second major building block of the global financial system. The United States, for example, has an extremely well-developed set of financial markets. Similar financial markets have developed in the United Kingdom, France, West Germany, Switzerland, Japan, and most other industrialized countries.

Financial markets are usually classified either as *intermediated* or as *direct*. Intermediated markets are those in which financial intermediaries, such as commercial banks, savings and loan associations, or postal savings systems, receive funds from savers in the form of deposits and then lend those funds to other intermediaries or final borrowers. In direct markets, borrowers issue securities directly to savers, usually with the assistance of an investment bank or a similar facilitating financial institution.

The primary function of financial markets — the transfer of funds from savers to those needing capital — is performed more or less efficiently in most major countries. Of course, the institutional structure of these markets differs, sometimes quite materially, from country to country. In the United States, the commercial and investment banking functions have been legally separated since the Great Depression, and commercial banking has been restricted historically to operations in no more than a single state (although this aspect is changing rapidly). In West Germany, on the other hand, commercial and investment banking business can be carried on by the same firm, and both these areas have been dominated by the so-called Big Three (Deutsche Bank, Commerzbank, and Dresdner Bank), whose operations span the entire country.

Financial executives must be well acquainted with the major financial markets in which their firm's subsidiaries operate. These local markets are a primary source for short-term funding and trade financing. In developing countries, particularly, where foreign exchange restrictions and exchange risk management considerations impede the use of external financial resources, full use of local markets becomes overwhelmingly important, as we will see in Chapter 8.

International Operations in Domestic Financial Markets

As far as the global financial system is concerned, the existence of domestic financial markets and the foreign exchange market creates the possibility for two different kinds of international financial transactions:

1. Investors, seeking a more profitable outlet for their funds, may choose to convert their funds to foreign currency and either invest in securities issued by foreign firms or make deposits with foreign financial institutions.

2. Borrowers, seeking to reduce their borrowing cost, may go to foreign banks for loans or issue securities to foreign investors on the foreign market.

Foreign borrowing in a domestic market or domestic investment in foreign markets may be closely regulated by either the country of the investor or the country of the borrower. Such regulation may be designed to insulate the local money or capital markets from foreign influences or to prevent capital flows from moving the exchange rate from the level that the government desires.

Foreign Bonds

From a corporate viewpoint, the existence of foreign capital markets provides the opportunity to raise funds through the issuance of foreign bonds. A *foreign bond* is a bond issued on the bond market of an individual foreign country, subject to all regulations of the country of issue and usually denominated in the currency of the country of issue. A U.S.–based multinational has issued a foreign bond, for example, if it issues a Swiss franc bond on the domestic bond market of Switzerland.

Only a few domestic bond markets provide sufficient breadth to allow foreign firms to issue long-term debt and equity on a regular basis. In 1986, some $38.44 billion in foreign bonds were issued globally. The leading markets for foreign bonds are the United States, Switzerland, and Japan.

In the United States, foreign bonds are known as Yankee bonds and are subject to filing requirements of the Securities and Exchange Commission, just like issues of domestic firms are. In 1986, some $6.06 billion of Yankee bonds were issued, comprising 15.8 percent of the global issue of foreign bonds.

Switzerland has been a traditionally strong market for the issuance of foreign bonds, and issues by foreign borrowers there totaled $23.40 billion in 1986, or 60.9 percent of the global total of foreign bonds. Publicly traded foreign bonds are subject to stringent regulation, including the restriction that only resident Swiss institutions can participate in new issues. These issues must be approved by the Swiss National Bank, and the volume of new issues has at times in the past been restricted to maintain orderly market conditions. Private placement of corporate issues is common. Switzerland's prominence as a locus for foreign bond activity is in part explained by the traditional role of Swiss banks as recipients of substantial amounts of foreign capital; many of the foreign bonds sold in Switzerland enter the portfolios of nonresidents. The ability of Swiss banks to place (sell) securities has given them a traditional position of strength in international capital markets.

The third major foreign bond market is Japan. The very high savings rate of the Japanese results in a large supply of loanable funds; however, the Japanese bond market as a whole has been very closely regulated by the Japanese Ministry of Finance to keep interest rates low. As a result, foreign participation in Japanese financial markets has been far lower than one would otherwise expect. Nonetheless, some foreign governments, international organizations (such as the World Bank), and top-rated corporations (such as Sears Roebuck & Co.) have received permission from the ministry to issue yen-denominated foreign bonds, nicknamed *samurai bonds*, on the Japanese bond market. In 1986, $4.76 billion of foreign bonds were issued, comprising 12.4 percent of the global foreign bond total.

Foreign bonds are an important source of long-term capital for multinational corporations whose market name and creditworthiness are sufficient to ensure acceptance of the issue. However, in any given year, foreign bonds represent only about 15 to 30 percent (17.0 percent in 1986) of the long-term debt issues on the international capital markets. The primary source for long-term capital (other than a company's own domestic market) is the Eurobond market, one of a group of external financial markets whose development has revolutionized international finance since 1960.

EXTERNAL MARKETS

A complete system of direct and intermediated financial markets has developed since 1960 that is not directly linked to the national (domestic) market of any country. These markets are normally referred to as the *Euromarkets,* although they are more correctly known as the *external markets* because they are external to any one national market and external to the control of any one government. They are also called *parallel markets* because they function parallel to domestic markets.

External markets that are intermediated (with financial institutions standing between the ultimate lender and the ultimate borrower) are known as the *Eurocurrency markets.* Because the dollar is the most frequently used currency in these markets, they are somewhat incorrectly called the *Eurodollar markets.* Whatever they are called, they are enormous in size; dollar volume in these markets normally exceeds the expanded money supply (M2) of the United States.

In the Eurodollar market, banks take deposits from customers and lend them to other customers, just as in domestic markets. The significant difference is that the banks, borrowers, and lenders operate outside the direct control of the banking authority responsible for the currency in which these operations are conducted. When a French bank takes a U.S. dollar deposit from a German (or a U.S. national, for that matter), it has accepted a Eurodollar deposit, and when it makes a U.S. dollar loan to a Dutch firm, it has made a Eurodollar loan. The currency of the loan or of the deposit, the U.S. dollar, is not that of the home country of the bank (France).

Characteristics of an External Market

Four main characteristics define an external market:

1. The suppliers of funds to the market are usually not resident in the country where the transaction takes place.
2. The borrowers of funds from the market are also usually nonresident.
3. The currency in which the financial contracts are denominated is usually not the currency of the financial center.
4. The financial institutions intermediating the loan or underwriting the investment transaction are usually units of large multinational institutions.

The prefix *Euro-* is applied to these markets because they first developed in Western Europe. Despite their geographic origin, the external Euromarkets now involve participation by financial institutions, borrowers, and lenders of almost all nationalities.

Transactions in the Euromarkets frequently involve the use of financial institutions in so-called *offshore financial centers.* These centers provide both a limited regulatory environment favorable to a Eurocurrency business, as well as a low tax rate on profits from these transactions. Locations such as the Cayman Islands, the Bahamas, Luxembourg, and Panama, which have limited or nonexistent domestic financial markets, nonetheless have become important financial centers in which nonresident investors or depositors are brought into contact with nonresident borrowers by nonresident financial institutions.

However, external markets can develop only where the regulatory environment is favorable; London is the acknowledged center of the global external market because the Bank of England chose to allow British financial expertise to apply itself to the full development of an external market. As a leading external market center, London generates earnings from external financial transactions that have been a significant factor in the economy of Great Britain. Frequently, as well, transactions that are agreed on in London, New York, or other major financial centers are simply legally booked in the offshore financial center. The activity, and the people, stay in London or New York.

The Eurocurrency Market

The modern Eurocurrency market was developed as a direct result of the post-World War II confrontation between the United States and the Soviet Union. Soviet monetary authorities were afraid to hold their dollar balances at U.S. banks because of the potential claims that might be filed against them in the U.S. legal system. Consequently, the two Russian banks operating in Western Europe, the Moscow Narodny Bank in London and the Paris-based Banque Commerciale du Nord, were able to get banks in London to accept deposits from them but to denominate the deposits in dollars. Other European holders of dollar balances also discovered the convenience of depositing their dollar balances at European rather than U.S. banks. European central banks, which kept a portion of their foreign currency reserves in dollars, also moved funds into the incipient Eurodollar market.

How Eurocurrency Deposits Are Accepted

How can banks in Europe accept dollar deposits? Their capacity to take dollar-denominated deposits arises from the same correspondent banking system that makes the foreign exchange market possible. A European bank normally has a dollar bank account with a U.S. correspondent bank or with its own branch in the United States. Suppose that a customer wishes to deposit $1 million with the European bank. The customer transfers the $1 million into the correspondent dollar account of the European bank in the United States. This action creates an asset on the European bank's books of $1 million. The European bank credits the customer with a deposit of $1 million, and a million new Eurodollars have been created.

115

The customer has exchanged a $1 million deposit at a U.S. bank for a $1 million deposit at a European bank. The European bank has increased its assets by $1 million (the increase in its correspondent dollar account in the United States) and has increased its liabilities by $1 million, the amount placed on deposit by the European customer.

The Eurocurrency market is not restricted to dollars. Suppose that a British resident is receiving payment for an export shipment to Germany in the amount of DM 1 million. The British resident could have the DM 1 million transferred to the account of a British bank in Frankfurt and in turn receive a DM 1 million deposit at the British bank. The same mechanism has created *Euromarks*. The bank's correspondent balance in Frankfurt would increase by DM 1 million, and the bank's liabilities would increase by DM 1 million, the amount placed on deposit by the British exporter.

Any currency can become a Eurocurrency as long as it is freely convertible for most purposes. External markets have developed in the dollar, mark, Swiss franc, yen, sterling, French franc, Dutch guilder, and numerous other currencies. As Exhibit 6-1 shows, however, the largest market historically has been in U.S. dollars.

Banks active in the market, known as *Eurobanks*, bid for Eurocurrency deposits from their customers. Most deposits are made at fixed interest rates, with the bulk of the deposits having a maturity of three months or less.

Although most Eurocurrency deposits are for a specific term at fixed interest rates, Eurobanks also attract funds by issuing negotiable certificates of deposit, known as *Eurodollar CDs*. When issuing the CDs, banks set a specific face amount and interest rate for the CD and sell them on the market to as many buyers as they can attract at that rate. Because CDs are negotiable, they usually yield less than a Eurocurrency deposit.

Suppliers of Funds to the Eurocurrency Markets

The original rationale for the development of the Eurocurrency market, the safeguarding of deposits from the reach of potential U.S. claimants, still plays a minor role in the Eurodollar market. Arab investors, seeking liquid outlets for oil-generated dollar balances, tended in the late 1970s to channel their liquid funds through the Eurocurrency markets. The U.S. freezing of Iranian balances during the hostage crisis of 1979 to 1981 may have reinforced the belief that holding balances in the U.S. banking system is politically risky.

EXHIBIT 6-1 Size of the Euromarkets (in US $ billions)

	1971	1975	1980	1981	1982	1983	1984	1985	Sept. 1986
Eurocurrency liabilities*	150	485	1578	1954	2168	2278	2386	2846	3379
To nonbanks	30	90	278	372	432	479	497	585	662
To official monetary institutions	15	65	128	112	91	88	96	112	117
To other banks	105	330	1172	1470	1645	1711	1793	2149	2600
In dollars	114	378	1193	1539	1741	1846	1950	2147	2420
In other currencies	36	107	385	415	427	432	431	699	959
Total**	NA	NA	1858	2217	2418	2538	2666	3223	3843
To nonbanks			360	446	502	552	577	699	783
To banks and official institutions			1498	1771	1916	1986	2089	2524	3060
In dollars			1328	1665	1857	1981	2096	2316	2611
In other currencies			530	552	561	557	570	907	1232
Net market size***	85	255	957	1155	1285	1382	1430	1676	1910

*Eurocurrency liabilities of banks in major and offshore financial centers, including U.S. international banking facilities.

**Includes domestic currency liabilities to nonresidents.

***Net of interbank deposits.

SOURCE: Morgan Guaranty Trust Co. of New York, *World Financial Markets* (April 1987, July 1985, November 1983, August 1981). Reproduced with permission of the copyright holder.

However, the enormous growth of the Euromarkets since the early 1960s cannot be accounted for by political risk considerations. Instead, growth has come because interest rates on deposits in the Eurodollar market have been higher than rates on deposits of comparable maturity paid in U.S. domestic financial markets. Higher rates can be paid on Eurodollars because the Eurodollar system is unregulated. Banks are not required to hold a specific portion of their Eurodollar deposits in the form of noninterest-bearing reserves. Although prudence dictates that a certain proportion of these deposits can be maintained as reserves, a larger percentage of Eurodollar deposits can be loaned out than can domestic dollar deposits. Further, Eurodollar deposits have never been subject to interest rate ceilings. During the formative period of the Eurodollar market, U.S. banks were precluded from paying market rates of interest on deposits by the interest rate ceilings embodied in Regulation Q. Additionally, certain U.S. government policies, designed to stem the outflow of dollars from the United States in the late 1960s, encouraged corporate borrowers to seek dollar funding from non-U.S. sources.

The Interbank Market for Eurocurrencies

Banks pay for Eurocurrency deposits because they can lend these deposits out at a higher interest rate. Eurocurrency funds can be loaned to customers of the bank in search of dollar financing, to major corporations seeking large-scale, medium-term financing, or to foreign countries borrowing for national purposes. The final uses of Eurodollars are discussed later in this chapter. However, just as the bulk of foreign exchange transactions in the market are interbank transactions, most Eurocurrency transactions also take place in the *interbank market*. The active interbank market in Eurocurrencies provides a ready source of funds to banks whose loan commitments exceed their national deposit bases, and a ready outlet for profitable investments for banks whose Eurocurrency deposits are greater than their immediate needs for funds.

The London market is generally headquarters for the interbank Eurocurrency market, although New York, Paris, Zurich, and Singapore are also active trading centers. Banks active in the market quote a bid rate, the rate at which they would pay for funds, and an offer rate, the rate at which they would be willing to lend funds. The key market rate in the Euromarket is the London Interbank Offer Rate (LIBOR). Because many banks use the LIBOR rate as a basis for pricing loans to customers, LIBOR takes on the same importance in the Eurocurrency markets as the prime rate does in U.S. financial markets.

Approximately three-quarters of all Eurobank deposits are interbank deposits. Banks engage in interbank trading primarily for trading profits. Eurocurrency deposits also can be used to create foreign exchange positions. Traders can borrow Eurocurrencies short and lend long, anticipating a decline in short-term interest rates, or they can lend short and borrow long, anticipating an increase in short-term interest rates. The extent to which traders are allowed to mismatch maturities for trading gains is closely controlled by bank management. Unlike the foreign exchange market, where the primary risk is nondelivery of the foreign currency, the interbank market in Eurocurrency deposits is a credit market. As a consequence, banks are judged on their ability to repay. Banks with a higher credit standing tend to be able to borrow funds at lower cost; this phenomenon is known as *tiering*. Major U.S. banks have historically tended to be in the first, or most creditworthy, tier, although recent problems associated with a high level of lending by these banks to Latin American countries have created changes in the relative credit ranking of some U.S. money center banks.

Because the creditworthiness of the bank on the other side of the transaction is important, the interbank market usually works through brokers, who receive a commission of ⅟₃₂ percent on each transaction. By using a broker, the bank can decline to make a deposit at another bank whose credit limit might be reached, without direct contact with the bank that is being turned down.

The interbank Eurocurrency markets are unregulated, and concerns regarding the absence of a lender of last resort have been frequently raised. In 1974, the Bankhaus Herstatt in Germany failed as a result of aggressive foreign currency and Euromarket trading. This failure caused a significant reassessment of Eurocurrency trading practices and a tightening of limits for particular financial institutions. Also, the Basle Committee, composed of representatives of central banks of the major industrialized countries, was established to develop some oversight of these markets. Gradually, most countries have established reporting requirements that allow early detection of routine problem situations.

The Asia Currency Market

Since 1969, financial institutions in Singapore have been authorized to accept deposits and make loans denominated in dollars and other convertible currencies. This external market is known as the *Asia currency market*. It operates in precisely the same fashion as the Euromarkets. In essence, the Asia currency market is really a component of the global external market, segmented from Europe primarily by differences in time zone.

U.S. Bank Activities in Eurocurrency Markets

U.S. banks have been very active in the Euromarkets and many banks have established branches or subsidiaries in offshore financial centers in order to operate a Eurocurrency business. Although banks have established legal entities in these offshore centers, their Eurocurrency business is effectively conducted in New York.

In 1981, banks operating in the United States were allowed to set up *international banking facilities* (IBFs). In essence, the IBF concept represents an attempt by U.S. banking authorities to create the same conditions that fostered the development of the Eurocurrency market elsewhere. A number of U.S. banks have set up IBFs in New York, with the result that New York has become one of the leading centers for Eurocurrency dealing.

Interest Rate Relationships in the Eurocurrency Market

Because the Eurocurrency market is unregulated, banks accepting Eurocurrency deposits are not normally subject to official reserve requirements. Eurobanks can thus lend out a larger proportion of a Eurocurrency deposit than they could of a domestic deposit. Further, banks can pay a market rate for Eurocurrency deposits and are not subject to interest rate ceilings or other restrictions on interest payments. For this reason, Eurobanks can afford to pay interest rates higher than those normally available on bank deposits in the domestic market for the same currency.

Similarly, Eurobanks must charge less on loans in a particular currency than the rate charged in the domestic loan market in order to attract loan business. The unrestricted nature of the Eurocurrency markets and, particularly, the absence of reserve requirements enable Eurobanks to operate on narrower spreads (the difference between the price at which money is lent and the bank's cost of funds). Exhibit 6-2 shows the hierarchy of the rate structure of the Eurocurrency market.

Eurocurrency Lending

Because of the broad deposit base that the Eurocurrency markets provide, international banks have been able to lend funds to multinational

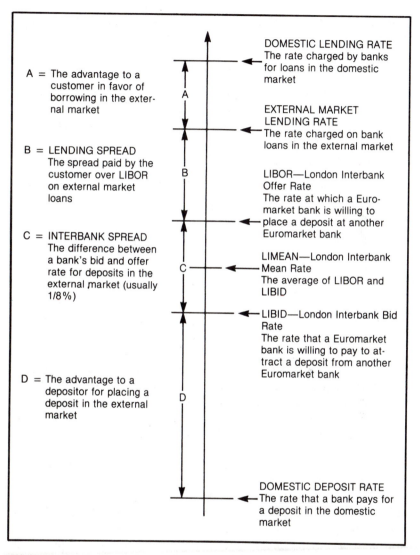

EXHIBIT 6-2 Rate Structure in the Eurocurrency Market

corporations, domestic clients, and sovereign governments. Unlike traditional financial markets, where loans are priced in terms of a fixed interest rate, from its inception, Eurocurrency loans have been priced on a floating interest rate basis. Rates on loans are usually quoted at a *lending spread* over the London Interbank Offer Rate (LIBOR). At periodic intervals, determined in the loan agreement, the interest rate charged to the borrower is changed to reflect changes in LIBOR.

Suppose, for example, that Agfolk Industries agrees to borrow $2 million for two years at a rate for LIBOR plus ⅜ percent, with adjustment in the interest rate to take place every six months. At the time the loan agreement is made, let us suppose that LIBOR is 9¼ percent. For the first six months of the loan, the interest rate charged is LIBOR plus ⅜ percent, or 9.25 percent plus 0.375 percent, equal to 9.625 percent. After six months, suppose that LIBOR falls to 8½ percent. The rate on the loan for the second six-month period is 8.50 percent plus 0.375 percent = 8.875 percent. At the end of the first year, a new rate would be set for the next six months, and at the end of the eighteen months, a new rate would be set for the final six months of the loan.

The Impact of Floating Interest Rate Pricing

LIBOR pricing shifts the risk of changes in interest rate to the borrower. If interest rates rise over the life of the loan, the borrower may end up paying more in interest than anticipated. On the other hand, if interest rates fall, the borrower can take advantage of lower rates.

The floating interest rate system allows the lending institution to match its interest earnings to the cost of its funds. The deposit base for Eurolending is generally short-term in nature. A lending institution normally would not obtain a substantial volume of two-year Eurodollar deposits. Using LIBOR pricing eliminates the interest-rate risk that arises from borrowing short-term at changing interest rates and lending long-term at fixed interest rates.

Returning to the example above, suppose that the bank can fund the original loan with six-month money. When its six-month deposits mature, it can go into the Eurocurrency market and buy funds from other banks at the current LIBOR rate. Because the bank receives LIBOR plus a spread and because its cost of funds is at most LIBOR, the bank ensures that it will make a profit on the loan transaction equal to the spread. Of course, a bank may choose to mismatch maturities between its assets and liabilities, depending on its view of interest rates. Nonetheless, the LIBOR pricing system would allow a conservative bank, which always borrowed at or below LIBOR and loaned at LIBOR plus some spread, to make the spread as its profit.

Utilization of Euromarkets for Term Credit

Multinational corporations find Eurocurrency loans to be a flexible method of financing. Loans on this floating rate basis are readily available for maturities ranging from three months or shorter to as much as ten years. Banks can also offer *standby Eurodollar lines of credit*, where the bank agrees to lend the borrower, as needed, up to a fixed limit at the prevailing LIBOR rate plus spread. Banks generally charge a commitment fee for this standby line of credit. Also, the bank may create a *revolving credit facility*, also called a *rollover facility*. The bank commits to lend funds for a three- to five-year period. The borrower evidences indebtedness by issuing six-month notes that are renewed, or rolled over, at maturity. The interest on the new notes is calculated at LIBOR plus the agreed spread. A fee is charged on the unused portion of the revolving credit facility.

Syndicated Eurocredits

The credit needs of a particular corporation or country often far exceed the capacity of an individual bank to lend prudently. In order to accommodate these large credit needs, banks form syndicates to provide the required funds. Loans of Eurocurrencies by a syndicate of banks are known as *syndicated Eurocredits*. Although some syndicated Eurocredits are relatively small and involve only a few banks, large sums of money have been raised in this fashion. Syndicated credits of over $1 billion (known as *jumbos*), involving 200 or more banks, have been arranged. Syndicated loans to corporate borrowers normally fall in the range of $50 million to $250 million, although in 1985 Texaco arranged two syndicated credits of $500 million and $750 million, respectively. Most borrowing in the syndicated Eurocredit market is done by sovereign borrowers—that is, by national governments or public-sector agencies borrowing with a guarantee from the national government. In particular, developing countries, such as Brazil, Mexico, Argentina, South Korea, and Venezuela, have been very active borrowers. Communist bloc countries, particularly Poland and Romania, have also borrowed heavily.

How Eurocredits Are Arranged   The banks involved in a syndicated credit can be classified according to their function. One bank receives a *mandate* from a prospective borrower to put together a syndicate of banks that will lend on specified terms and conditions. This mandated bank then puts together a group of *managing banks* that agree that each will be responsible for a certain portion of the loan. Between them, the managing banks guarantee that they will provide the entire amount of the credit on the terms specified. Normally, much negotiation takes place between the mandated and managing banks regarding the terms of the credit.

The mandated and managing banks then attempt to involve other banks in the syndicated credit. They prepare a description of the loan and supporting information regarding the borrower, the so-called *placement memorandum,* and they circulate it to other banks. The mandated bank generally invites participation from other banks by telex. Banks that decide to become *participating banks* subscribe to purchase a certain share of the syndication. Up to half the loan may be taken by participating banks, with the mandated bank retaining about 10 percent of the credit and other managing banks taking their respective portion.

In deciding whether to participate in the syndicated credit, it is the responsibility of the participating bank to perform its own credit analysis. Mandated banks theoretically make no guarantee as to the creditworthiness of the loan, although their own participation would indicate that the borrower is creditworthy. Participating banks also recognize that these loan participations are not readily liquid assets; although it is possible to sell off participation in a particular loan, it is a rather lengthy process.

Front-End Fees   All banks participating in a syndicated credit receive interest payments on the funds that they have committed. However, fees charged to the borrower at the time that the credit is syndicated are a major source of compensation to managing and participating banks. These *front-end fees* range from ½ to 1 percent of the entire amount of the credit, depending on the negotiating power of the borrower at the time the syndication mandate is given. A participating bank generally receives ¼ to ½ percent of the amount of its participation. The managing banks receive ⅛ to ¼ percent of the amount of the loan for which they have taken responsibility. The mandated bank receives ⅛ to ¼ percent of the amount of the entire credit as compensation for originating the loan.

Front-end fees materially increase the rate that banks earn on syndicated credits. For this reason, the competition to receive the mandate to syndicate a loan for a good credit risk is intense.

Euronotes and Eurocommercial Paper

In recent years, a new approach to borrowing, the Euronote and Eurocommercial paper (Euro CP), has begun to replace the syndicated Eurocredit as the primary vehicle for floating rate funding, at least for prime corporate and sovereign lenders. Euronotes are essentially short-term issues of promissory notes by corporate and sovereign borrowers, which are distributed to ultimate purchasers through an underwriting and a sales distribution agreement with either commercial banks or investment banks.

Euronote Issuance Facilities   A *Euronote issuance facility* is arranged with a bank or bank syndicate (either commercial or investment) and extends several years into the future, allowing the corporate borrower to have promissory notes outstanding up to the limit of the facility. The arranging banks usually receive a front-end fee. These facilities are underwritten, in the sense that a group of *underwriting banks* agrees to purchase any paper that is not otherwise sold, up to the limit of the facility. Banks agreeing to participate in underwriting the facility receive a *facility fee.*

Because the Euronote market is relatively new, widely varying practices in placing the promissory notes with the final investor have appeared in the market. Most early Euronotes utilized a *tender panel*, a group of banks that would bid for the notes when the borrower decided to issue them and resell the notes to private investors. More recently, facilities have used one financial institution to act as a *sole placing agent*; the placing agent undertakes the responsibility of selling the entire Euronote issue to investors.

The development of the Euronote market provides, essentially, a long-term funding commitment at short-term floating interest rates. The corporate borrower can borrow only as much as is needed at any point in time and has some flexibility in maturity (one, three, or six months) when using the facility. From the viewpoint of the corporate issuer, the cost of funds is usually lower than what it might find in the syndicated credit market.

There are two reasons for the relatively low cost of Euronote financing. First, competition among investment and commercial banks for position in the Euronote marketplace has led to extremely low facility fees. For example, the average facility fee of the Unilever Capital Corp. issue in May 1985 was only 5.01 basis points (0.0501 percent). Second, there is a significant demand by ultimate investors for corporate paper in their portfolios. Because commercial banks are carrying large amounts of suspect sovereign debt, arising from loans to developing countries, investors who usually buy Euro CDs to put funds on deposit with Eurobanks have been aggressively seeking to diversify their risk. Corporate promissory notes are not viewed to be as risky as bank debt, from the investor's viewpoint.

As a consequence of these factors, corporate borrowers have secured funds by issuing Euronotes at rates below LIBOR. Indeed, when Unilever issued the first $100 million of paper under the $1 billion facility mentioned above, the average cost of three-month funds was 13.25 basis points below LIBID, the London Interbank Bid Rate. Savings by issuance of Euronotes rather than utilizing syndicated credit financing are estimated at 10 to 50 basis points.

From a modest beginning in 1978, the number of announced note issuance facilities grew dramatically; some 230 note issuance facilities were arranged in 1985 alone, totaling $38.9 billion. Large sovereign facilities (a $4-billion facility arranged for Sweden in 1984 being the largest) are now being replaced in the market by large facilities for corporations, such as the $1-billion Unilever facility and the $1.3-billion facility for John Deere. As Euro CP emerged, the number of new facilities fell; in 1986, there were only 148 new facilities, totaling $25.5 billion.

Although as of mid-1985 there were some $40 billion of note issuance facilities in effect, only about $7 billion of Euronotes had been issued. In some cases, borrowers were using the note issuance facility as a cheap backup to a program of issuing commercial paper in the United States. In others, firms were taking advantage of the flexibility of the note issuance facility concept to borrow only the funds required for the moment, while retaining the right to increase loans at a later date, as needed.

The Emergence of Eurocommercial Paper   Because Euronotes are rather new, the market is evolving dramatically. Prime borrowers are eliminating the underwriting component of the facility, marking the emergence of a parallel Eurocommercial paper market with a system of dealers similar to the domestic U.S. market. General Motors Acceptance Corporation (GMAC), the world's largest corporate borrower, had approximately $1 billion in Eurocommercial paper outstanding as of August 1986, compared with $34 billion in U.S. commercial paper.

From only three Eurocommercial paper dealerships announced in 1984, with a total amount of $281 million, sixty-three new programs (with a total value of $13.0 billion) were launched in 1985; and in 1986, 256 new programs, with an announced value of $49.8 billion, were begun.

Bank regulators appear to be worried about the growth of bank contingent liabilities from the underwriting commitments of Euronote deals; so far, only the Bank of England has acted, including underwriting commitments of banks in the calculation of their contingent liability position. Regulation of the market would increase the cost to the borrower, erode the cost advantage that Euronotes currently offer when compared to syndicated credits, and spur the further development of nonunderwritten Eurocommercial paper.

Medium Term Notes   In 1986, prime corporate borrowers (led by Pepsico) issued *medium-term notes* — corporate promissory notes with a one- to five-year maturity sold through an investment bank acting as dealer—on the Euromarkets. These medium-term note facilities represent an extension of the Euro CP approach to marketing corporate liabilities to investors and essentially complete the maturity spectrum for direct corporate borrowing on the Euromarkets as follows:

Maturity	*Vehicle*
1 year or less	Eurocommercial paper or Euronotes
1–5 years	Medium-term notes
5 years or more	Eurobonds

Multi-Option Funding Facilities

With the wide range of potential funding vehicles available to the borrower, many borrowers would like to create a flexible funding arrangement that leaves open the possibility of borrowing from alternative sources at the best possible rate. Commercial and investment banks have responded by developing the concept of *multi-option funding facilities*, which offer the borrower the choice of up to six different funding options. In these arrangements, the bank provides access to the funds and the borrower can select the way the funds are provided. Typical options include borrowing at LIBOR plus a spread, issuing Euronotes, or having banks bid on short-term advances to the borrower.

The Eurobond Market

A *Eurobond* is a bond issued in an external capital market. Just as external intermediated markets have developed since 1960, an external market for the direct medium- and long-term debt issues of corporations and government entities has also developed. From a modest volume of $164 million in 1963, the market saw new Eurobond issues total $188 billion in 1986, as shown in Exhibit 6-3.

The distinguishing characteristic of a Eurobond is that it is issued outside the country in whose currency the bond is denominated. Bonds denominated in dollars are the predominant type issued in the market (60 to 75 percent), but issues are made in the German mark, British pound, Japanese yen, composite currencies such as the Special Drawing Right (SDR) and the European Currency Unit (ECU), and a number of others, in significantly smaller amounts. Euromark bonds are somewhat difficult to classify because the relative openness of the German capital market allows foreign borrowers to place mark bonds with German residents and nonresidents through both German and non-German securities firms; for statistical purposes, German mark issues of non-German borrowers are classified as Euromark issues.

Eurobond issues are not subject to the control of the regulatory authorities of the country in whose currency they are issued. Thus, Eurodollar bonds are not subject to registration with or regulation by the Securities and Exchange Commission. Consequently, Eurobonds can be brought to market rather quickly; the ability to time issues flexibly to take advantage of favorable market conditions has been a major reason for Eurobond market growth.

Fixed-Rate Eurobond Issues

The typical size of Eurobond issues of major corporations ranges from $50 million to $300 million. Issues are normally made in the form of the bearer certificates with an annual coupon. Issues are made in jurisdictions that are free of withholding taxes on interest payments. Withholding taxes are taxes on dividend and interest payments that are

EXHIBIT 6-3 International Bond Issues and Bank Credits (in US $ billions)

	1982	1983	1984	1985	1986	Jan-Mar 1987
International bond issues	78.042	76.329	107.411	167.756	226.393	58.493
Eurobonds	51.645	48.501	79.458	136.731	187.952	49.304
U.S. dollar	43.959	38.428	63.593	97.782	118.220	17.601
German mark	2.588	3.817	4.604	9.491	16.870	7.505
British pound	0.748	1.947	3.997	5.766	10.510	5.369
Japanese yen	0.374	0.212	1.212	6.539	18.673	8.168
ECU	1.980	2.019	3.032	7.038	6.965	3.377
Other	1.996	2.078	3.020	10.114	16.713	7.284
Foreign bonds	26.397	27.828	27.953	31.025	38.441	9.189
U.S. dollar	5.946	4.545	5.487	4.655	6.064	1.550
German mark	2.952	2.671	2.243	1.741	—	—
British pound	1.214	0.811	1.292	0.958	0.322	—
Swiss franc	11.432	14.299	12.626	14.954	23.401	5.992
Japanese yen	3.418	3.772	4.628	6.379	4.756	0.981
Other	1.435	1.730	1.677	2.339	3.898	0.666
International bank credits	92.585	82.074	125.922	116.964	91.164	15.610
Eurocurrency credits	85.015	74.222	112.605	110.317	82.755	13.793
Foreign credits	7.570	7.852	13.317	6.647	8.409	1.817

SOURCE: Morgan Guaranty Trust Co. of New York, *World Financial Markets* (April 1987, February 1986). Reproduced with permission of the copyright holder.

withheld at the time that the interest or dividend payment is made. Because the United States had a 30-percent withholding tax on interest paid to foreign nationals until mid-1984, U.S. corporations issuing Eurobonds created special international financing subsidiaries to issue the bonds, and backed them with a parent guarantee. Repeal of the withholding tax in July 1984 has led to direct borrowing on Euromarkets by U.S. firms. Maturities range from two to twenty years.

Most Eurobonds with a maturity of seven years or more have either a *purchase fund* or a *sinking fund.* Under a purchase fund agreement, issuers are required to purchase a portion of the issue on the secondary market, as long as the secondary market price is below par. A purchase fund provides price support in the market if interest rates rise but requires the issuer to refund that portion of the debt at a higher interest rate. A sinking fund obligates purchase by the firm of a portion of the debt each year, either in the secondary market if the bond is trading below par or through random selection and call at par if the bond is trading above par.

When contemplating a Eurobond issue, the corporate treasurer selects a leading financial institution to serve as lead manager for the issue. The lead manager's responsibility begins with providing advice regarding the timing, amount, interest rate, and currency of denomination for the proposed issue. The lead manager perhaps may bring in several other investment firms to serve as comanagers. Together they assemble a syndicate of investment houses to underwrite the issue; the underwriting syndicate actually buys the securities from the issuer at a specified price. Each underwriter arranges with a larger number of investment firms to sell, or distribute, the issue to the investor. A lively *grey market* has developed, where bonds not yet issued are actively traded.

Lead managers are judged on their ability to price an issue properly, distribute the issue broadly, and stabilize the price of the issue in the secondary market. Depending on the size and maturity of the issue and the state of competition among potential lead managers, fees and commissions range from 1.5 percent to 2.5 percent of the amount issued. Typically, the lead manager or lead management group receives ⅜ to ½ percent, the underwriters receive ⅜ to ½ percent, and the selling group receives 1.25 to 1.75 percent.

Investors and Borrowers in the Eurobond Market

For the investor, the Eurobond market offers investor anonymity (through the use of bearer securities), no taxation of income at the source, and a certain degree of marketability. Although the secondary market in Eurobonds is not as deep as some investors would like, a total of $3.57 trillion in international securities transactions (primarily Eurobonds) were cleared through the two market clearing firms, Euroclear and Cedel, in 1986.

For the borrowers, the primary incentive to use Eurobonds is cheapness. Commissions and fees in the Eurobond markets are lower than in national markets. Other issuing expenses are lower because of the absence of regulatory requirements. Further, because of the advantages of Eurobonds to the investor, they are willing to accept a lower yield on these instruments.

Because a large portion of the Eurobonds outstanding are held by individuals rather than institutions, the Eurobond market is a "name" market in which the name recognition or brand identity of the borrower is an important consideration. Firms without name recognition must be introduced to the market gradually, accompanied by a substantial public relations, or "roadshow," effort. Firms with wide recognition may achieve terms not obtainable in the New York bond market because their name outweighs purely financial considerations. On the other hand, preservation of a positive corporate image becomes very important; for example, Texaco, a major borrower, saw an extensive secondary market sell-off in its Eurobond issues in November 1985, shortly after a negative judgment in the Pennzoil litigation.

Variations on the Fixed-Rate Eurobond

The Eurobond market, in its unregulated state, offers the opportunity for almost unlimited experimentation and innovation. Each innovation must offer advantages both to the borrower and to the investor. In many cases, the borrower achieves a lower cost by offering the investor a sweetener of some sort. One variation is the so-called *retractable bond*. For example, a bond might be issued with a maturity of fifteen years, with a coupon fixed for the first five years. At the end of five years, the issuer sets a new coupon rate for the next five years, and the investor has the right to redeem the bond at par. The borrower, unless seeking to reduce indebtedness, would set the new coupon high enough to prevent redemption but in line with market rates; the borrower saves the expense of refunding the debt by a new issue on the market. From the investor's viewpoint, he or she has purchased a five-year bond that can be rolled over for another five years (and rolled over again at ten years) at market interest rates.

Extendable bonds offer the opportunity to the investor to extend the maturity of the bond at a new interest rate; these bonds are usually issued with a short-term horizon but with the opportunity for numerous annual extensions. Other issuers attach warrants to fixed-interest bonds, either to purchase debt or equity. The typical *debt warrant* allows the holder to purchase a bond of the issuer at par or at some other price that carries a particular coupon. For example, at the same time that Standard Oil issued $150 million in four-year notes with a 10.5-percent coupon in December 1985, it also sold 150,000 warrants at $25 each. Each warrant allows the holder to buy a $1,000 note carrying a 10 percent coupon with a December 1992 maturity. The warrant exercise price varies so that the final yield to the investor is always 11.5 percent.

Zero-coupon bonds have been very popular in the Eurobond market from time to time. Maturities for these issues tend to be longer than for typical Eurobonds, on the order of ten to twenty years.

Floating-Rate Notes

The Eurobond market also offers the opportunity to secure long-term funding at floating interest rates. Since the first floating-rate issue in 1970, debt securities with periodically adjustable interest rates have become a major component in the Eurobond market, totaling more than half the value of Eurodollar bond issues in 1984.

The typical *floating-rate note* changes the interest rate every six months. Interest is normally tied to the six-month London Interbank Offer Rate (LIBOR); interest is paid LIBOR plus some spread fixed over the life of the security. The spread depends on the creditworthiness of the borrower and market conditions. The primary issuers of floating-rate notes have been financial institutions, whose asset positions typically include floating rate loans to customers. Issuing expenses on floating-rate notes are generally lower than on fixed-rate issues (¼ to 1 percent of face) because the floating interest rate minimizes the risk to the underwriter.

Numerous variations of the floating-rate approach are available. These are usually designed to offer either the issuer or the investor protection against extreme interest rate movements. Many issues have a *minimum coupon*, which will be paid if the floating rate falls below it. A variant of this approach is the so-called *drop-lock* floating-rate note, where the issue converts to a fixed-rate issue if the floating rate falls below a certain threshold. Also, floating-rate notes are now issued that allow conversion to fixed-rate bonds in the early part of the bond's life, at the option of the bondholder.

On the upside, borrowers have sought interest-rate protection through the issuance of floating-rate notes with a capped interest rate. In a typical *capped floating-rate note*, interest payments do not exceed a maximum coupon, typically set at approximately 3 percent over LIBOR at issue; in exchange, the investor receives a more generous spread over LIBOR. In many cases, financial institutions that issue floating-rate notes with caps do not need the protection afforded by the cap and sell the cap to another floating-rate borrower in exchange for a lump-sum payment or for a payment stream over the life of the loan (typically about ⅜ percent of face over the life of the loan). Floating-rate notes within both minimum and maximum coupons have also been issued.

Maturities for floating-rate notes are typically longer than those for fixed-rate issues because the interest rate does float. Sweden has issued notes, for example, with a forty-year maturity. In late 1984, perpetual floating-rate notes, with no fixed maturity date, began to be offered.

Equity Linked Eurobonds

Eurobonds with equity features made an early appearance in the Eurobond market. Convertible bonds have been offered since an issue by Monsanto in 1965. Convertible bonds are essentially analogous to convertibles issued in the U.S. domestic bond market, although conversion by Eurobond investors may lead to broadening the international basis of stock ownership.

A wide variety of pricing opportunities exist in Euroconvertibles. Essentially, the issuer can put a coupon on the issue slightly below market rates and maintain a high conversion premium (up to 30 percent). Texaco took this approach with its massive $1-billion, ten-year convertible issue of March 1984, which had an 11⅛ percent coupon and a conversion premium of 28.6 percent. Other issues have featured substantially below-market coupons and conversion premiums in the 15 to 20 percent range.

Bonds with equity warrants have also been issued. Typically, firms sell these issues at par, with a below-market coupon rate set so that the value of the warrant is 5 to 20 percent of the value of the issue. Japanese firms, in particular, have been heavy users of this form of funding.

Global Equity Markets

To a much greater extent, equity markets have remained outside the process of globalization of international capital markets. Usual approaches by corporations have been to list shares of the company on exchanges outside the home market or to use local equity markets for equity issues of the local subsidiary. Often, such local equity issues have been designed to meet local requirements for equity participation by local nationals rather than as purely financial operations. Many multinationals prefer 100 percent ownership of their subsidiaries and consequently have not used local equity markets for subsidiary funding.

Nonetheless, since 1983, truly international share offerings have begun to appear with increasing frequency. In 1986, 102 new Euroequity issues, valued at $9.4 billion (a total almost three times that for 1985), were brought to market. A limited number of global investment banks underwrite equity issues or sell shares on a best effort basis at sales commissions or concessions of 2.5 to 6.5 percent of the market price of the stock. In some issues, the international share offering is a component of a multiple market offering. For example, in September 1983, Swiss Bank Corporation headed a syndicate placing internationally 1 million shares of Alcan Aluminum, Limited at $39.50. Simultaneously, 3.3 million shares were sold in Canada and another 3.3 million in the United States.

Typically, Euroequity issues have been syndicated among investment banks, much like Eurobonds. The capacity of the market was tested with unfavorable results by the secondary offering of $2.09 billion of Fiat equity in September 1986, which left underwriters with losses estimated at $100 million to $250 million. Although the Fiat issue's full ramifications are as yet unclear, it has established at least a temporary upper limit on the size of Euroequity issues.

Swaps

The emergence of the interest-rate swap market in the early 1980s materially enhanced the ability of corporate finance executives to secure funding that meets corporate requirements at very inexpensive rates. Basically, a liability swap is an exchange of debt obligations between two borrowers; that is, Borrower A assumes Borrower B's repayment obligation, and Borrower B assumes Borrower A's repayment obligation. The transaction is normally funneled through a commercial or investment bank, so that each party to the swap has the bank as the credit risk rather than the other party. For standing in the middle of the transaction and taking on the credit risk of both parties, the bank receives compensation from one or both parties to the transaction. The size of the market in liability swaps is not known with accuracy; estimates are that $150 billion to $200 billion were written in 1985 and about $300 billion in 1986. Seven financial institutions, Citicorp, Bankers Trust, Salomon Brothers, First Boston, Chemical Bank, Morgan Guaranty, and Chase Manhattan, are estimated to have each written more than $20 billion in swaps over the twelve-month period July 1985 through June 1986, as market growth accelerated.

Liability swaps are of two kinds: interest-rate swaps and currency swaps. In an interest-rate swap, one borrower has fixed-rate funding and seeks floating-rate funding, and the other has floating-rate funding and seeks fixed-rate funding. In a currency swap, one borrower might have dollar funding and seek Swiss franc funding, while the other might have Swiss franc funding and seek dollar funding. Because the debt issues in each of the currencies may be fixed or floating, there are actually three kinds of currency swaps:

1. *Fixed-to-fixed:* both are fixed-rate fundings.
2. *Fixed-to-floating:* one loan is at a fixed rate, and the other floats.
3. *Floating-to-floating:* both loans have floating interest rates.

Many international financial deals are swap-driven, in the sense that the borrower has no specific use for the currency in which a funding takes place but is simply taking advantage of a relative borrowing advantage in a particular market. The liabilities created in this manner are then swapped as attractive swap opportunities present themselves. The dramatic explosion in floating rate note funding by banks in 1984 was swap-driven, in this sense, because most of these liabilities were swapped for corporate fixed-rate fundings. Banks received long-term fixed-rate financing and corporations received floating-rate funds, frequently at rates below LIBOR. Liability swaps are a major component in the development of global funding strategies for the multinational corporation. Their use in this regard is explained in detail in Chapter 7.

THE INSTITUTIONAL STRUCTURE
OF THE GLOBAL FINANCIAL SYSTEM

Thus far, the discussion in this chapter has been limited to the financial markets that comprise the global financial system. In Chapter 7, we will explore in detail how corporations can meet their global funding needs by accessing these markets. However, a discussion of the global financial system would be incomplete without introducing the major financial institutions that are participants in these markets. They are

1. major commercial banks with international capabilities
2. major investment banks active on international securities markets
3. specialized financial institutions, such as merchant banks, that offer international financial services
4. development finance institutions
5. government and supragovernment financial institutions (such as the International Monetary Fund) that manage the global financial system.

Global Commercial Banks

Commercial banks are a major force in the global financial system. Exhibit 6-4 shows the top thirty banks in the world in 1985, ranked by assets. From their strong bases in the financial markets of their home country, these banks have developed a substantial international presence. Most commercial banks active globally have adopted a strategy of international involvement that includes the establishment of a global network of branches, subsidiaries, correspondent relations, and other vehicles for participation in various global financial markets. Although many banks went international to meet the international needs of their corporate clientele, participation in international lending and other operations has, in many ways, become more market-opportunity than client-service based. As commercial banks have become more competitive for corporate international business, a premium has been placed on the ability to innovate, particularly in the area of financial services and creative funding mechanisms.

Global banks typically have a specific geographical base of operations where they secure retail deposits. However, the majority of funds used by these banks internationally are bought funds; that is, deposits from other financial institutions and other investors paid for at market interest rates.

Foreign Financial Market Presence

Banks can achieve a presence in a particular country's financial market in six different ways:

EXHIBIT 6-4 The World's Largest Banks

Rank	Name of Bank	Assets (US $ millions) 1985	Capital (rank)	
1	Citicorp United States	$167,201	$7,765	(1)
2	Dai-ichi Kangyo Bank Japan	157,614	3,126	(18)
3	Fuji Bank Japan	142,088	3,206	(17)
4	Sumitomo Bank Japan	135,349	3,326	(14)
5	Mitsubishi Bank Japan	132,901	3,253	(16)
6	Sanwa Bank Japan	122,973	2,731	(22)
7	Banque Nationale de Paris France	120,859	2,396	(32)
8	Caisse Nationale de Credit Agricole France	120,672	5,136	(2)
9	Bank America Corp. United States	114,751	4,547	(4)
10	Credit Lyonnais France	109,445	1,274	(67)
11	Norinchukin Bank Japan	106,724	506	(156)
12	National Westminster Bank United Kingdom	103,498	4,263	(8)
13	Industrial Bank of Japan Japan	102,741	2,146	(35)
14	Societe Generale France	95,864	1,944	(37)
15	Deutsche Bank West Germany	93,855	3,740	(9)
16	Barclays United Kingdom	93,108	4,724	(3)
17	Tokai Bank Japan	90,397	1,843	(40)
18	Mitsui Bank Japan	88,476	1,653	(47)

(*continued*)

EXHIBIT 6-4   continued

Rank	Name of Bank	Assets (US $ millions) 1985	Capital (rank)	
19	Chase Manhattan Corp. United States	84,865	4,459	(6)
20	Midland Bank United Kingdom	82,941	2,637	(24)
21	Mitsubishi Trust and Banking Corp. Japan	80,546	1,663	(46)
22	Sumitomo Trust and Banking Co. Japan	79,180	1,705	(43)
23	Long-Term Credit Bank of Japan Japan	78,859	1,618	(51)
24	Bank of Tokyo Japan	78,172	1,632	(49)
25	Dresdner Bank West Germany	74,890	2,197	(34)
26	Taiyo Kobe Bank Japan	74,477	1,349	(62)
27	Manufacturers Hanover Corp. United States	74,334	3,546	(11)
28	Mitsui Trust & Banking Co. Japan	72,901	1,455	(59)
29	Cie. Financiere de Paribas France	71,586	3,389	(13)
30	Hongkong and Shanghai Banking Corp. Hong Kong	68,833	2,802	(21)

SOURCE: *Institutional Investor* (June 1986).

1. A *subsidiary bank*: a wholly owned incorporated bank located in a foreign country, subject to the banking laws of that country and able to conduct a full range of banking business in that country.

2. An *affiliate bank:* a locally incorporated bank owned in partnership

with other foreign banks or with local shareholders, conducting a full range of banking business.

3. A *branch bank:* a branch of the parent bank not legally separate from the parent and subject to the banking regulations of the parent's country *and* the host country. Branch deposits are legal obligations of the parent, and consequently the credit of the parent bank backs deposits at branches. Branches can carry out all banking business permitted by local and parent country authorities.

4. An *agency:* an establishment similar to a branch that cannot accept deposits from the public.

5. A *representative office:* an office established to develop business relationships in a country but that cannot conduct a banking business within the host country.

6. A *correspondent bank relationship:* a correspondent relationship established with a local bank, which handles the banking activities of the foreign bank on a compensated basis. A bank may prefer this arrangement over establishing its own presence in the foreign country.

U.S. Banks in the International Financial Market

There are several aspects of the banking system of the United States that affect how banks based there structure their international banking operations. U.S. banks are authorized to set up international banking facilities (IBFs), which allow them to conduct a Eurocurrency business from a U.S. base. These IBFs offer time deposits to foreign banks and foreign residents (including corporations) and may lend to these same groups. They may borrow and lend to other IBFs, so that an interbank Eurocurrency market may develop. IBFs are not subject to reserve requirements, interest-rate ceilings, or federal taxes.

Because the finance of the international trade of the United States has historically been centered in New York, the Federal Reserve Act, as early as 1916, contained a mechanism for banks to conduct an international banking business across state lines. A bank could set up a subsidiary in another state after agreeing with the Board of Governors of the Federal Reserve System to restrict their activities to those related to the conduct of an international banking business; for this reason, these subsidiaries were called *agreement corporations.* Another amendment, in 1919 (known as the Edge Act, after its author), allowed chartering of subsidiaries for international banking and financing operations. Many banks have, since 1960, chartered one or more *Edge Act subsidiaries* to provide a geographical presence in major trading centers. Banks not based in New York have set up Edge Act subsidiaries in that city; however, money center banks have used the Edge Act vehicle to set up international banking operations in the emerging trade centers of the Sun Belt. Edge Acts are also used to provide ownership of foreign subsidiaries because U.S. banks cannot own overseas subsidiaries directly.

Foreign Banks in the U.S. Financial Market

Foreign banks operating in the United States did so with great flexibility prior to the passage of the International Banking Act of 1978, which regulated their activities for the first time. Foreign banks are no longer able to set up retail banking operations in more than one state or to mix commercial and investment banking business. As U.S. financial markets are increasingly deregulated, foreign banks will be able to expand their U.S. operations. They have proven to be strong competitors, particularly in the corporate loan sector. Their competitiveness is based, in part, on access to Eurocurrency funding and on lower capital adequacy ratios imposed by their home governments.

International Services of Commercial Banks

Corporations approach global commercial banks both for funding and for services. A corporation seeking funding for local subsidiary operations may borrow from the local branch of its lead bank. Commercial banks have been the primary source for the finance of international trade transactions. As has been shown, commercial banks have also played a major role in the syndicated credit and Euronote market. Where regulatory authorities allow, some commercial banks have established subsidiaries or entered joint ventures to participate in underwriting and distributing Eurobonds and foreign bonds.

In Chapter 2, we saw that global commercial banks are the primary market makers in foreign exchange. Expertise in the movement of money across national boundaries has led banks to offer cash management services. With the enhanced technological capability of electronic funds transfer systems, banks have developed sophisticated online global funds management systems, allowing the customer to obtain reports on account balances, initiate global funds transfers, make short-term investments, repay loans, and take other financial measures on a timely basis. Banks also offer advisory services for foreign exchange risk management and exchange rate forecasting services; set up netting systems (see Chapter 8); and, in general, provide international financial expertise that the corporate client may not be able to generate internally.

Global Investment Banks

Traditionally, investment banks offer services to corporations and others wishing to sell debt and equity securities to individuals and institutions. The emergence of the Eurobond market in the 1960s was the occasion for many investment banks in the United States to develop their international business. As U.S.-based multinational corporations sought offshore capital, their U.S. investment houses worked with investment banks in Europe to bring these issuers to the emerging Eurobond market. Because the major financial institutions in Germany and Switzerland combine both the investment and commercial banking function, U.S. commercial banks, as well, began to establish an investment banking capability in Europe, usually in London. These global investment banks underwrite and distribute securities in home country and external (Euro-) capital markets. As we have seen, the primary external market vehicle is the Eurobond, but beginning in 1983, the number of Euroequity issues began to grow. In addition to public offerings, these investment banks may also place external market securities privately.

Once securities have been placed, global investment banks are very active in the secondary Euromarkets. They make markets for specific securities, particularly those for which they served as lead managers. They serve as brokers in secondary market transactions and trade on their own account. On an international basis, investment banks are free of U.S. regulations separating commercial and investment banking, and so they engage in money market operations, as well. Investment banks have become prominent in the swap market and the market for Euronotes.

Consortia Banks and Bank Groups

Many commercial banks, anxious to diversify their international product lines in the late 1960s and 1970s, formed *consortium banks*, also called *multibanks*. These banks were formed to participate in the Eurocurrency and Eurobond markets. The typical consortium bank is owned by a number of other banks (usually, five to ten); no one partner owns a controlling share of the equity. Some are geographic in origin. For example, Scandinavian Bank is owned by seven different banks from five different Nordic countries; Japan International Bank, by four Japanese commercial banks and three Japanese securities firms. Others have broad European membership, and some include U.S.-based banks.

The consortium bank was and is a strategic response to the market opportunity offered by the emergence of the Euromarkets. As commercial banks develop other Euromarket opportunities, participation in consortia may no longer fit bank strategy. The early 1980s have seen some consortia bank divestment; for example, Orion Bank, a major early consortium, was sold by its owners to the Royal Bank of Canada.

Banks in the various European countries have formed so-called *banking clubs*, associations of European banks that provide a Europewide set of financial services for each member bank's clients. These banking clubs may also establish joint ventures to pursue opportunities in specific financial markets, such as leasing.

Merchant Banks

The concept of a *merchant bank* has its origin in the British banking system. Merchant banks are specialized financial institutions that conduct a banking type business (acceptance of deposits and making loans) but whose primary function is the provision of financial expertise in exchange for payment of fees. Merchant banks typically serve as advisors in major merger and acquisition activities, as catalysts in major project financings, arrangers of large-scale cross-border leases, and other specialized financial engineering beyond the skills of other institutions.

The merchant bank concept is the assembling of financial expertise and the application of that expertise to a wide variety of client funding needs in exchange for a fee. Merchant banks can be viewed as the financial engineers of the global financial system.

British merchant banks were uniquely situated to take advantage of the development of the Euromarkets in London. In fact, in its early days, the Eurodollar market was called the *merchant bank market*. Many merchant banks have been acquired by large commercial or investment banks as a method of bringing their global expertise to bear on client problems. Other financial institutions have set up merchant banking subsidiaries.

Many of the larger commercial banks have, in essence, become multiple-product merchant banks in the sense that they have moved rapidly into the provision of global financial expertise on a fee basis to clients. Bankers Trust, one of the largest U.S. money-center banks, has announced its strategy to become a global merchant bank.

Development Finance Institutions

Developing countries have a continuous need for external capital to be used in the process of economic development. Although a portion of this external capital may come in the form of direct grants from the developed countries, most comes either from borrowing at commercial rates from financial institutions or borrowing from institutions especially created to assist in the development process.

Most countries have their own national development bank or banks, which provide local currency financing for projects and may also pass through foreign currency funds from external institutions. Some countries, particularly the Middle Eastern countries of Kuwait, Abu Dhabi, and Saudi Arabia, have loan funds (created from oil revenues) that are made available for the economic development of other countries.

Regional Development Banks

A number of major regional development banks raise funds from members and from world capital markets, and lend them on to developing nations within the region. Among the most important are

1. The Inter-American Development Bank (IDB) (which makes development loans primarily to Latin America; members include twenty-seven western hemisphere nations and sixteen nonregional developed countries)
2. The Asian Development Bank (ADB)
3. The African Development Bank (AFDB)
4. The Caribbean Development Bank (CDB)
5. The Central American Development Bank of Economic Integration (CABEI)
6. The European Investment Bank (EIB)
7. The Nordic Investment Bank
8. The Islamic Development Bank
9. The Arab Fund for Economic and Social Development (AFESD)
10. The OPEC Special Fund for International Development (OFID).

143

These regional development banks or funds make loans for various types of development projects. Projects may receive funding from a number of different development banks, should the host country be eligible.

The World Bank Group

The World Bank Group plays the most important role in providing official funds for economic development. The World Bank itself, organized in 1944 as the primary postwar development finance institution, makes loans on market terms for the economic development of its member nations. Most loans are for infrastructure activities (agriculture, energy, transportation, water, and so forth), but the World Bank also lends to local development banks to fund their local activities. The World Bank funds its operations by the contributions of its member countries and by substantial borrowing on world financial markets, backed by pledges of additional contributions by members. World Bank loans are priced to cover the cost of funds to the bank, so borrowing countries are paying market rates on funds provided by the World Bank. However, an affiliate of the World Bank, the International Development Association, makes loans on a highly concessionary basis; IDA loans may run as long as fifty years, feature extended grace periods before repayment begins, and require little or no interest payments. These loans are earmarked for critical projects in the poorest countries.

World Bank financing is not common in most corporate project financings, unless an infrastructure component of the project is present. The World Bank has included cross-default clauses with other financings related to World Bank projects, stipulating that default on any loan in the project means default on the World Bank loan, as well. Because countries value their access to World Bank funds, they are not likely to default on these loans, which adds protection to other project loans.

The area of the World Bank Group most likely to be involved in funding corporate investment projects is the International Finance Corporation (IFC), which makes loans to the private sector in developing countries. IFC will also take a minority equity position in a project, although ultimately the IFC will attempt to divest to local investors. IFC participation in a project is generally viewed with favor by other project lenders because the IFC has a reputation for careful analysis of the market and operating risks of its projects.

National and Supranational Institutions

Understanding of the development of global financial markets is incomplete without an awareness of the role played in the international monetary system by the finance (treasury) ministries and central banks of the countries of the world. In particular, policy decisions taken by the monetary authorities of the leading economic powers determine what market and funding opportunities are available to the multinational corporation. For example, it was the benevolent attitude of the Bank of England toward the taking of foreign currency (nonsterling) deposits by British banks that led to the development of the Euromarkets as they are known today. The monetary authorities, among other ways, directly affect global financial markets by their

1. money supply policies
2. exchange rate policies
3. controls on foreign portfolio and direct investment
4. regulation of financial markets and institutions
5. policy toward access to external financial markets by residents
6. policy toward access to domestic financial markets by nonresidents.

There is no Eurobond market in Swiss francs, for example, because the Swiss National Bank actively discourages its development as a matter of policy.

Sovereign Borrowing

The treasuries and other government agencies of developed countries are active borrowers on external markets. In 1984, the United States Treasury issued bonds specifically targeted for the foreign investor, as part of its strategy for funding the U.S. government's increasing deficits. Government agencies, such as the Federal National Mortgage Association (FNMA) and the Student Loan Marketing Corporation (SLMC), have issued tailored securities on external markets.

Borrowing by governments or their agencies is known as *sovereign borrowing*. Countries with reasonable external credit standing have been able to access both the Eurocredit/Euronote and the Eurobond markets. Developing nations such as Mexico, Brazil, Argentina, and Korea have raised vast amounts through syndicated credits. Although these borrowings in part went to specific development projects, many countries used Eurocredits to meet the balance-of-payments problems created by oil price increases. Because OPEC nations invested significant amounts in Eurocurrency deposits in the period 1977 through 1981, funds were readily available to Eurobanks to support large syndicated Eurocredits. Because competition to make loans was severe, the spread over LIBOR on these loans narrowed substantially during the period. The dramatic increase in interest rates in the United States and the accompanying rise in LIBOR, coupled with the effect of the global economic downturn of 1981 through 1982, have created substantial repayment problems for most developing sovereign borrowers. Although outright default on repayment obligations has generally been avoided, banks have been called on to extend additional credit and to delay the dates of payment of interest and principal.

Rescheduling Sovereign Debt

Rearrangement of payment terms for a borrower because of an inability to meet original terms is known as *rescheduling*. The process of rescheduling the debts of the developing countries has almost monopolized the attention of the international banking community since August 1982, when Mexico indicated that it could not meet the original terms of its debt. Overextension of credit to developing countries and to Eastern bloc countries has created a position in which the very stability of the international banking system has been questioned. Although some argue that the debt problems of developing nations are analogous to temporary liquidity problems, most believe that major structural issues in these economies must be addressed before creditworthiness can be reestablished. Initiatives for a combined public- and private-sector extension of additional credit, such as the proposals made in September 1985 by U.S. Secretary of the Treasury Baker, along with a multiyear rescheduling of existing debt, may provide a long-term solution.

The International Monetary Fund (IMF) has taken a leading role in the rescheduling process. Originally created to provide financial resources and policy guidance toward the maintenance of fixed exchange rates, the IMF has applied its resources and expertise toward providing funding for debtor nations attempting to reschedule their commercial bank debt. The absolute amount of IMF funding in an individual country rescheduling is not usually large, but IMF participation is evidence that the debtor nation has promised to implement economic policies designed (hopefully) to develop creditworthiness on external markets. For this reason, reschedulings may be delayed until the IMF has signed an agreement with the developing nation; failure to meet IMF economic targets usually leads to another round of rescheduling.

CHANGES AND IMPLICATIONS: A SUMMARY

The decade of the 1980s has seen major changes in the global financial markets, which will affect the approach that corporations will take toward developing a global funding strategy. Deregulation of many financial markets has led to a multitude of new opportunities for accessing funding on a global basis. Corporations that have access to a number of different domestic and external markets can seek funds at the lowest rate globally. Removal of exchange restrictions allows transfer of funds within the developed world, leading to a greater degree of market integration. Exchange financing techniques such as swaps take advantage of the differential pricing of risk in various markets and indeed are a form of arbitrage that, if unfettered, will reduce significantly the risk-pricing differential that now prevails.

The distinction between commercial and investment banks is blurring. As has been shown, in many countries these two functions have never been legally separated. However, investment banks are moving into commercial banking activities in the Euronote market, and commercial banks are establishing a prominent position in the Eurobond market. Both groups are scrambling for the types of business that characterize merchant banking activity. For the corporate borrower, the enhanced competitiveness for corporate business may lead to lower borrowing costs and transactions fees.

Commercial banks are being forced to move in the investment banking direction because of the increasing securitization of lending, particularly evident in the replacement of the syndicated Eurocredit by Euronotes and Eurocommercial paper, at least for top credits. In other words, a smaller proportion of corporate borrowing is being intermediated.

The global debt crisis has also enhanced the demand for corporate securities issued directly to the investor. Commercial banks with extensive developing country debt portfolios are viewed by investors as possibly riskier than prime corporate borrowers. For this reason, corporate names can borrow on the Euromarkets at or below LIBOR. Commercial banks, to maintain earnings, are looking more to fee-based activities for income generation, rather than the spread earned from relending bought money.

The advent of global electronic funds transfer capabilities, corporate computer ties with bank information systems, and more timely data on funds borrowing and investment opportunities has led to a more aggressive corporate posture in mobilizing global financial resources. Indeed, many multinational corporations have set up their treasury units as financial profit centers, expecting them to be active in a number of financial markets, seeking out the lowest possible cost of funds and taking advantage of arbitrage opportunities to enhance corporate profitability. Japanese firms, with large cash positions and a ready access to cash-rich Japanese financial markets, have provided the financial markets with a new term, *zaiteku*, to signify aggressive profit-seeking corporate activity on international financial markets.

The global financial system has changed dramatically in the 1980s. Its numerous financial markets have become more highly developed and integrated. Multinational corporations generally have become more aware of the opportunities that global financial markets offer for reducing funding costs and for diversifying funding sources, and are moving aggressively to take advantage of these alternatives.

DISCUSSION QUESTIONS

1. What types of international financial operations use domestic financial markets? How does the existence of the foreign exchange market make these transactions possible?

2. What are LIBOR and LIBID? (Answer with respect to the Eurodollar.) How do they relate to Eurodollar lending rates, domestic lending rates, and domestic deposit rates?

3. On September 1, 1986, Popson Enterprises takes out a one-year Eurocurrency bank loan priced at three-month LIBOR plus 1½ percent. Over the next few months, LIBOR behaves as follows:

Date	LIBOR
September 1, 1986	8⅛%
October 1, 1986	8⅝%
November 1, 1986	8¾%

Date	LIBOR
December 1, 1986	8¼%
January 1, 1987	8⅛%
February 1, 1987	7¼%
March 1, 1987	7½%

What interest rate on the loan is Popson charged for the period December 1, 1986 through February 28, 1987? What interest rate will be charged for the period March 1, 1987 through May 31, 1987? How can the bank making the loan to Popson fund the loan to make at least 1½ percent per annum profit on the loan (unless Popson defaults)? In a loan of this type, who bears the risk that interest rates may change?

4. What are the major differences between

   a. a note-issuance facility (NIF) and Eurocommercial paper?

   b. a sole placing agent and tender panel (both with respect to NIFs)?

   c. a Eurobond and a foreign bond?

   d. fixed-rate Eurobonds and floating-rate notes (FRNs)?

5. What roles do each of the following play in a syndicated Eurocredit?

   a. mandated bank

   b. managing bank

   c. participating bank

   What role do front-end fees play in compensating the banks involved in the credit?

6. What role do each of the following play in the global financial system?

   a. commercial banks

   b. investment banks

   c. merchant banks

   d. development finance institutions

   e. government and supragovernmental financial institutions.

7. What entry alternatives are available to a bank that seeks to enter a foreign banking market? What is an Edge Act subsidiary? What is an international banking facility (IBF)?

8. What is sovereign borrowing? Why have sovereign borrowers encountered repayment difficulties since 1982? How have these difficulties been managed?

9. What are the implications of financial market deregulation and increased competition between commercial and investment banks for global financial markets?

10. In the Eurocurrency markets for most major currencies, banks calculate interest on short-term loans and deposits according to the following formula:

$$\text{Interest} = \text{Principal} \times \frac{\text{Stated interest rate}}{100} \times \frac{\text{Days to maturity}}{360}$$

For example, the interest on a $10 million deposit for ninety-one days at 7¼ percent is

$$\$10,000,000 \times \frac{7.25}{100} \times \frac{91}{360} = \$183,263.89$$

Interest is paid at the maturity of the loan or deposit.

a. What would the bank earn on a $10 million loan for 275 days at 7¾ percent?

b. Suppose that a bank loaned $10 million for 275 days at 7¾ percent and initially funded the loan by taking a $10 million deposit for ninety-one days at 7¼ percent. In ninety-one days, this deposit matures, and the bank must take another deposit of $10 million to fund the loan. Suppose that LIBOR for 184-day deposits at the time the loan must be refunded is 8 percent and the bank accepts a $10 million deposit and agrees to pay this rate.

    i. How much interest would the bank pay on this 184-day deposit?

    ii. Assume that the interest paid for the first ninety-one-day deposit is also funded by a 184-day deposit. Does the bank make a profit by lending long for 275 days at 7¾ percent, borrowing short for ninety-one days at 7¼ percent, and refunding at the maturity of the short deposit at 8 percent? How much does the bank earn or lose?

    iii. How high can LIBOR on 184-day deposits be before the bank loses money by lending long, borrowing short, and refunding? This interest rate is known as the *implied forward rate* and is used to develop the interest-rate risk management tool, the *future rate agreement*.

SUGGESTED READINGS

1. Bankson, Lloyd, and Michael Lee (editors). *Euronotes*. London: Euromoney Publications, 1986.

2. Business International. *Financing Foreign Operations*. New York, New York: Business International, various issues.

3. Fisher, III, Frederick G. *International Bonds.* London: Euromoney Publications, 1981.

4. George, Abraham M., and Ian H. Giddy (editors). *International Finance Handbook*, Vols. I and II. New York, New York: John Wiley & Sons, 1983. Parts 3–5.

5. Grabbe, J. Orlin. *International Financial Markets.* New York, New York: Elsevier Science Publishing Co., 1986. Chapters 12–20.

6. Khoury, Sarkis. *Dynamics of International Banking.* New York, New York: Praeger Publishers, 1980.

7. Macdonald, Robert P. *Syndicated Loans.* London: Euromoney Publications, 1983.

8. Park, Yoon S., and Jack Zwick. *International Banking in Theory and Practice.* Reading, Massachusetts: Addison-Wesley Publishing Company, 1985.

9. Ugeux, Georges. *Floating Rate Notes*, 2nd Edition. London: Euromoney Publications, 1985.

10. Zenoff, David B. *International Banking Management and Strategies.* London: Euromoney Publications, 1985.

In addition, the following periodicals are primarily devoted to recent developments in global financial markets:

Annual Report of the Bank for International Settlements
Banker
Business International Money Report
Euromoney
Euromoney Corporate Finance
Financial Market Trends (OECD)
International Banking and Financial Market Developments (Bank for International Settlements)
World Financial Markets (Morgan Guaranty Trust Co.)

CHAPTER 7

▼

Global Funding Strategy
and Capital Structure

▲

INTRODUCTION

Multinational corporations (MNCs) derive both advantages and disadvantages from the international status of their operations. In Chapter 5, we saw that multinationals must develop measures to manage the risk of currency fluctuation. In Chapter 9, we will see how they are subject to the political risks inherent in operating under the political jurisdictions of rarely harmonious national governments. Plus, multinationals must adapt to the variety of cultures that complicate how companies approach specific product and financial markets. Much of the remainder of this book addresses the issue of how these particular problems should be addressed by the financial manager.

The Financial Advantages of Being a Multinational

Multinationality has its advantages, however, for both the firm as a whole and the financial manager. The very fact that a multinational firm is able to invest directly in a number of different national environments may offer the investor the benefits of international diversification of risk. To the extent that investors in the parent company are precluded from such diversification by any other means, they are sometimes willing to pay for the advantages of such international diversification by accepting a lower rate of return. Thus, the cost of equity capital to the multinational firm can be lower than that of an equivalent but purely domestic company.

Second, by having operations in a number of different countries, multinationals have ready access to a wide variety of local financial markets. Often, by its overall name recognition and innate financial strength, the local subsidiary of a multinational is one of the best credit risks available to local financial institutions. Although some countries restrict borrowing in local markets by multinationals, the multinational normally has access to local sources of funds at interest rates possibly not available to the equivalent domestic firm.

Third, multinational corporations typically are involved in some degree of international trade. Over many decades commercial banks with international operations have developed an extensive system for the financing of goods involved in international trade. Multinational corporations with trade activities can access this highly developed and structured market for international trade finance.

Fourth, by their very size and diversity of operations, multinational corporations have ready access to the emerging and ever more integrated global capital markets. Plus, multinationals can access their own large domestic money and capital markets; this advantage accrues, in particular, to firms based in the United States and Japan. Further, the external (Euro-) and foreign bond, Euronote, Eurocommercial paper, and syndicated Eurocredit markets, described in Chapter 6, offer many opportunities to tap a variety of markets on a global basis for funding, with a swap into the desired currency. Because of the multinational scope of their operations, the names of these corporations become familiar to retail investors in the foreign and external markets.

The fifth advantage of multinationality is the ability to move funds from one unit in the corporate system to another and thus from one market to another. The availability of channels for such funds movement theoretically allows the multinational to borrow in one financial market and move funds to a unit in another country that has a funds need. If exchange control regulations or other barriers to the movement of funds from one market to another exist, the financial markets involved are, to some extent, segmented. Depending on the degree of financial market segmentation that exists and the availability of funds transfer channels within the multinational's financial system, the multinational can take advantage of the discrepancies in interest rates among markets to secure funds at relatively lower rates. Yield and interest rate differentials, which arbitrage would be certain to eliminate if world financial markets were fully integrated, may remain and be exploited by multinationals.

Financial market segmentation is created in great measure by government regulation, although other barriers, particularly those of culture and of information, also may be contributing factors. However, the creativity of man and the necessities of finance often find inventive ways to circumvent the regulatory framework. Whether it be the market for corporation-to-corporation loans in Brazil (which developed after severe restrictions on lending by Brazilian banks to foreign-owned corporations were imposed) or the much more massive Eurocurrency markets (which flourished initially because U.S. banks were subject to interest rate ceilings on their time deposits), we find that financial markets do arise to meet specific funding needs and provide needed financial services. In the case of the Eurocurrency system, removal of the regulatory actions that created the market failed to eliminate the market: the financial institutions that created the market developed extensive alternative functions that ensured the market's continued existence.

The development of new international financial markets and institutions has strengthened, on the whole, the position of multinational firms. Although the existence of these markets and institutions does tend to break down — to some extent, at least — the market segmentation that provides opportunities for the multinational, the wide range of new financial services and the presence of expert, efficient financial institutions active on a global basis have been of significant advantage to multinational corporations.

Global Funding Strategies for the MNC

To make the most of the advantages multinationality confers, the funding strategy of the multinational should be global in scope. Briefly stated, the objective of a global funding strategy is to meet the funds needs of the various global units of the firm at the lowest possible cost, with due regard for the currency and political risk engendered by the funding strategy, and with the provision of flexibility for meeting unanticipated or uncertain funding needs without excessive delay or cost. The global funding strategy of a multinational firm usually employs the following components:

1. the emerging global equity markets
2. global debt markets
3. uniquely international funding mechanisms, such as trade finance, project finance, and cross-border leases
4. local financial markets where a firm has subsidiaries
5. the internal financial system of the multinational for unit-to-unit funds transfers.

This chapter looks at the first four components of a global strategy for mobilization of financial resources — those that deal with how the multinational firm accesses external markets. Chapter 8 then deals with the fifth component, the opportunities for intersubsidiary and parent/subsidiary transfers that exist in the internal financial system of the multinational corporation and how they are used in cash and working capital management.

INTERNATIONAL DIVERSIFICATION AND EQUITY FINANCING

The advantages of portfolio diversification for the investor are well known. By holding a well-diversified portfolio of securities, the investor can achieve a higher return for a given level of risk or, stated another way, reduce the risk needed to secure a specific return.

The opportunity for a domestic firm to diversify internationally clearly offers the investor the possibility of financial gains. Empirical evidence tends to confirm the risk-reduction potential of foreign portfolio investment. The systematic, or nondiversifiable, risk of an internationally diversified portfolio can be reduced primarily because of low correlations between returns in various national markets.

In an ideal world, where capital would be free to move from country to country without restriction, one could envision the existence of a completely integrated world capital market. Each company's securities would be priced on the basis of its relationship to a world market portfolio. Although the theoretical basis for the pricing of securities according to an international capital asset pricing model has been established, empirical research has not demonstrated that securities are priced in reference to a world market portfolio.

Significant barriers to international portfolio diversification remain. In many countries of the world, exchange controls limit the acquisition of foreign securities. In more advanced countries, key institutional investors are precluded by law from investing in foreign securities or from expanding their investments overseas. The inability of investors to acquire adequate information about foreign securities, the relative narrowness (in terms of number of different securities available) and the relative shallowness (in terms of volume of securities issued) of foreign financial markets, and the risk of political action against foreign portfolio investors all have been advanced as reasons why international portfolio investment does not take place to the extent necessary for securities to be priced internationally.

Because obstacles to international portfolio diversification exist, the investor might be able to achieve diversification by including multinational firms in the investment portfolio. If multinationals provide such diversification benefits, they should, if properly priced, require a lower return than an equivalent but purely domestic firm.

Empirical research to establish that investors recognize the international diversification benefits offered by multinationals has achieved mixed results, although much of the problem in obtaining a clear conclusion may arise from the use of index portfolios for comparison, which themselves contain multinational firms. Research studies that have corrected for that problem show that the international diversification effects of investing in multinationals exist and can be realized by investors.

Implications for Financial Strategy

Several implications for corporate financial policy are evident from a review of the concept of international portfolio diversification. First, there is no strong empirical evidence to indicate that world equity markets are unified. Therefore, the possibility exists that a multinational can find situations where it would have access to certain sources of capital, simply because it is a multinational, to which other firms would not have access. To the extent that the internal funds transfer channels of the multinational are available, the opportunity exists to source funds for a particular venture at a marginal cost lower than otherwise possible.

Second, there is a positive advantage to the multinational from international diversification of its own activities because such diversification may be rewarded by investors in its home country. Thus, it may not be appropriate to demand a higher return from foreign investment projects than from domestic projects with the same general risk characteristics. Indeed, although it is difficult to see this point being argued successfully in application, foreign investment projects may well deserve to be evaluated at a lower rate. In any event, multinational corporations offer investors in their home country an opportunity to diversify, and this opportunity should result in the ability to issue equity on the home country market at a lower cost than if the company were purely domestic.

Internationalizing a Firm's Ownership

To the extent that either insufficient information about a company or a lack of ready access by foreign nationals to home country equity markets exists, multinationals can benefit by making the advantages of foreign portfolio diversification more readily apparent and available to foreign investors. Many U.S.-based multinationals have secured listing of their companies on foreign stock exchanges, and a number of foreign companies are actively traded on the New York Stock Exchange. Although such listings may offer convenience to the potential investor, their primary benefit to date seems to have been the publicity and name recognition gained by meeting local listing requirements. The continued fragmentation of European stock exchanges, coupled with the increasing expense of listing on these exchanges, makes a strategy of a large number of foreign listings expensive.

Instead, firms may try to take advantage of the predicted emergence of a larger global equity placement capability to reach new potential investors. Firms might join an international equity tranche to a domestic equity issue; both primary and secondary offerings can be used for this purpose. Because the cost of international equity issues may be high (2.5 to 6.5 percent of the proceeds), companies should work with investment bankers that can provide significant offshore final retail placement in new markets, rather than have the new issue immediately sold back into the issuer's home country.

Despite the increasing availability of international equity issuance opportunities, the bulk of offshore equity is still raised by the issuance of convertible bonds and bonds with equity warrants on the Eurobond market. Conversion of the bonds or exercise of the warrants will eventually lead to a wider holding of the company's shares. Warrants have been used heavily by Japanese corporations in particular, although the primary purpose appears to have been obtaining more favorable access to fixed-rate funding.

An alternative to seeking international ownership through listings or through parent securities issuance is the issuance of equity by local subsidiaries. Some countries require levels of minority or even majority ownership by local nationals. Firms typically have difficulty in achieving a broad-based ownership of their subsidiaries in the very thin capital markets of most developing countries. Where local equity ownership is not required, equity issues by local subsidiaries of U.S. multinationals are rare. U.S. firms, in particular, prefer the flexibility of operations that sole ownership affords. Firms that are technology based are concerned with the loss of control over proprietary technology that taking on an equity partner or partners might portend. Multinationals of other countries, however, sometimes want to take on local equity, especially in their U.S. subsidiaries, taking advantage of the remarkably broad and sophisticated U.S. equity market.

To summarize, the predominant source of equity investment in a multinational is the equity market in the firm's home country. Because global financial markets are neither totally integrated nor wholly segmented but fall somewhere in between, multinational corporations offer a vehicle whereby domestic investors, otherwise precluded, may realize some of the benefits of portfolio diversification. Firms seek to expand global ownership of parent equity through listing shares on foreign stock exchanges or through utilization of equity or equity-related debt issues on global capital markets. Sale of subsidiary equity, while common because of governmental regulation, is not usually initiated by U.S. multinationals.

APPROACHING THE GLOBAL DEBT MARKET

From a strategic point of view, the global financial markets of the 1980s offer a significant advantage that was not available to previous generations of financial managers because of the development of liability swaps, long-dated forward contracts, Eurocommercial paper, and Euronotes. In assessing medium- to long-term funding needs, the international financial manager needs to determine the kind of funds to borrow — their maturity, amortization terms, whether they are at fixed or floating interest rates — and the currency of denomination of the debt. As in all such fundings, the maturity and amortization of the debt is determined by the volume and duration of projected funding needs. The advisability of fixed-rate funding versus floating-rate funding depends on the relative cost of the two alternatives and the sensitivity of the firm's cash inflows to changes in interest rates.

The initial impact of the development of external financial markets was to make available a great many more funding options for the financial executive. The development of LIBOR-plus pricing and of the syndicated Eurocredit market offers the typical multinational access to floating-rate financing analogous to a term loan. The development of the Euro CP and Euronote markets offers prime credits great flexibility in access to funds at a very small level of commitment fees. Most important, the development of the interest-rate swap allows firms to borrow in floating-rate markets even when their needs are for fixed-rate funds. Conversely, firms that need floating-rate funding can use the fixed-rate market and swap into floating-rate funds.

Using Interest-Rate Swaps

Interest-rate swaps can arise when the market for floating-rate debt and the fixed-rate market provide different risk evaluations for firms. For example, suppose that two firms, Alpha Corp. and Beta Corp., require $50 million each in funding for a seven-year period. When Alpha and Beta approach their investment banker, they learn that they can raise seven-year money under the following terms:

	Alpha Corp.	Beta Corp.	Differential Favoring Alpha
Fixed rate	10.00%	11.00%	100 basis points
Floating rate	LIBOR + ¼%	LIBOR + ¾%	50 basis points

These terms are typical, in that the interest differential favoring the stronger credit, Alpha, is wider in the fixed-rate market than in the floating-rate market.

The possibility for a profitable swap exists because the interest differential in the fixed-rate market (100 basis points) is not the same as in the floating-rate market (50 basis points). Alpha can reduce its cost of floating-rate funds by borrowing in the fixed-rate market, where it has a relative advantage, and swapping into a floating-rate loan. Beta can reduce its cost of fixed-rate funds by borrowing in the floating-rate market, where it has a relative but not absolute advantage, and swapping into the fixed-rate market.

An investment bank or a commercial bank intermediates the swap. Alpha borrows $50 million at 10 percent in the fixed-rate market; Beta borrows the same amount at LIBOR + ¾ percent in the floating-rate market. Exhibit 7-1 shows how the swap might be arranged.

Alpha pays the bank LIBOR; Beta has borrowed at LIBOR + ¾ percent; it uses the LIBOR + ¾ percent inflow from the bank to make its floating interest payments. Beta pays the bank 10⅞ percent fixed interest; the bank in turn pays Alpha 10 percent, which Alpha uses to completely pay the interest on its outstanding fixed-rate debt.

As a result of the transaction, Alpha has effectively borrowed floating-rate funds at LIBOR, 25 basis points below the LIBOR + ¼ percent that the market requires. Alpha has swapped a 10 percent per annum interest charge for a LIBOR interest charge.

Through the swap, Beta has borrowed fixed-rate funds. It pays the bank 10⅞ percent, saving 12.5 basic points on the market required fixed rate of 11 percent.

Default Risk and Bank Fees

What would happen if Beta defaulted on its obligations? Alpha is protected by the swap agreement with the bank. Alpha could continue

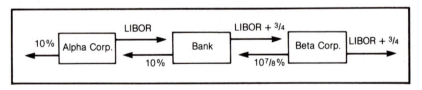

EXHIBIT 7-1 Structure of an Interest-Rate Swap

paying the bank LIBOR and continue to receive fixed-interest payments of 10 percent from the bank. To compensate the bank for the risk of default by either party, the bank earns a fee derived from the fact that the interest paid into the bank by the swap participants exceeds the interest paid out by the bank by ⅛ percent. The income to the bank of 12.5 basis points in this example is lower than the 15 to 20 basis points that banks seek to earn from the typical swap. However, banks have booked swaps with fees of 6 to 8 basis points; fees at this level may not compensate the bank adequately for the risk that they assume.

Reconciling the Savings from a Swap

The amount of the savings to the two participants and the fee income to the intermediating bank is determined by the difference between the fixed-market interest rate differential of the two swap parties and the floating market differential. Exhibit 7-2 provides a reconciliation showing how this amount is divided among participants.

Interest-rate swaps can be used to take advantage of corporate borrowing capacity in a particular market or to take a view with respect to the direction that interest rates will go. Suppose, for example, that a firm with substantial floating-rate debt anticipates a significant rise in short-term interest rates over the next few years. Rather than refund the existing debt, with the expenses associated with such an activity, the firm can swap for fixed-rate financing. If the firm anticipates a decline in interest rates over the medium term, it could swap into floating-rate debt.

Fixed market differential	100 basis points
− Floating market differential	− 50 basis points
= Total savings from swap	50 basis points
Allocated as follows:	
Savings to Alpha	25 basis points
+ Savings to Beta	12.5 basis points
+ Fee to arranging bank	12.5 basis points
= Total savings from swap	50 basis points

EXHIBIT 7-2 Division Savings from a Swap

Currency Liability Swaps

Just as interest-rate swaps allow a firm to separate the decision of whether to use fixed-rate or floating-rate funding from the decision to borrow in fixed or floating markets, currency swaps allow a firm to maximize its use of the debt markets in various currencies. External markets, particularly in nondollar issues, are still relatively small, and the markets can be quickly saturated by the issues of a borrower that comes to them repeatedly. Companies may find themselves needing Swiss francs or German marks, but if they have what the market views as substantial debt outstanding in these currencies, they may not be able to issue bonds directly in these markets. The currency swap allows indirect access to these markets through another borrower.

The currency swap can be illustrated by the following example. Suppose that Agfolk needs to borrow DM 100 million for ten years to fund a new investment in Germany at a time when the exchange rate is DM 2.5 per dollar. Agfolk has been expanding German operations substantially over the past several years and has issued DM 250 million in bonds over the past two years. Agfolk's investment bankers believe that the Euromark market is somewhat saturated with Agfolk issues and that a new issue could be placed with some difficulty at 6¾ percent, well above the prevailing 6 percent fixed rate for prime corporate credits in the Euromark market. Agfolk has not been a frequent issuer of Eurodollar bonds, however, and could readily issue them at 9⅞ percent fixed rate for ten years.

Agfolk's investment bank is also trying to raise funds for a Dutch food processing company, Nederkooken, which needs dollars for a U.S. investment. Because Nederkooken is a rather small company, it can borrow in the Eurodollar segment of the Eurobond market at 10¼ percent for ten years. However, a large portion of its sales are in West Germany, where it has established a wide consumer base; for this reason, the investment bank believes that Nederkooken, which has never borrowed marks, could issue ten-year Euromark bonds at the prevailing 6 percent.

Agfolk and Nederkooken can achieve substantial savings by borrowing in the market where each has a relative advantage and then engaging in a currency swap through the intermediation of the investment bank. We can see that a currency swap is feasible by looking at the following comparison:

	Agfolk	Nederkooken	*Differential Favoring Agfolk*
Eurodollar bond	9.875%	10.250%	37.5 basis points
Euromark bond	6.750%	6.000%	−75.0 basis points
Total savings from swap			112.5 basis points

Agfolk should thus issue $40 million in Eurodollar bonds for ten years at 9⅞ percent. Nederkooken should issue DM 100 million in Euromark bonds for ten years at 6 percent.

Configuring the Currency Swap

Exhibit 7-3 shows one possible configuration of a swap wherein the two firms swap the proceeds of the loan. Agfolk agrees to pay the investment bank 6¼ percent interest in marks on a principal of DM 100 million and, at the end of ten years, will pay the investment bank the principal amount. The investment bank pays Nederkooken 6 percent in marks per annum and, at the end of ten years, pays Nederkooken DM 100 million, so that Nederkooken can repay the principal amount. Nederkooken pays the bank 9⅞ percent interest on $40 million for ten years, which the bank passes on to Agfolk to pay holders of its Eurobonds. At the end of ten years, Nederkooken pays the investment bank $40 million, which is then paid to Agfolk to allow it to repay the principal.

Agfolk has borrowed fixed-rate Euromarks at 6¼ percent, a savings of 50 basis points. Nederkooken has borrowed fixed-rate dollars at 9⅞ percent, a savings of 37.5 basis points. The investment bank, which stands in the middle of the transaction, earns a fee of 25 basis points (the difference between the 6¼ percent it received from Agfolk and the 6 percent it pays to Nederkooken). The total of the interest savings of

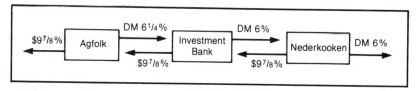

EXHIBIT 7-3   Structure of a Foreign Currency Swap

the two participants plus the bank's fee (50 bp + 37.5 bp + 25 bp = 112.5 bp) equals the difference in the market differentials in favor of Agfolk [37.5 bp − (−75 bp) = 112.5 bp].

It is important to note that in the currency swap the intermediating bank once again takes the risk of nonperformance by either party. In our example, if Nederkooken defaulted, Agfolk would continue to pay marks to the intermediating bank and would continue to receive dollar payments from the intermediating bank. Should Nederkooken default, the bank would have a substantial currency exposure; for this reason, bank fees on currency swaps are a bit higher than on interest-rate swaps.

Using Swaps to Minimize Borrowing Costs

Liability swaps are thus a powerful tool for corporate financial executives to use in minimizing borrowing costs. To take advantage of the opportunities they offer, finance officers must clearly identify the firm's borrowing capacity in the various sectors of the Eurobond and foreign bond markets. U.S.-based corporations have been able to take advantage of foreign investor demand for prime U.S. corporate paper to expand their borrowing into a wide variety of currencies. In many recent cases, however, bond deals in nondollar currencies have been done solely for the purpose of swapping the liability into a dollar liability. Essentially, U.S. corporations have taken advantage of their placing power offshore to lower the cost of dollar financing through swaps.

Alternate Methods of Using Borrowing Capacity

The currency swap is just one method for using a firm's borrowing capacity in various sectors of the Eurobond and foreign bond markets. Two important alternate methods also exist:

1. long forward contracts
2. dual currency bonds.

Covering with Long Forward Contracts

Suppose that Agfolk borrows Sfr 50 million for five years at an annual coupon rate of 5 percent. Agfolk has committed itself to a repayment stream of Sfr 2.5 million per year for the next five years and a final repayment of Sfr 50 million five years hence.

If Agfolk could purchase Swiss francs forward for each interest payment date, it could fix its funding cost in dollars. Because they have clients who have cash flows in Swiss francs that they are willing to sell forward, the very largest commercial and investment banks have been able to create a market in long-dated forwards, which are forward exchange contracts with a maturity of more than one year. On occasion, forward purchase of foreign currency interest payments and principal repayments has resulted in a lower borrowing cost measured in dollars than could have been achieved by funding in dollars.

Exhibit 7-4 calculates the dollar cost of Agfolk's five-year Swiss franc funding on the assumption that Agfolk's investment bank will sell it Swiss francs at a 3 percent per annum premium from the current spot rate of $0.45 per Swiss franc. Column 2 shows the amount of the payment to be made each year, and Column 3 shows the forward rate at which the purchase takes place. Once Agfolk has agreed to enter into a forward purchase contract, it has essentially fixed its payments in dollars at the level shown in Column 4. The dollar cost of the Swiss franc loan (completely covered by forward purchases of Swiss francs) is found by determining the discount rate that equates the present value of the dollar outflows in Column 4 with the current dollar value of the Sfr 50 million, $22.5 million (= Sfr 50.0 × 0.45, the current spot rate). That discount rate is 8.15 percent.

Agfolk can thus borrow Swiss francs and completely eliminate the exchange risk by forward purchase. By doing so, Agfolk can lock-in a dollar borrowing cost of 8.15 percent. This fully covered Swiss franc borrowing may be cheaper than any available dollar source of fixed-rate funding, and many U.S.-based multinationals have been able to lower their dollar borrowing costs by borrowing foreign currency on a fully hedged basis.

A fully hedged borrowing requires two basic forms of long forwards. To hedge the principal, it is necessary to purchase one very large amount of foreign currency at the medium- to long-term maturity date of the loan. To hedge the interest, it is necessary to find a counterparty with foreign currency cash inflows on a regular basis; the borrower must purchase a stream of foreign currency flows.

Covering with Dual Currency Bonds

The *dual currency bond* is a mechanism to eliminate the necessity for hedging the principal of a foreign currency loan. The dual currency bond is denominated in a foreign currency, and interest is paid in

EXHIBIT 7-4 Covering a Bond with Long-Term Forwards

Year	(1) Type of Payment	(2) Amount of Payment		(3) Forward Rate	(4) Dollar Equivalent
1	Interest	Sfr	2,500,000	0.4635	$ 1,158,750
2	Interest	Sfr	2,500,000	0.4774	$ 1,193,500
3	Interest	Sfr	2,500,000	0.4917	$ 1,229,250
4	Interest	Sfr	2,500,000	0.5065	$ 1,266,250
5	Interest	Sfr	2,500,000	0.5217	$ 1,304,250
	Principal	Sfr	50,000,000	0.5217	$26,085,000

NOTE: Current spot is US $0.45/Sfr. The original Swiss franc principal is worth $22,500,000. The bond carries a 5-percent annual coupon. Forward rates assume a compound 3-percent per annum premium. That is, the forward rate for year 1 is (0.45) (1.03), for year 2 is (0.45) (1.03)^2, and, in general, for year t, (0.45) (1.03) (1.03) (1.03)^t. The dollar cost of the Swiss franc loan is 8.15 percent.

foreign currency at the coupon rate. However, the rate of exchange to be applied to the principal is fixed in advance, usually at a substantial premium above the current spot exchange rate if the coupon rate is lower than the coupon rate for equivalent issues in the dollar market. In effect, the borrower has incorporated the forward contract on the principal into the terms of the bond. By varying the coupon and final exchange rates, borrowers can create instruments that reduce the level of interest expense and initial cash flows to service the debt. Dual currency bonds primarily have been denominated in Swiss francs, but approval of issuance in Japanese yen in 1985 led to numerous issues in that currency, as well.

Illustrating the use of dual currency bonds is the Gillette Co., which has placed a dual currency feature on a convertible Swiss franc issue. Use of the dual currency feature will retard conversion if there is a rapid appreciation of the Swiss franc. And Minnesota Mining and Manufacturing Co. has issued a reverse dual currency bond, with interest (9¾ percent) payable in dollars but with redemption of the bond in pounds at a fixed exchange rate of $1.3065.

Issuers of dual currency bonds can hedge the interest payments through forward contracts and lock-in a known dollar cost of funding. Issuers of reverse dual currency bonds can hedge the final principal payment and achieve the same objective.

Currency Composites

Financial operations in particular currencies are subject to the impact of exchange-rate changes, as we clearly saw in Chapter 4. Since 1970, a mechanism has developed known as the *currency composite,* or *currency cocktail,* which has been used to provide some diversification of the currency risk associated with funding operations. The two most used currency composites are the Special Drawing Right (SDR) and the European Currency Unit (ECU).

Currency composites are artificial units composed of blends of various different real currencies. The SDR is made up of various amounts of five major world currencies (see Exhibit 7-5 for composition); on January 15, 1987, the SDR was worth $1.25863, the market value of its constituent currencies. The ECU is made up of various amounts of the ten currencies of the European Economic Community (EEC) currencies, as seen in Exhibit 7-6; the value of the ECU on January 15, 1987, was $1.11790. When new nations enter the EEC, their currencies

EXHIBIT 7-5 Valuation of the SDR

One Special Drawing Right (SDR) consists of the following:

Currency	Number of Currency Units
U.S. dollar	0.452
German mark	0.527
Japanese yen	33.4
French franc	1.02
British pound sterling	0.0893

are included in the formulation of the ECU, and the amounts of the other currencies are adjusted to preserve the ECU's external value.

The value of a currency composite is wholly determined by the value of the currencies that it contains. As the values of these constituent currencies change, the value of the currency composite changes.

Both the SDR and the ECU have their origin in official multilateral institutions. The SDR is a creation of the International Monetary Fund, developed to provide a replacement for the U.S. dollar as a way of measuring value and as a vehicle for creation of new reserves by the IMF. The ECU has its origin in the European Monetary System (dis-

EXHIBIT 7-6 Valuation of the ECU

One European Currency Unit (ECU) consists of the following:

Currency	Number of Currency Units
Belgian franc	3.71
Danish krone	0.219
French franc	1.31
German mark	0.719
Irish pound	0.00871
Italian lire	140.0
Luxembourgian franc	0.14
Netherlands guilder	0.256
British pound sterling	0.0878
Greek drachma	1.15

cussed in Chapter 3), the arrangement for stabilizing exchange rates within the EEC.

Despite their official origin and usage, the private sector has adopted both the SDR and the ECU as units of accounts. Banks treat these composites as if they were real currencies; they are bought and sold in a manner similar to foreign exchange. Banks will accept SDR and ECU deposits and make loans in them; SDR and ECU certificates of deposit (CDs) have been issued; and ECU travelers checks are now available. Both the SDR and the ECU have been used as the currency of denomination for Eurobonds and syndicated credits.

The SDR Eurobond market in recent years has been moribund, with only a few floating-rate issues in 1981. On the other hand, the ECU became the third-largest currency of issue in the Eurobond market in 1985, with most ECU issues being fixed-rate issues. The coupon rate is supposed to be a weighted average combination of the coupon rates of the constituent currencies, although some currencies in the ECU have no real external bond market with which to measure the component coupon rate. In general, the ECU has found a market niche as a currency weaker than the German mark or Swiss franc but stronger than the French franc, Italian lira, and Belgian franc. The nominal coupon rate for ECUs is thus higher than those of mark or Swiss franc bonds; it offers investors in Belgium, France, and Italy a higher yield than these two currencies, and a chance for currency appreciation.

The primary reason for the currency composite, however, is that it offers an opportunity for currency diversification to both the borrower and the lender. If the borrower does not prefer to remain exposed to the residual currency risk of the ECU, the swap or long forward market can provide an alternative currency configuration.

Euromarkets and U.S. Capital Markets

A primary decision faced by the finance executives of multinationals is how to use both the Euromarkets and the U.S. markets simultaneously. Traditionally, the Euromarkets have offered numerous advantages for the U.S. multinational borrower, including

1. flexibility in issuance because Eurobonds are not subject to registration with the Securities and Exchange Commission (SEC) or to waiting periods typically imposed on U.S. domestic issues

2. no withholding tax on payment of interest, allowing purchasers of bearer instruments to avoid taxation

3. the appetite for U.S. corporate names in the Euromarkets, resulting in very low borrowing costs and (occasionally) the ability to increase the size of the issue

4. relatively low issuance costs.

The provision for shelf registration by the SEC in 1982 and the repeal of the U.S. withholding tax on interest payments to nonresidents in 1984 have, to some degree, weakened these advantages. Nonetheless, U.S. corporations can still count on the Eurobond and foreign bond markets as an alternative source of dollar funds and as the major source of nondollar funds. These markets do provide both speed and flexibility when compared with the U.S. domestic market.

SPECIALIZED FUNDING FOR MULTINATIONALS

Trade Finance

Firms that engage in cross-border trade can call on the well-developed mechanisms of trade finance as an additional source of funds. Historically, the trade finance mechanism arose because exporters wanted payment when the goods were shipped and importers wanted to make payment when the goods were received, or even later. Because the sale of the underlying goods in the trade transaction would provide an obvious means of repayment, trade finance became an early specialty of commercial banks, which saw trade finance as the classic self-liquidating short-term loan.

Financial Terms of International Trade Transactions

There are five ways in which the importer can pay the exporter in a trade transaction. Ranked in order of their decreasing credit risk to the exporter, they are as follows:

1. *Open account:* The exporter ships the goods and sends an invoice on standard commercial terms to the importer. The importer makes payment as specified by the exporter. Until payment is made, the exporter has extended unsecured credit to the importer.

2. *Documents against acceptance (D/A):* The exporter ships the goods to

the importer. The exporter draws a time draft on the importer and attaches the time draft to the documents that allow the importer to take possession of the goods. The exporter's bank mails the documents and draft to a correspondent bank in the importer's country. The foreign bank presents the draft to the importer. When the importer accepts the draft (writes *accepted* on the draft and signs and dates it), the importer receives the documents conveying title to the physical goods. Usually, time drafts are drawn for thirty, sixty, or ninety days after sight, indicating how long the importer has before the draft must be paid. When the draft matures, the foreign bank presents it to the importer, who must pay it; proceeds are then transferred to the exporter. In a D/A transaction, the exporter provides credit to the importer from the time that the documents are mailed to the payment of the draft. Once the draft is accepted, the exporter may usually discount it with the foreign bank. In any event, it is the credit standing of the importer that determines the value of the accepted time draft.

3. Documents against payment (D/P): This method is the same as the D/A method, except that the draft drawn on the importer is a sight draft. When the sight draft is presented to the importer, it must be paid immediately, or the title documents will not be given to the importer. Under D/P payment terms, physical possession of the goods is not surrendered until after payment is made. The exporter must finance the sale only up to the date that the documents are presented.

4. Letter of credit (L/C): Under these terms, the credit standing of a commercial bank is substituted for the credit of the importer. Although there are numerous ways of using letters of credit in trade transactions, we shall review the use of a confirmed irrevocable letter of credit. The importer approaches his or her local bank and asks the bank to open a letter of credit on behalf of the exporter (the beneficiary). The importer's bank contacts its correspondent (or branch or parent) in the exporter's country, notifying the correspondent that a letter of credit has been opened for the exporter, asking the correspondent bank to confirm the letter of credit and to advise the exporter of the letter of credit. The letter of credit is then sent by the bank to the exporter.

Typically, the letter of credit specifies that if certain documents evidencing shipment of goods and giving title to the goods are presented to the confirming bank, along with a time or sight draft, before a specified date (the expiration date), the confirming bank will accept the time draft or pay the sight draft. The letter of credit is irrevocable when the confirming bank states that it will not revoke its obligation to accept or pay before the expiration date.

In essence, the confirming bank is extending a loan to the importer's bank, which is in turn extending a loan to the importer. As far as the exporter is concerned, the credit of the confirming bank has been substituted for the credit of the importer. As long as the documents are in order and presented to the confirming bank, the attached draft will be accepted or paid. Because a time draft accepted by a major bank arising from international trade is eligible for rediscount at the Federal Reserve, the banker's acceptance created by an L/C transaction is highly marketable at a very favorable rate of interest. The exporter may discount the acceptance in the market for prime banker's acceptances and secure short-term financing at the lowest possible rate. The importer, on the other hand, must compensate its bank both for the use of funds (when credit is extended) and for the use of the bank's creditworthiness. The importer's bank pays a fee to the exporter's bank for confirming the L/C.

5. *Cash in advance:* The safest method of selling overseas is to demand cash payment in advance, which eliminates the credit risk to the exporter entirely and places the entire burden of financing the transaction on the importer.

The terms of payment and credit outlined above offer firms engaged in export transactions the opportunity to access short-term funds, often at attractive rates. They have been developed over decades for the careful allocation of credit and commercial risks between the participants in a trade transaction. As in any transaction, terms of payment are negotiable between buyer and seller and may affect whether a sale is made.

To facilitate extension of credit to overseas buyers and thereby to promote exports, most developed countries have an export credit insurance capability, which typically provides insurance against nonpayment by buyers for both political and commercial reasons. In the United States, the Foreign Credit Insurance Association (FCIA) markets export credit insurance.

Official Export Credit

Competition for export sales is often intense between nations, particularly for sales of capital goods. Most developed countries have a governmental or quasi-governmental agency that facilitates the extension of medium- to long-term credit in support of exports. In the United States, a government corporation, the Export-Import Bank (Eximbank), provides moderately subsidized direct loans to foreign borrowers to finance purchases in the United States. Eximbank also operates a program guaranteeing the repayment by foreign borrowers of obligations issued to U.S. exporters that have been purchased by U.S. banks.

Eximbank also guarantees the loans of the Private Export Funding Corp. (PEFCO), a joint venture of U.S. financial and industrial firms that raises funds in U.S. capital markets and uses them for loans in support of large-scale long-term export transactions.

Official export lending agencies such as Eximbank are supposed to finance transactions that are not normally fundable by commercial sources of credit. In reality, subsidized export credit has become a major marketing tool in the market for sales of capital goods to developing nations. In response, major exporting countries negotiated in 1978 the International Arrangement on Officially Supported Export Credits, which prescribes maximum lending maturities (8½ to ten years, depending on the country), minimum down payment (15 percent), and formulas for developing minimum export credit interest rates. Nonetheless, when countries seek to secure contracts for the sourcing of large projects, and the decision depends on the financing package for the project, countries have been known to link direct government-to-government aid to the selection of their country for sourcing.

Project Finance

Frequently, multinational corporations, particularly those in extractive industries such as mining or petroleum, have investment projects that require massive amounts of capital. The classic investment project risks, such as altered marketing conditions, cost overruns, and political risk, are greatly magnified when the price tag of the project tops the billion dollar mark.

Over the past fifteen years some twenty to thirty financial institutions have developed specialized capabilities to pull together financing packages for large-scale investment projects. Originating primarily in the U.S. petroleum extraction sector and taken international by the massive capital requirements for ventures such as exploitation of North Sea oil resources, project financings are characterized by

1. legal separation of the project from the sponsoring firm
2. extensive use of direct project debt to finance a large proportion of the capital required
3. multiple providers of debt, particularly firms supplying capital goods and construction/engineering services to the project, government and development finance entities of the various countries, and commercial banks

4. commitments for purchase of the project output, which are used to provide security to project lenders.

Project financing arrangements are carefully designed to allow project participants to share in the project risk. In developing country environments, political risk can be reduced by obtaining local government financial support and project approval.

Developing the Project Finance Plan from Cash Flow Projections

Once the cash flow and capital requirements of a project have been developed, a plan for financing the project can be developed. Usually a large portion of the equipment and other components of the final project are imported into the host country. Also, most projects rely on firms in the developed world to provide construction and engineering services. Suppliers of materials, equipment, and services to the project are one source of credit; typically, they offer the project extended payment terms. A significant portion of the credit extended by suppliers to the project comes from export financing agencies of the suppliers' home countries, such as Eximbank in the United States.

Many projects include loans from local development banks to meet the local portion of the project expenses. Regional development banks, discussed in Chapter 6, provide nonrecourse financing of a medium- to long-term nature at market rates. The World Bank may provide funding for project-related infrastructure, and the International Finance Corporation (IFC) may put in long-term debt or take an equity position. Purchasers of the output of the investment often will make advance payment for output as a method of funding the project. Project sponsors may also lend to the legally separate project and must supply (perhaps with the IFC and other investors) the equity needed for the project.

Bank Components of Project Financings

Even with these diverse suppliers of capital, there usually remains an amount that is financed by commercial banks, usually through the vehicle of a syndicated credit. Where the banks are not willing to accept the commercial risk of the project itself, they look to the sponsoring multinational for some sort of financial guarantee. Of course, project sponsors prefer to finance the project in such a way that lenders do not have recourse to the sponsor in case the project does not generate sufficient cash flow to service the debt.

Rather than guarantee repayment of the bank credit to the project, which might cause the loan to appear on the project sponsor's balance sheet, the sponsor may be able to offer alternative guarantees. Usually, these involve an agreement to purchase the project's output; they may take the form of a *take-and-pay contract*, agreeing to purchase the project output if available. Sometimes, a so-called *hell-or-high-water contract* is used, obligating payment for the output whether or not it is available. Lending banks may also require a *completion guarantee* from the project's sponsor to proceed with a nonrecourse funding.

When properly arranged, a complicated project finance structure can provide a large amount of funding with due regard for matching the risk of each funding component with the reward of the project. Although many firms will not find themselves directly engaged in putting together a large-scale project, participation as a supplier or customer in a financing of this type is quite common. Because credit extension is such an important point in sales to project sponsors, corporate finance executives are apt to be called on to engage in project financing activities as a supplier of credit.

Cross-Border Leasing

Leasing is a viable and frequently utilized international financing technique. Many countries have more or less developed leasing markets, although leasing does not always offer the tax advantages in foreign markets that it does in the United States.

Cross-border leases, where the lessor is located in one country and the lessee (and presumably, the leased object) is located in another, can be done for particular types of equipment with a number of countries as a base. Changes in tax laws and regulations open and close cross-border leasing windows of opportunity frequently. The ability to lease some types of equipment can depend on seemingly trivial details; for example, commercial jet aircraft can be leased cross-border from a U.S. base because U.S. taxing authorities consider an aircraft as located in the United States if it lands there once every two weeks.

USING LOCAL FINANCIAL MARKETS: FUNDING
SUBSIDIARY WORKING CAPITAL NEEDS

Access to the financial markets of the various countries in which a multinational operates can be advantageous in lowering the overall cost of capital to the firm. Thus, the financial decision maker must be able to evaluate the forms of financing that each local market offers, as well as the local opportunities for the investment of surplus funds.

Certain key policy decisions affect the way that a firm approaches local financial markets. Some multinationals prefer to decentralize their control over the financial operations of their subsidiaries and give significant autonomy in subsidiary financial decisions to regional or local management. If such a policy is adopted, and the local subsidiary is, in a sense, operated as a relatively independent business, its financial structure should be viable in the eyes of local providers of funds.

Other firms may seek to centralize financial operations to take complete advantage of the channels for interunit funds movement that might be available. Such an approach might find the German affiliate of a multinational borrowing because the French affiliate needed funds. In such a case, the debt carried by the German unit might be far larger than would be prudent if the unit were viewed as a separate entity.

The Capital Structure of a Local Subsidiary

The nominal capital structure of a particular firm is often strongly influenced by how the parent contribution to the subsidiary is structured. As we shall see later, a parent may be reluctant to designate the entire amount of its investment in a subsidiary as equity. Rather, it may prefer to treat a large portion of it as a loan. Repayment of loan principal by the subsidiary to the parent provides a convenient mechanism for withdrawing funds, significantly less subject to exchange controls and host country interference than actual capital repatriation. Thus, a subsidiary may be carrying two, three, or even four times its equity in the form of parent debt. As viewed by an external provider of funds, the local subsidiary may appear to be grossly undercapitalized, and the lender might be reluctant to proceed without a parent guarantee or other protective measure.

Firms that generally create locally appropriate capital structures for their subsidiaries give up the opportunity to exploit their own mul-

176

tinational character and take advantage of the potential for profitable interunit funds movements. On the other hand, they cannot be accused of using local capital to finance operations in other countries, which is a frequently heard criticism of multinationals.

Firms that tend to deviate too far from local structural norms are apt to have the parent called on to issue guarantees for the debt of the local subsidiary. The issue of whether to guarantee formally the debt of a subsidiary is, of course, a separate one from whether to allow a subsidiary to default on its debt when the occasion arises. Very few companies have allowed local units to go bankrupt. However, many firms refuse or are reluctant to guarantee their subsidiaries' debt.

Accessing Local Financial Markets

Regardless of whether funds are used for local operations only or become part of a globally active pool of funds, the responsible financial executive must understand the principles and nuances of financing in each of the local financial markets available to the multinational. Although in some countries financial practices are similar to those encountered in the United States, they are affected by local cultural and economic conditions.

A number of short-term financing techniques are common in local financial markets but may be unfamiliar to U.S. financial managers accustomed to securing short-term funds through bank loans evidenced by promissory notes. The international financial manager must understand each of these techniques.

In many countries, banks lend on the basis of an *overdraft*. In essence, the borrowing firm is permitted to overdraw its account at the bank up to a limit agreed on by the firm and its bank. Interest is charged only on the actual amount overdrawn and is usually computed on the daily balance owed. An overdraft facility offers a very flexible method of meeting short-term funds needs and particularly assists in smoothing out any minor temporary shortfall in funds.

The extension of trade credit to customers frequently becomes a source of short-term financing. In many countries, the *discounting of bills of exchange* that arise in the course of domestic trade transactions is widely practiced. In general, the seller of the goods draws a time draft on the buyer for the amount owed. When the draft is presented to the buying firm, it accepts the draft; the accepted draft is taken by the selling firm to its bank and discounted. Although the discounting of trade bills involves a significant amount of paperwork to all parties to the transaction, both legal and cultural factors continue to make it a common financing methodology in countries such as France and Italy. Short cuts in the process, such as the bank discounting the trade bill prior to acceptance by the buying firm, have emerged, but in many countries the use of trade bills in financing is decreasing in favor of term loans and overdrafts.

In addition to the less familiar form of financing available in local markets, multinationals will also find that cultural considerations may affect how familiar financing methods are used. The use of collateral for term loans varies from country to country and depends on local banking practices. In Germany, the bank loans that are the most common are essentially signature loans; in Japan, on the other hand, most bank loans are secured.

Practices with regard to compensating balances also vary substantially. In a number of countries, compensating balances are not used, and the bank receives its compensation solely from the interest rate charged and the various commissions and fees associated with the form of financing. In some cases, banks take advantage of the *float*, the difference between the time when the bank receives credit for a payment and the time the recipient receives credit. Banks may also reduce customer account balances several days before payment is actually made. Yet in other countries, the compensating balance system has been instituted, particularly in Latin American countries such as Mexico, Brazil, and Colombia.

As might be expected, interest rates on local loans vary dramatically from country to country and depend on local inflation and currency trends. In extremely inflationary countries, interest rates have run higher than 200 percent. Although such high rates may be shocking, inflationary effects on asset values may still allow profitable operations, even at these rates. In some countries, bank loan rates are indexed to the rate of inflation.

Local Financing for Subsidiary Working Capital

If a multinational has substantial local sources of raw materials or other inputs, it will most likely be able to take advantage of credit extended by its suppliers. Country-to-country differences in the terms of supplier credit and the extension of discounts for early payment are to be expected. The basic determination of whether to use credit from suppliers is completely analogous to that in the domestic case.

The services of receivables factors have become available in the past fifteen years in many developing nations. Factors can be used for credit services and collections only or they may be used, in addition, to extend credit at appropriate interest rates. In countries where internal trade transactions use bills of exchange, commercial banks may discount trade bills without recourse to the seller, a technique that competes with the factor's method of nonrecourse purchase of receivables.

Commercial paper, the unsecured promissory notes of large corporations sold at a discount in the open market, is not particularly common outside the United States and the emerging Euro CP external market. Yet, especially in Latin America, direct loans are often made from one corporation with excess cash to another requiring cash. Despite legal restrictions designed to prevent *intercompany loans,* firms in Brazil, for example, have developed a complicated method of having firms with excess funds lend appropriate financial instruments to firms needing funds, which then sell the instruments via a dealer back to the firm with excess funds; at the maturity date of the arrangement, the borrowing firm purchases the financial instruments. Although disguised as a loan of financial instrument rather than a loan of funds, the net effect is that cash is transferred to the borrowing entity. The creativity contained in the method outlined here results from a desperate desire for Brazilian cruzado-denominated funds on the part of the borrower and a corresponding need for highly profitable investment outlets by the firm with excess funds. Such complicated intercorporate transactions are sometimes necessary but are also subject to unfavorable intervention of local financial authorities.

Meeting Subsidiary Needs for Term Credit

Medium- and long-term funds are also available in local markets; although details differ from country to country, most developed countries offer the multinational subsidiary the opportunity to secure medium-term bank loans and lease financing on terms very similar to those encountered in the U.S. market. Even venture capital firms have emerged in most European countries.

Depending on the historical development of the country's financial system, firms may encounter a greater predominance of public sector, quasi-governmental institutions providing medium- and long-term bank credit. The commercial banking system itself may be composed primarily of nationalized banks, as in the case of France prior to privatization. Further, the French financial system contains a number of specialized public and semipublic institutions, such as the Credit National, which is a major supplier of loans up to twenty years in maturity to industry. Although governmental control of the institutions granting medium- and long-term credit does not of necessity lead to direct governmental control of the allocation of credit, in general, the greater the control of the banking system through ownership, the more likely it is that government lending priorities will be reflected in the actual loans made by the bank. If governmental policies include restrictions of the activities of foreign investors in local markets, multinationals with local operations may find it difficult to find local sources of funding.

Some traditional sources of financing in most financial markets may not be readily available in the local market. In Germany, for example, the issuance of bonds by even the strongest domestic industrial companies is almost nonexistent. Instead, long-term fixed-interest loans for industry are provided by German state banks (Landesbanken), which in turn issue long-term fixed-interest bonds as their source of funding. On the other hand, bond markets in Switzerland are a primary source of funds for industrial firms, including foreign firms.

Medium- and long-term financing in developing countries is much more restricted; capital formation locally may be very low compared to the financial demands of national development programs, and state-dominated or -subsidized agencies often crowd out private-sector borrowers. Multinationals are often the target of severe credit restrictions, primarily because they are expected to supply external capital to their subsidiaries and not to use up scarce local capital. For example, in 1980, in their search for local financing denominated in cruzeiro (the predecessor to the cruzado), the Brazilian subsidiaries of a number of multinationals began to use the Brazilian market for debentures; once the Brazilian authorities saw that the issuance of cruzeiro debentures by multinationals was being used as a mechanism to avoid bringing in foreign capital, they began withholding approval for the issuance of debentures until new equity capital equal in amount to the debenture issue had been supplied by the parent. As might be expected, issues of cruzeiro debentures by multinationals were rarely even considered thereafter.

Both developing and developed countries may offer incentives to encourage certain types of investments that are deemed to be in the national interest. Subsidized local financing, with softer-than-market terms, such as grace periods and reduced interest rates, may form part of the capital structure of any new investment project. The specialized national financial institutions, such as local development banks, which engage in making these subsidized loans, do, however, tend to preempt funds that would otherwise flow through the local financial markets, further reducing the depth of these markets.

SUMMARY

Multinationals theoretically should have a lower cost of capital than purely domestic firms. The cost of equity should be lower because multinationals offer home-country investors the opportunity to diversify across national boundaries. The reputation of the multinational allows it to access global capital markets on favorable terms. The development of liability swaps provides a mechanism for adjusting the currency and type (fixed or floating) of financing to corporate needs while raising debt on a global basis at the lowest possible cost. A highly developed internal funds movement mechanism provides a bridge between global and local money and capital markets. Within local markets, the subsidiaries of multinationals may appear to local lenders as extremely creditworthy, especially when their borrowings are supported by a parent guarantee. On the other hand, local government regulation and intervention in the capital allocation process limit the use of local sources.

DISCUSSION QUESTIONS

1. What are the financial advantages of being a multinational corporation? How does the multinational offer the local investor the opportunity to diversify internationally? Are there advantages to internationalizing the firm's equity investor base? How might this internationalization be accomplished?

2. Alford, Ltd., a British computer software house, has the opportunity to issue a floating rate six-year Eurobond at LIBOR plus ½ percent or fixed-rate six-year Eurobonds at 9¾ percent. Broadway, Inc., a prime U.S. corporate borrower, needs six-year money; it can negotiate a floating-rate loan from a bank at LIBOR plus ⅛ percent or fixed-rate six-year Eurobonds at 8⅝ percent.

a. Demonstrate that the potential for an interest-rate swap between Alford and Broadway exists.

b. In which market should Broadway issue debt in order to participate in a swap?

c. In which market should Alford issue debt in order to participate in a swap?

d. Because Alford's long-term future may depend on the vagaries of the software market, Broadway requests that its lead bank, the Bank of Lancastria, intermediate the swap transaction. The bank requires a fee of ⅛ percent to do so. Structure a swap in which Alford saves ⅛ percent on its borrowing cost, the Bank of Lancastria receives its ⅛ percent, and the remaining interest savings from the swap is passed on to Broadway.

e. How much does Broadway save using the swap? How much does Alford save? Reconcile the potential savings demonstrated in part *a* with the actual savings of Broadway, Alford, and the fees charged by the Bank of Lancastria.

3. As swaps manager of Credit Belge Third Chicago (CBTC), a leading investment bank, it is your responsibility to make swaps recommendations to your clients and to enter into swaps as an intermediary. One client, Brickfill Corp., a major construction engineering firm, needs to borrow six-year Swiss francs; Brickfill can issue Swiss franc bonds to yield 5 percent or can borrow six-year dollars at 8 percent. A second client, Schweizermilch, a Swiss chocolate company, is planning an expansion in the United States and needs six-year dollar funding. Schweizermilch can also borrow six-year francs at 5 percent, but because it has never issued long-term debt in dollars, it would have to pay 9 percent for dollar funds.

a. Demonstrate that the potential for a swap exists between Brickfill and Schweizermilch.

b. On the assumption that CBTC would charge ¼ percent for intermediating the swap, structure a swap between Brickfill and Schweizermilch that reduces Brickfill's cost of borrowing by ½ percent. In which market does each company borrow? What are the payments between firms? How does CBTC earn its ¼ percent?

c. Show that the potential for the swap mentioned in part *a* has been completely fulfilled in the transaction that you structured.

4. Billbert Enterprises, a well-known U.S. multinational, can issue $100 million face amount of five-year U.S. dollar Eurobonds at par with an annual coupon of 9 percent. It also has the opportunity to issue a dual currency Swiss franc/U.S. dollar bond according to the following terms:

a. Issue amount: Sfr 200 million at par

b. Annual coupon: 5 percent, payable in Swiss francs

c. Principal repayment: $120 million, the equivalent of Sfr 200 million at the fixed exchange rate of Sfr 1.6667 per U.S. dollar.

The current spot exchange rate is Sfr 2 per dollar. Billbert plans to cover the Swiss franc annual interest payments by buying them forward at the following forward rates:

Year 1	1.9400
Year 2	1.8700
Year 3	1.8000
Year 4	1.7300
Year 5	1.6600

Ignoring taxes and issuing expenses, what is the dollar cost (annual discount rate equating issue proceeds with future interest payments and principal repayments) of the Swiss franc/U.S. dollar dual currency issue? Should Billbert issue dual currency bonds, or should it issue dollar bonds?

5. Suppose that the dollar exchange rates for the constituent currencies of the Special Drawing Right (SDR) were as follows:

German mark	$0.5300
Japanese yen	0.0070
French franc	0.1800
British pound sterling	1.6000

What is the value of the SDR? Use Exhibit 7-5 for the composition of the SDR.

6. What are the major financial terms on which goods are sold in international trade? How do these terms affect the risk to the exporter that the importer will not pay?

7. What are the major characteristics of the finance of large-scale international projects?

8. What alternatives are available for the capital structure of the local subsidiary of a multinational firm? How does this capital structure affect access to local financial markets?

9. What is an overdraft? How are bills of exchange used to finance a local subsidiary? What other sources of short-term capital should be reviewed by local subsidiary management?

SUGGESTED READINGS

1. Antl, Boris (editor). *Swap Finance Service*, Vols. I and II. London: Euromoney Publications, 1986. (Also, loose-leaf service.)

2. Bankers Trust Company. "The International Swap Market," *Innovation in the International Capital Markets*, supplement to *Euromoney* (January 1986). Pp. 93–104.

3. Folks, William R., and Ramesh Advani. "Raising Funds with Foreign Currency," *Financial Executive*, Vol. 48, No. 2 (February 1980). Pp. 44–49.

4. George, Abraham M., and Ian H. Giddy (editors). *International Finance Handbook*, Vols. I and II. New York, New York: John Wiley & Sons, 1983. Parts 6 and 7.

5. Jacquillat, Bertrand, and Bruno H. Solnik. "Multinationals Are Poor Tools for Diversification," *Journal of Portfolio Management*, Vol. 4, No. 2 (Winter 1978). Pp. 8–12.

6. Johnson, R. Stafford, Charles W. Hultman, and Richard A. Zuber. "Currency Cocktails and Exchange Rate Stability," *Columbia Journal of World Business*, Vol. 14, No. 4 (Winter 1979). Pp. 117–126.

7. Lessard, Donald R. "World, Country, and Industry Relationships in Equity Returns: Implications for Risk Reductions through International Diversification," *Financial Analysts Journal*, Vol. 32, No. 1 (January/February 1976). Pp. 32–38.

8. Smith, Jr., Clifford W., Charles W. Smithson, and Lee M. Wakeman. "The Evolving Market for Swaps," *Midland Corporate Finance Journal*, Vol. 3, No. 4 (Winter 1986). Pp. 20–32.

9. Solnik, Bruno H. "Why Not Diversify Internationally Rather Than Domestically?" *Financial Analysts Journal*, Vol. 30, No. 4 (July/August 1974). Pp. 48–54.

10. Stanley, Marjorie T. "Capital Structure and the Cost of Capital for the Multinational Corporation," *Journal of International Business Studies*, Vol. 12, No. 1 (Spring/Summer 1981). Pp. 103–120.

CHAPTER 8

▼

Global Mobilization
of Financial Resources

▲

INTRODUCTION

The ability of a multinational corporation to source funds in a wide
variety of financial markets (discussed in Chapter 7) is complemented
by its ability to move funds from one unit to another. This chapter
provides an introduction to the channels by which a multinational corporation can move funds from one unit to another and discusses some
of the obstacles MNCs encounter in funds transfers. Its perspective is
that of a parent company with a number of subsidiaries operating globally.

Some channels of funds movement require a parent/subsidiary legal
relationship:

1. The parent provides the initial capitalization of the subsidiary, which
   may be in the form of

   a. capital investment in subsidiary equity

   b. parent loans to the subsidiary.

2. The subsidiary returns funds to the parent via four available channels:
   a. repayment of loans from the parent
   b. return of capital to the parent
   c. payment of interest on loans from the parent
   d. payment of dividends to the parent.

Other channels require the existence of patterns of movement of goods, services, or technology between units:

1. payments arising from the use of patents, trademarks, technology, or management skills of another unit, as
   a. royalties
   b. licensing fees
   c. management fees
2. acceleration or delay of payment for goods (leads and lags)
3. funds movements arising from alteration in the transfer prices on interunit transactions.

Other methods of funds movement arise simply from the extension of credit from one unit to the other in the form of *interunit* (sometimes referred to as *intracorporate*) *loans*. Such loans can be any of the following:

1. direct loans
2. back-to-back loans, intermediated through a bank
3. parallel loans, intermediated through another corporation.

Restrictions and taxations are major complicating factors in developing a system for global cash management. Nevertheless, significant opportunities for efficient use of cash balances remain.

OBSTACLES TO FUNDS TRANSFERS WITHIN A MULTINATIONAL CORPORATION

The very factors that give rise to opportunities for profit from moving funds from one unit to another also conspire to complicate the financial manager's effort to carry out the funds transfer. In particular, exchange controls and taxation policies must be closely monitored. Both may conceivably alter the feasibility and profitability of any planned funds move.

Certain desired financial transactions simply may not be allowed by regulatory authorities. For example, although the United States now allows its resident companies virtually unrestricted opportunities to move funds in and out of the country, in 1968, as part of its defense of the dollar's overvalued exchange rate, the United States imposed strict controls on the ability of direct investors to make new overseas investments or to add to existing investments with funds generated in the United States, *preventing funds outflows*. Indeed, U.S. firms were forced to repatriate funds from foreign investments to meet targets set by the government.

Countries sometimes act to *prevent funds inflows*, as well. From time to time, in the early 1970s, Germany imposed a cash deposit requirement (the *bardepot*) on foreign holdings of deutsche marks, where a certain portion of incoming foreign investment was required to be deposited in noninterest-earning accounts.

In developing countries, *restrictions on transfers*, particularly transfers of funds out of the country, are frequently stringent. Countries that are chronically short of foreign exchange, or that have borrowed heavily from external sources, are reluctant to allow multinationals to remit dividends from the subsidiary to the parent because the subsidiary's local currency dividend would be converted by the parent into foreign exchange. Recent debt reschedulings have occasionally given public-sector debt repayment preference over private-sector obligations. When exchange controls are such that the funds generated by local operations cannot be transferred at all, these funds are called *blocked funds*.

Tax considerations play an important role in transfer management. Most transfers out of a country, such as dividends, interest payments, or royalties, are subject to a *withholding tax* by a local government. The burden of these withholding taxes is often mitigated by a bewildering array of bilateral tax treaties, providing for a reduction in the tax rate or in the outright elimination of the tax for residents of the two countries involved. When received by the parent, dividends, interest, and fees are treated as taxable income and possibly further reduced by parent country tax.

PARENT/SUBSIDIARY LEGAL RELATIONSHIPS

Capitalization of the Subsidiary

The initial capitalization of a local subsidiary by the parent need not consist entirely of equity funds. Indeed, it is frequently advantageous to inject a significant portion of the original capitalization in the form of a parent loan to the subsidiary. The parent loan may have a fixed repayment schedule, carry a stated interest rate, and, if the parent company is U.S. based, normally be denominated in dollars. The use of the loan mechanism for capitalizing a subsidiary has several advantages:

1. It provides an additional method, through the repayment of the principal and payment of interest, of bringing funds back to the parent. The repayment of principal is not taxable.

2. Local authorities may be more inclined to permit loan repayment than repatriation of equity capital. If the entire amount of the initial capitalization were equity, the parent would have more difficulty in withdrawing any of it once the subsidiary became a cash generator.

3. Exchange restrictions and taxation factors frequently favor interest payments over dividends. Interest payments are a tax deduction for the subsidiary, even if they are made to the parent.

In most conceivable situations, then, companies find that parent debt should form a component of the initial capitalization of the subsidiary. In any event, an analysis should be undertaken to determine if debt offers advantages.

Companies using this approach must be careful not to make their initial equity investment too thin. Developing countries are anxious to secure permanent foreign direct investment. Authorities are aware that thin equity capitalization is evidence of anticipated rapid funds withdrawal and may well move to restrict repatriation of funds that appears to be exploitive in nature. Further, because the receipt by the parent of a loan principal repayment is not taxable in the parent's country, the use of a high percentage of debt might be viewed by the taxing authorities as a method of avoiding taxation that would ensue on the payment of dividends. The U.S. Internal Revenue Service, with its broad powers, may simply view the loan repayment as the same as a dividend and tax it accordingly.

Subsidiary Dividend Policy

Once a subsidiary is in place, it is expected to generate local profits, and from these profits it may seek to pay dividends. Receipts of subsidiary dividends form a major component of funds flow from the subsidiary to the parent.

There are numerous factors to consider when determining the appropriate level of dividend payment by a subsidiary. Among the most important are

1. relative needs of the subsidiary and parent for funds
2. exchange rate prospects of the local currency
3. effect of the dividend on the firm's global tax bill
4. short- and long-term attitudes of local authorities toward and legal restrictions on the level of dividend payments.

Approaches to Subsidiary Dividend Policy

Firms may use several different approaches in determining subsidiary dividend policy. At one extreme a firm may require each subsidiary, wherever located, to remit a dividend based on a formula. The normal approach is to set subsidiary dividends as a percentage of local after-tax earnings; formulas based on local net or fixed assets also have been used. Firms may seek to have each subsidiary pay a level dividend, with infrequent adjustments, on a quarterly or annual basis. At the other extreme, parents might adopt an entirely flexible policy, calling for dividends in highly variable amounts and only at times when the factors outlined above lead to favorable results for the company. Most companies tend to combine the two approaches, trying to create a pattern of dividend payment that balances off a host of complex objectives.

The Impact of Funds Availability

Clearly, the funds position and the needs of the local subsidiary play a major role in setting subsidiary dividends. If the local unit required major additional funding, particularly for capital expansion, declaration of a dividend would cause a funds drain at an inopportune moment; it would make little sense to withdraw funds from the subsidiary via the dividend route, paying the potentially extensive additional taxes triggered by the dividend and then reinvesting the funds as equity. Even if local funds were available to finance the subsidiary's funds requirement, governments of many nations look askance at the use of local financial markets to fund, as it were, a dividend payment to the parent. Some reduction of local funds needs could be achieved by relending the dividend back to the subsidiary or by extending the time between declaration and payment date, but these measures do not escape the tax burden that dividend declaration may impose. Still, firms seeking to establish a track record with regulatory authorities may declare a dividend even in the face of substantial local needs. Or, if the parent is in urgent need of funds, increasing the local subsidiary's dividend may provide a mechanism for obtaining them.

The Impact of Anticipated Currency Movements

The prospects of the local currency against the dollar also may be an important factor in determining the dividend. If the local currency is anticipated to depreciate, an increase in the level of dividend or the scheduling of a large extra dividend may provide a way to reduce local currency assets and convert funds legitimately to the parent's currency. But, the dividend would have to be paid, not just declared, prior to the anticipated currency depreciation. And exchange control authorities would be far more likely to question whether the dividend declared was done so for legitimate business purposes or whether it is simply a form of speculation against the local currency. It is unlikely that the subsidiary would receive permission to remit the dividend, in the latter case. Nonetheless, quick payment of dividends should be explored as a potential funds adjustment measure when local currency depreciation is anticipated.

If the local currency is expected to appreciate, it might be possible to skip or delay declaration of a dividend. Or, even if the dividend has been already declared, funds so generated could be reloaned to the subsidiary. Countries whose currencies are strong enough to be able to dispense with extensive controls generally pay little attention to dividend payments that are within any reasonable range.

The Impact of Corporate Tax Situation

The corporate tax situation is often the controlling factor in determining the timing and amount of subsidiary dividends. In many countries, dividend payments are subject to significant withholding tax by the host country. Although tax treaties sometimes reduce or eliminate the withholding tax, and despite the fact that a tax credit is given in the United

States for the amount of withholding tax paid, dividends are usually not costless. U.S. taxation on foreign source income is deferred until dividends are declared; tax is then due on the amount of the local income needed on a before-tax basis to earn the after-tax amount of a dividend (known picturesquely as "grossing up the dividend"). Because a tax credit is also given for the foreign taxes already paid on the earnings being remitted, the U.S. tax liability is negligible or nonexistent when the foreign tax rate is approximately the same as the U.S. tax rate. But, if the foreign tax rate is higher than that of the U.S., the dividend generates an excess foreign tax credit and, on the other hand, if the foreign tax rate is lower, the dividend may incur a U.S. tax liability.

Because dividend policy clearly affects the tax bill of the multinational, some firms approach the subsidiary dividend decision from a tax minimization viewpoint and try to select those dividend payments that reduce the overall tax bill.

Resolving Conflicting Goals in Dividend Policy

Evaluation of a dividend decision using the criteria discussed above (funds position, exchange risk exposure, tax payments) could lead to conflicting or complementary results. Firms that approach dividend policy on the basis of these short-term financial considerations would tend to operate a highly variable dividend policy, with high payout from any particular subsidiary in some years and low payouts or omitted dividends in others. Such variability may attract the attention of exchange control authorities in highly restricted countries and may lead to negative results ranging from unpleasant public relations to blockage of the proposed dividend. Dividends of multinationals are closely watched by exchange authorities and are very often subject to quantitative restrictions or to punitive taxes. In Brazil, for example, dividends cannot exceed 12 percent of registered capital (an officially defined measure of the value of the foreign portion of the company's investment base); dividends beyond that level are subject to a stiff supplementary income tax.

The establishment of a steady record of dividend payments may well provide the local subsidiary with an argument for continuation of payment at the same level, even in the face of new dividend remittance regulations. However, in a particularly severe foreign exchange crisis, it is unlikely that such an argument would prove effective in justifying dividend payments. For this reason, financial managers would be well advised to manage dividends actively from a funds requirement, exchange exposure, and tax minimization viewpoint, although companies may also wish to avoid extreme swings in dividend payout. One U.S. auto manufacturer reinvested local profits in its Australian subsidiary for thirty years without paying a dividend; when a large dividend was finally declared, the local press and government officials noted with disapproval that the dividend was several times larger than the company's original investment.

The flow of dividend payments must follow ownership patterns; dividends are, after all, the compensation given to providers of equity capital for the risks that they bear. Although we have viewed multinational corporations as though they consist of one parent providing equity capital to a number of separate subsidiaries, legal and tax considerations usually require the establishment of a much more complicated ownership pattern in which subsidiaries, in turn, own other subsidiaries or two or more subsidiaries jointly own another. The patterns can be even more complex. These legal structures also help determine the equity/dividend linkages between units of the multinational system.

MOVEMENT BETWEEN UNITS OF GOODS, SERVICES, OR TECHNOLOGY

Royalties, Licensing Fees, and Management Fees

When one firm allows another firm to use its technology, patent rights, trademarks, or other intangibles, it normally receives compensation from the other firm. In many cases, when a firm has proprietary technology or trademarks, it will deliberately choose to license its technology or trademarks as a means of exploiting technology in a country that it considers inappropriate for direct investment. The licensing agreement normally requires payment for each unit manufactured or sold by the licensing firm.

In a similar fashion, when one unit of a multinational (usually but not always the parent) allows other units to use similar intangibles, the opportunity to move funds by payment of royalties and licensing fees exists. To simplify this discussion, assume that the parent owns the intangibles and the subsidiary licenses the technology or trademark.

Unlike remittances by dividends, the remittance of royalties and of fees is not subject to great flexibility. Countries require a formal agreement between the licensing parent and the licensee subsidiary that stipulates the amount of the royalty (usually a fixed percentage of sales or a fixed amount per unit). Exchange control authorities monitor any changes in this agreement very carefully. Countries that are trying to conserve their holdings of foreign exchange are reluctant to see those holdings used in payments for intangibles. In general, they try to discourage this form of remittance by placing a quantitative restriction on the level of the royalty or refusing to allow the subsidiary to deduct it as an expense on its local corporate income tax return. Royalties and licensing fee payments by subsidiaries are viewed as just a way of disguising profit remittances; where controls on other forms of remittances are in place, companies will probably have little flexibility in the use of royalties.

For this reason, the financial manager must analyze with great care the initial level of royalty payments from a subsidiary. Whatever level is chosen, the subsidiary will be responsible for payment regardless of its local funds needs.

Royalties and fee payments are often subject to withholding taxes by the government of the licensee's country and represent foreign source income to the parent. But, because royalties usually are tax deductible to the subsidiary and because the withholding tax rate on royalty payments usually is below both the U.S. and host country corporate tax rates, royalties are a particularly advantageous method for remitting profits for the parent.

Because royalty payments are usually advantageous, it is sound practice to build them into the financial plan of the subsidiary. The fixed flow of funds from subsidiary to parent generated by the imposition of the royalty can be offset, if desired, by loans or other financial operations causing funds to flow from parent to subsidiary.

Parent companies may also charge their subsidiaries fees for other activities, such as the provision of technical assistance or specific managerial skills. The technical assistance and management fees are similar to royalties in their structure, regulation, and financial impact.

Leads and Lags

An important possibility for funds movement between units of the multinational corporation arises from the flow of real goods between units and so multinationals may seek to rationalize their global production. A plant in Hong Kong, for example, may supply one product to sales subsidiaries in all of Asia while a plant in Korea sells subassemblies to the plant in Hong Kong. The complex pattern of goods movement gives rise to a complex pattern of funding and funds shifting alternatives.

Suppose, for example, that the French subsidiary of Agfolk Industries sells $500,000 worth of goods monthly to the German subsidiary. If the German unit is given sixty days to pay, the French unit has on its books an account receivable of $1 million due from the German unit. In essence, the French unit has loaned $1 million to the German subsidiary.

Suppose that the German subsidiary requires an additional $1 million in funding. The French subsidiary could provide this additional funding by giving the German subsidiary 120 days to make payment. The German unit would not make the monthly payment of $500,000 for the next two months; at the end of the two months it would have an account payable to the French subsidiary of $2 million.

Suppose, on the other hand, that the French unit requires funds. The French subsidiary could change its payment terms to cash on delivery, and the German unit could immediately prepay the existing $1 million account payable to the French unit, providing the needed funds.

The technique of changing the date of payment of a trade account to change the time at which funds are transferred is called *leads and lags*. Making payment on an account prior to its normal due date is referred to as *leading* the payment. Making payment on an account after its normal due date is referred to as *lagging* the payment. Leads and lags are among the most frequently used, flexible, and powerful methods of moving funds between units of the multinational corporation. All that is required is the existence of trade flows between the subsidiaries.

In the Agfolk example, the change in terms between the French and German subsidiaries from 60 to 120 days results in a two-month delay in payments by the German subsidiary. This example shows that a lag transaction moves funds from the selling subsidiary to the buying subsidiary.

On the other hand, if the German subsidiary prepays the account payable to the French subsidiary, we have a lead transaction. A lead moves funds from the buying subsidiary to the selling subsidiary.

Even if current terms call for cash on delivery, the buying unit can transfer funds to the selling unit by paying for goods in advance. Trade credit in many countries can be extended up to six months without difficulty. The U.S. Internal Revenue Service allows the extension of trade credit in the usual fashion for six months without the imposition of an interest charge. Theoretically, leading and lagging offer great flexibility for funds movement.

Government Restrictions on Leads and Lags

As might be expected, governments place substantial restrictions on the ability of multinationals to utilize leads and lags. From the government's point of view, there are four types:

1. *Export lead:* advanced payment by a foreign buyer for exports from a local supplier
2. *Export lag:* delayed payment by a foreign buyer for exports from a local supplier
3. *Import lead:* advanced payment by a local buyer for imports from a foreign supplier
4. *Import lag:* delayed payment by a local buyer for imports from a foreign supplier.

From the point of view of a country that is trying to manage its holdings of scarce foreign currency, export leads and import lags are encouraged. The export lead causes funds to be received by the local supplier at an earlier date and thus provides an earlier receipt of foreign exchange. An import lag delays use of foreign exchange to pay for imports; Brazil, for example, required at one time that at least 180 days in credit be extended to Brazilian buyers of foreign goods.

Exchange authorities are more reluctant to allow export lags and import leads. The extension of additional trade credit to foreign buyers (the export lag) delays the date at which the foreign currency proceeds of the export sale become available to the seller. The prepayment of foreign purchases (the import lead) accelerates the date when foreign exchange is needed by the local buyer. Both cause a drain on the local country's exchange holdings.

Thus, a local subsidiary that seeks to lead a payment to a sister subsidiary elsewhere or that seeks to extend additional trade credit to that subsidiary may encounter restrictions that vary in severity depending on the extent to which the local country is having foreign exchange difficulties.

Payments Netting

Closely allied in practice to leading and lagging is the concept of *netting*. The basic idea of netting is quite simple. If the German unit owes the French unit $3 million and the French unit owes the German unit $2 million, the debts are discharged by having the German unit pay the French unit $1 million ($3 million minus $2 million) — the net amount due. When netting is done between two subsidiaries, it is referred to as *bilateral netting*.

Netting requires that the subsidiaries involved have payments moving in both directions. The primary advantage of netting arises from the fact that it reduces the actual volume of funds that flows through the payment system. Despite the relative ease and speed with which payments can be made between most major countries, the transfer of funds still leads to transfer expenses from the bid/ask spread in the foreign exchange market, the loss of use of funds while they are in transit, and the bank commissions and fees associated with the transfer. In the bilateral netting example above, only the net amount of $1 million in funds is transferred; without netting, $5 million would have to enter the payments system.

Multilateral Netting   The advantage of bilateral netting can be extended by the application of the netting approach to the interunit transactions for a larger number of subsidiaries. Exhibit 8-1 shows the anticipated payments between the units of Agfolk Industries for September 1987. For example, the German subsidiary is scheduled to pay the Dutch subsidiary $1.5 million, while the Dutch subsidiary is scheduled to pay the German unit $2 million. If each subsidiary engaged in bilateral netting with every other subsidiary, the total volume of payments made could be reduced from $63.8 million to $24.4 million, a substantial reduction.

It is possible to reduce the total volume of payments even further by using the technique of *multilateral netting*. The first step in applying this technique is to determine the total receipts and payments of each subsidiary. Germany, for example, is scheduled to receive $10.5 million from the four other units and is expected to pay out $9.8 million. After all payments have been made, Germany would receive a net amount of $0.7 million. The Dutch unit, on the other hand, is expected to pay out $1 million on a net basis.

Under a multilateral netting system, the deficit units in the system

EXHIBIT 8-1 Agfolk Industries Interunit Payments, September 1987 ($ millions)

Receiving Unit	Paying Unit					
	Germany	Netherlands	Switzerland	United Kingdom	United States	Total Receipts
Germany	–	2.0	1.5	4.0	3.0	10.5
Netherlands	1.5	–	4.0	3.5	3.0	12.0
Switzerland	2.1	1.0	–	–	3.0	6.1
United Kingdom	1.2	4.0	3.0	–	4.0	12.2
United States	5.0	6.0	10.0	2.0	–	23.0
Total payments	9.8	13.0	18.5	9.5	13.0	63.8

Net Position

Unit	Receipts	Payments	Net Position
Germany	10.5	9.8	+ 0.7
Netherlands	12.0	13.0	– 1.0
Switzerland	6.1	18.5	– 12.4
United Kingdom	12.2	9.5	+ 2.7
United States	23.0	13.0	+ 10.0

EXHIBIT 8-2   Agfolk Industries Payment Schedule ($ millions)

Paying and Receiving Units	Payment
Netherlands pays Germany	$ 0.7 million
Netherlands pays United Kingdom	0.3 million
Total	$ 1.0 million
Switzerland pays United Kingdom	$ 2.4 million
Switzerland pays United States	10.0 million
Total	$12.4 million
Total payments	$13.4 million

pay the surplus units. Once the net positions of the units have been determined, a payments schedule can be drawn up, and units can make the required payment. Exhibit 8-2 gives one of a number of possible payments schedules. The Dutch unit pays the $0.7 million that Germany is to receive on a net basis. The U.K. unit receives $0.3 million from the Dutch unit and the remaining $2.4 million from Switzerland. Switzerland pays the U.S. unit $10.0 million. Multilateral netting has further reduced the total volume of funds moving through the international payments system to $13.4 million. The total amount of funds not transferred is $63.8 million − $13.4 million = $50.4 million. If the cost of moving funds through the payments system is ½ percent of the amount transferred, the use of multilateral netting would save $252,000 ($50.4 million × 0.005) in the month of September 1987.

Restrictions on Netting   Although netting technically should not reduce the net amount of foreign exchange that a country receives, exchange control authorities sometimes limit or prohibit netting. Some countries allow the netting of trade transactions but prohibit netting of financial transactions. Others allow bilateral netting, where evidence of transactions involving payments to and from the specific country is clear, but prohibit participation in multilateral netting schemes, where payments are sometimes made even though no direct trade occurs between the local unit and the unit receiving payment. Exchange controls may limit to some extent the opportunity for multilateral netting, but many companies have established systems that have been exceptionally cost effective.

Third-Party Netting   An extension of the concept of netting inter-subsidiary flows is that of third-party netting, where payments to and from units of other companies are included in the netting program. Suppose, for example, that a Swedish company sells Agfolk's U.K. subsidiary $2.0 million worth of parts and, in the same month, buys $2.5 million from Agfolk's Swiss unit. The Swedish company would benefit if it would net out its transactions with Agfolk, paying only a net amount of $2.5 million − $2.0 million = $0.5 million to Agfolk's Swiss unit. The U.K. unit would be responsible for the remainder of the Swedish company's payment of $2.0 million to Switzerland. Because Switzerland is scheduled to pay the U.K. $2.4 million anyway (see Exhibit 8-2), the U.K. subsidiary's payment to the Swiss unit could be netted out, and Switzerland would end up paying only $2.4 million − $2.0 million = $0.4 million to the U.K. unit. It would be even more advantageous for the Swedish company to pay the $0.5 million net amount to the U.K. subsidiary, which could then net out the $2.5 million that it needed to pay the Swiss unit with the $2.4 million that it is scheduled to receive, for a final payment of $0.1 million.

Reinvoicing Centers   Many firms that have set up netting systems have found it useful to set up reinvoicing centers to handle interunit and third-party trade transactions. In trade between subsidiaries, the selling subsidiary effectively sells the goods to the reinvoicing center, which in turn resells the goods (at a slightly higher price, usually) to the purchasing unit. In third-party transactions, the reinvoicing center buys the goods from the selling unit and then resells them to the third-party buyer. The actual goods go directly from the selling subsidiary to the final buyer; only legal title to the goods is vested in the reinvoicing center.

The use of reinvoicing centers actually predates the technique of payments netting. Such centers are usually located in low-tax-rate countries, so-called tax havens. Goods are billed to the reinvoicing center at one price and resold to the ultimate customer at a higher price. The profit earned by the reinvoicing center is taxed at a much lower rate than it would have been if earned by the selling subsidiary.

The use of reinvoicing centers in tax haven countries allows a multinational to capture profits at a much lower rate than otherwise would be possible. However, U.S. firms have not been able to take significant advantage of the tax avoidance opportunity since passage of the Tax

Reform Act of 1962, which eliminated deferral on taxes of subsidiaries that engage in this type of transaction. As a result, U.S.-based companies now use reinvoicing centers primarily to facilitate bilateral and multilateral netting. Also, since the introduction of the functional currency concept of *FASB Statement No. 52* (see Chapter 5), companies have had to rethink the normal U.S. practice of billing interunit sales in dollars because a dollar receivable or payable on the books of a subsidiary represents transaction exposure; movement in the dollar exchange rate with the local currency brings a transaction gain or loss that enters earnings. For this reason, it may be appropriate to bill the reinvoicing center in the currency of the selling subsidiary and bill the purchasing unit, in turn, in its functional currency. The reinvoicing unit can then take the appropriate action to manage the resultant positions; in effect, the reinvoicing center can assume and centralize the management of the transaction exposure of subsidiaries.

Further, development of a netting system and reinvoicing center allows prompt identification of units in the system that have funds needs and provides a mechanism for the centralized provision of funds to these units through the mechanisms of leads and lags. Suppose, for example, that after determining the payment pattern of Exhibit 8-2, Agfolk identifies that the Swiss subsidiary needs an additional $5.0 million for the next month. The Swiss unit could obtain these funds by lagging $5.0 million in anticipated payments to the U.S. parent.

Transfer Pricing

The discussion thus far has assumed that the transfer price—the price charged by one unit of the multinational to another unit for goods—has been constant. However, within very circumscribed boundaries, these transfer prices may be varied in such a way as to both move funds from one unit to another and to allocate taxable income between the two countries involved. Transfer pricing can thus be used as both a funds movement and a tax minimization technique.

The essence of the approach is that transfer prices are set to allocate as much income as possible to low-tax-rate countries and as little income as possible to high-tax-rate countries.

Suppose that Agfolk France ships 10,000 subassemblies per month to Agfolk Germany. The cost of each subassembly in France is $50. Agfolk Germany buys the subassemblies at the stated transfer price, adds $40 in local value, and sells the final product to third parties at $200 per unit. The French subsidiary's marginal tax rate is 50 percent and the German's, 40 percent (these rates are hypothetical).

Exhibit 8-3 compares the results of adopting a transfer price of $80 per subassembly with the results of applying a transfer price of $100 per subassembly to the transaction. At the transfer price of $80, the French subsidiary has a before-tax contribution of $300,000; on an after-tax basis, the contribution is $150,000. The German unit's cost of goods sold arises from the transfer price of $80 per subassembly and the local cost of $40 per subassembly, for a total cost of $120; with a marginal tax rate of 40 percent, the after-tax contribution is $480,000. Adding the German and the French subsidiaries' after-tax contribution together, the total after-tax contribution is $630,000.

EXHIBIT 8-3 Example of Transfer Pricing

	Transfer Price = *$80*	*Transfer Price =* *$100*
French Subsidiary		
Sales	$ 800,000	$1,000,000
Cost of goods sold	500,000	500,000
Contribution	300,000	500,000
Tax on contribution (50%)	150,000	250,000
After-tax contribution	150,000	250,000
German Subsidiary		
Sales	2,000,000	2,000,000
Cost of goods sold	1,200,000	1,400,000
Contribution	800,000	600,000
Tax on contribution (40%)	320,000	240,000
After-tax contribution	480,000	360,000
Total after-tax contribution	$ 630,000	$ 610,000
Consolidated Statement		
Sales	2,000,000	2,000,000
Cost of goods sold	900,000	900,000
Contribution	1,100,000	1,100,000
Taxes	470,000	490,000
Total after-tax contribution	$ 630,000	$ 610,000

Raising the transfer price to $100 raises the level of sales and before-tax income in the French subsidiary; it also raises the cost of goods sold to the German subsidiary and lowers the German before-tax contribution to $600,000. In effect, the higher transfer price increases taxable income in France by $200,000 and decreases taxable income in Germany by the same amount. Because more income is earned in France and the French tax rate is higher, the total tax bill of the entire firm increases, and total after-tax income decreases to $610,000. Clearly, Agfolk would prefer the $80 transfer price because it provides a larger after-tax contribution to the firm as a whole.

The consolidated statement at the bottom of Exhibit 8-3, which eliminates the interunit sale, shows that the total before-tax contribution is $1.1 million. Use of an $80 transfer price allocates $300,000 of this contribution to France and $800,000 to Germany; the total tax bill is $470,000. Use of the $100 transfer price allocates $500,000 of the contribution to France and $600,000 to Germany; the total tax bill is $490,000. The increase in tax bill at $20,000 can be viewed as a result of allocating $200,000 in income to France where the tax rate is 10-percent higher; $200,000 × 0.10 = $20,000, the incremental tax bill.

The Impact on Income Allocation of Transfer Pricing Decisions

Thus the level of the transfer price effectively allocates income between the selling and buying subsidiaries. In general, when a subsidiary in a higher-tax-rate country is selling to a unit in a lower-tax-rate country, the transfer price should be set as low as possible. This action captures the profits in the unit in the lower-tax-rate country. When the tax rate applied to the selling subsidiary is lower than that of the buyer, the transfer price should be set as high as possible, capturing profits for the seller. Where tariffs are charged on the transaction, their effect also should be included in the analysis.

Revenue authorities of all countries are acutely aware of the ability of multinational companies to allocate profits by use of the transfer price mechanism. Corporate latitude for altering transfer prices is circumscribed by what is acceptable to the government. In the United States, the Internal Revenue Service has broad latitude under Section 482 of the Revenue Code to reallocate gross income if it is found that a transfer pricing policy results in the evasion of taxes. The implementing regulations call for arm's-length prices between units of a multinational, and develop a number of methods for determining the appropriate arm's-length prices. For these reasons, transfer price management as a means of tax minimization is useful only within fairly narrow limits.

The Impact on Funds Flow Allocation of Transfer Pricing Decisions

Transfer pricing decisions also have a funds flow allocation impact. At the $80 transfer price level, Agfolk Germany has a monthly funds inflow of $480,000, and Agfolk France, only $150,000. When the transfer price is changed to $100, Germany's flow is reduced to $360,000, and France's flow is increased to $250,000. An increase in transfer price allocates more funds to the selling unit; decreasing the transfer price allocates more funds to the buying unit. If Agfolk France was in need of funds and Agfolk Germany had excess funds, one method of moving funds would be to raise the transfer price that the French unit charges the German unit. Of course, this technique would incur, as shown earlier, an additional tax burden of $20,000; in countries where alternate channels of funds movement are readily available, this approach would not be the most cost effective because of the substantial tax penalty.

Transfer pricing is much more likely to be used in countries where barriers to profit remittance exist, as a means of withdrawing funds. Goods produced by the local subsidiary are priced at a relatively low level, and goods sold to the local subsidiary are priced at a relatively high level. Because these transfer price actions both reduce the foreign currency proceeds from a country's exports and increase the import bill, they are extremely unpopular with local authorities and typically are monitored closely. Nonetheless, where funds would otherwise be trapped in a country whose currency is suspect, companies may choose to endure the administrative review of their transfer pricing decisions and pay whatever additional taxes might be incurred to use this mechanism.

INTERUNIT, OR INTRACORPORATE, LOANS

Direct Lending between Units

In major financial markets where restrictions on funds movements are minimal, one unit in the multinational's financial system can make funds available to another through the simple mechanism of a direct loan. These loans carry a stated rate of interest, may be denominated in the currency of either unit or in a third currency, as exchange restrictions allow, and typically have a fixed repayment schedule. Because the interest rate on the direct loan serves as the transfer price for funds, companies find it difficult to set artificially high or low interest rates on these interunit loans.

Back-to-Back Loans

In some countries, current exchange restrictions or the risk of their imposition in the future may lead a company to use a commercial bank or other financial institution as an intermediary in a *back-to-back loan.* The parent (or other unit that serves as the source of funds) deposits its funds at the intermediating bank; the bank, in turn, or its local branch, lends the recipient subsidiary the equivalent amount of funds, either denominated in the parent's currency or in the local currency. The bank pays interest at a negotiated rate on the parent's deposit; the subsidiary pays interest on the loan that it receives. The bank profits on the interest differential (adjusted for exchange rate changes) between what it pays the parent and what it receives from the subsidiary, as well as on any fees that it might charge for arranging the financing. The bank's loan is as close to riskless as is possible because if the subsidiary defaults, the deposit of the parent functions as collateral for the loan.

Corporations that use the back-to-back loan approach do so for several reasons. First, direct loans to the subsidiary may be banned, heavily restricted, or subject to differential tax rates, particularly withholding taxes. Second, because developing nations depend on banks for significant offshore funding, it is sometimes thought that loan repayments to external banks might be allowed, even if loan repayments to private firms become restricted. Given the difficulty in repaying bank loans that many developing nations encountered beginning in 1982, even loans from banks may not be allocated in foreign exchange for repayment. Nonetheless, private firm borrowings are still considered to be at a relative disadvantage.

Parallel Loans

A second intermediated method of advancing funds to a subsidiary is the *parallel loan.* Through a bank or other third party, a company needing to fund its local subsidiary is brought into contact with a company whose local subsidiary has excess cash. Suppose, for example, that Agfolk's subsidiary in Colombia needs 219.2 million Colombian pesos (equivalent to US $1 million). Agfolk learns that BBB Industries has a Colombian subsidiary that owns substantial excess Colombian pesos and that is precluded by exchange controls from remitting them. Agfolk can then lend BBB Industries $1 million at an agreed interest rate, while at the same time BBB's Colombian subsidiary lends Agfolk Colombian P 219.2 million for the same maturity at local Colombian interest rates. When the loans mature, Agfolk's Colombian subsidiary repays the pesos to BBB Colombia, while BBB's parent company repays the $1 million to Agfolk.

In effect, Agfolk has provided funding for its subsidiary without becoming exposed to the risk that repayment will be restricted by the Colombian exchange authorities. BBB has effectively remitted pesos from Colombia, temporarily; it gives up pesos in Colombia in exchange for use of dollars over the life of the loan. Typically, the credit risk of both sides is minimized by arranging for a right of offset; if one party fails to repay, the other party may offset its claim against the amount it owes. The financial intermediary that arranges the parallel loan receives a commission from each side. Because the company that has excess local funds generally wants access to dollars for some period of time, parallel loans normally have a relatively long (five- to fifteen-year) maturity.

UTILIZING BLOCKED FUNDS

The parallel loan transaction outlined above is one of a number of creative ways in which multinationals employ funds that they are unable to remit to their parent or to other units. These funds are referred to as *blocked funds* because their conversion to other currencies is blocked by local financial regulations. Local subsidiaries that are highly profitable generate funds; when these funds are blocked, they must be used locally. To the extent permitted, excess funds can be invested in local money market instruments or placed on deposit with local banks. The problem with these alternatives is that yields are not usually sufficient to keep pace with local inflation or the rate of local currency depreciation. Investment in real assets may permanently tie up funds. Thus, companies seek strategies that minimize the accumulation of blocked funds by providing as many remittance channels as possible and by designing strategies for the utilization of blocked funds in ways that minimize inflationary impacts, such as the parallel loan discussed in the previous section.

An emerging methodology for the use of blocked funds has developed from the growth of barter or *countertrade*. The firm with blocked funds uses them to acquire physical goods for which it may have no specific need. These goods are then exchanged for other goods that can be sold on the world market or used by the parent or other units in production. An early example of this creative use of blocked funds was the so-called Volks-steaks; Volkswagen of Brazil used its blocked funds to purchase significant quantities of beef for export to West Germany. Blocked funds usually can be spent locally, and firms use them to pay for local expenses of sales meetings, for airline tickets on the national carrier, or for other corporatewide expenses that can be sourced in the local market.

GLOBAL CASH MANAGEMENT

Just as the framework of funds transfer channels in the multinational allows the firm to source funds where they are cheapest and make efficient use of them to meet the global funds needs of the corporation, substantial economies can be achieved in meeting the liquidity needs of the various units of the multinational.

Cash and readily marketable assets are held to meet the uncertain cash flows that confront the various units of the multinational. If each unit is called on to hold assets for its own needs, the total amount of assets held for liquidity purposes is substantially larger than if some central asset pool could be created to meet the liquidity needs of a number of units. This thought is the driving force behind the concept of *asset pooling.*

An asset pool is an identifiable group of liquid assets held to meet the liquidity needs of a number of subsidiaries. Whenever a subsidiary has a shortfall in cash flows, it can call on the unit holding the asset pool to provide funds, usually in the form of an interunit loan. Because the random component of each subsidiary's cash flows is not perfectly correlated with the cash flows of the other subsidiaries, the total volume of assets held in the pool can be substantially smaller. Effective asset pooling requires a highly integrated financial information system to identify funds availability and funds need for each subsidiary. On a daily basis, excess cash is, whenever possible, placed in the asset pool.

The multinational corporation also has the usual range of securities available for short-term investment. External market instruments, such as Eurocurrency CDs, Eurocurrency deposits, Euronotes of major corporations, and government obligations of the major financial powers offer a wide range of maturity and credit risk.

SUMMARY

The existence of a number of funds flow channels between its various units allows the multinational corporation to source funds on a global basis and move them to their most profitable use. Interunit funds movements for intangibles (royalties and licensing fees), for payment for services (management and technical assistance fees), and for payment for real goods (trade credit, leads and lags, and transfer prices) are among the various funds flow channels used by multinationals. In addition, these firms have the flexibility to make direct loans between units and to reap rewards in liquidity management that accrue from the ready transferability of funds. They are, however, subject to constraints that limit the flexibility of interunit funds movements and that are imposed by local authorities to maintain the external value of their currency and counteract the tax avoidance potential inherent in these techniques. As financial markets become less regulated and as the financial information systems offered by large banks to their clients become more sophisticated, the scope for a more active rationalization of funds usage on a global basis will be enhanced.

DISCUSSION QUESTIONS

1. Identify the major channels for movement of funds between parent and subsidiary. What factors affect the policy that a firm adopts on dividend payment from subsidiary to parent?

2. What channels of interunit fund movements require the existence of underlying trade, service, or technology transactions between units of a multinational corporation? What factors should be considered in setting the appropriate level of royalties and licensing fees?

3. What is a parallel loan? What is a back-to-back loan? How do they differ?

4. Suppose that the German unit of Billbert Enterprises buys $500,000 per month of goods from the French unit and sells $1 million per month to the British unit. At present, all interunit sales require payment in thirty days. Using leads and lags, how can the following transfers of funds be made?

   a. from the German unit to the French unit
   b. from the British unit to the German unit
   c. from the British unit to the French unit
   d. from the French unit to the British unit

5. Norda Inc. has operations in four European countries and the United States. Because Norda is vertically integrated, it makes numerous shipments between these five units. In April 1988, the scheduled payments between these units are as follows (in $ millions):

Receiving Unit	Paying Unit				
	United States	Germany	France	Belgium	Denmark
United States	—	1.5	2.5	2.0	1.0
Germany	3.0	—	1.0	6.0	1.0
France	4.0	2.5	—	2.5	—
Belgium	5.0	1.0	6.0	—	1.0
Denmark	3.5	—	2.0	1.0	—

   a. If a multilateral netting program is utilized by Norda, what is the total volume of intercompany payments that will be made by Norda in April 1988? What would be the volume of payments made without netting? If Norda can save ¼ percent on each payment not made, what would be Norda's savings from using a netting system?
   b. Based on the information in the table, develop a payment schedule for Norda to follow in April 1988 (after netting). There is usually more than one feasible payment schedule.

6. Taxdodge, Inc. ships 300,000 dozen quidgets a month from their U.S. subsidiary to their Italian subsidiary. Taxdodge's marginal U.S. tax rate is 30 percent and its marginal Italian tax rate is 40 percent. Quidgets cost $10 per dozen to produce in the United States and sell in Italy for $25 per dozen. Taxdodge believes that it can set the transfer price on quidgets at any price from $15 to $18 per dozen.

   a. If Taxdodge wants to maximize after-tax income, what transfer price should it set? What would its consolidated monthly after-tax income on quidgets be? (Ignore other costs.)

b. In order to move funds to Italy quickly, Taxdodge adopts a transfer price of $15 per dozen. By how much is monthly after-tax income reduced? How much additional funding is made available to the Italian unit by the price reduction?

SUGGESTED READINGS

1. Burns, Jane O. "Transfer Pricing Decisions in U.S. Multinational Corporations," *Journal of International Business Studies*, Vol. 11, No. 2 (Fall 1980). Pp. 23–29.

2. Business International. *The BIMR Handbook on Global Treasury Management*. New York, New York: Business International, 1984.

3. Cohen, Fred L. "Accelerating Foreign Remittances and Collection," *Cashflow* (May 1981). Pp. 36–40.

4. George, Abraham M., and Ian H. Giddy (editors). *International Finance Handbook*, Vols. I and II. New York, New York: John Wiley & Sons, 1983. Parts 8.2, 8.3, and 8.11.

5. Kopits, George F. "Dividend Remittance Behavior within the International Firm: A Cross-Country Analysis," *Review of Economics and Statistics*, Vol. 54, No. 3 (August 1972). Pp. 339–342.

6. Kopits, George F. "Intra-Firm Royalties Crossing Frontiers and Transfer Pricing Behavior," *Economic Journal*, Vol. 86, No. 344 (December 1976). Pp. 791–805.

7. Sangster, Bruce F. "International Funds Management," *Financial Executive*, Vol. 45, No. 12 (December 1977). Pp. 46–52.

8. Shapiro, Alan C. "Payments Netting in International Cash Management," *Journal of International Business Studies*, Vol. 9, No. 2 (Fall 1978). Pp. 51–58.

9. Shapiro, Alan C. "International Cash Management—The Determination of Multicurrency Cash Balances," *Journal of Financial and Quantitative Analysis*, Vol. 11, No. 5 (December 1976). Pp. 893–900.

10. Simpson, H. Clay, Jr. "International Cash Management: An Introduction to the State of Current Practice," *Journal of Cash Management*, Vol. 2, No. 1 (March 1982).

CHAPTER 9

▼

International Investment Decisions

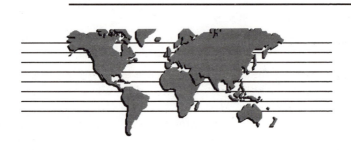

▲

INTRODUCTION

Foreign direct investment (FDI) is one of the most important vehicles for the international expansion of a firm. This chapter reviews the process that a firm uses to analyze and act on an opportunity for foreign investment. It examines the reasons for undertaking FDI and then presents considerations involved in assessing the climate for foreign investment. Finally, the chapter discusses the issues that distinguish the analysis of a capital budgeting proposal in a multinational setting.

REASONS FOR UNDERTAKING
FOREIGN DIRECT INVESTMENT

A number of theories have been advanced to explain foreign direct investment (FDI), including those based on (1) monopolistic advantage, where a firm uses its superior business knowledge, initially developed in its home market, to extend its product life cycle internationally; (2) oligopolistic reaction, where the firm reacts to competitive or cost structure changes in its industry by engaging in FDI; (3) financial factors such as the need to seek risk diversification and high rates of return; (4) the advantages of internalizing the international exchange of factors of production; and (5) the need to consider the interaction between firm-specific and country-specific factors to explain FDI. The following discussion of foreign direct investment is based on all of these theories as it combines elements from each of them at appropriate places in the discussion.

Alternatives to Foreign Direct Investment

Serving foreign markets can be an attractive way for a company to generate growth and higher profits and meet other corporate objectives. A company can serve international markets in a number of ways. For example, it can start out by serving foreign markets by export sales either directly through an export department in the company or indirectly through a foreign sales agent or an export management company. It also can serve foreign markets by licensing local manufacture of its products. In return for providing patented and/or another exclusive process, product technology, or management expertise, a company in return gets a stream of fees and royalty payments without having risked its own equity investment overseas. In countries with severe restrictions on the sale and conversion of their currency, a company may also consider some type of coproduction, barter, or countertrade deal. In some cases, a firm may sell its expertise to get a foreign producer started by means of a turnkey project or manage the foreign operation through a management contract.

In each of these cases, the firm is attempting to extend overseas its unique advantage in production, marketing, technology, or management without putting its capital at risk overseas. Although each of these approaches has certain advantages and may be the optimal approach for serving a given overseas market, each approach also has some disadvantages and limitations. One major disadvantage of selling expertise or another competitive advantage is that the company creates potential future competitors when it gives away its unique advantage. Such information often is resold after a few years to others or is otherwise exploited in foreign markets by the recipient company. Direct ownership of foreign operations circumvents these disadvantages.

Foreign direct investment, too, has its drawbacks. But, because total net global FDI keeps rising, we can assume that the advantages of foreign direct investment must be greater than its disadvantages in a large number of cases. FDI continues to be undertaken, probably because of its ability to generate extraordinary rates of return by successfully overcoming market imperfections and barriers to cross-border business transactions. If product and financial markets were perfect and internationally integrated, no extraordinary profit opportunities would exist, having been eliminated by competitive forces.

The Costs of Foreign Direct Investment

In order for foreign direct investment to take place, there must be extraordinary profit opportunities because managing foreign operations is more expensive than managing domestic businesses. Additional expense is incurred by the higher information costs of analyzing and understanding a distant and different business climate, higher telecommunication and travel costs, higher cross-border and local taxes, higher costs of overcoming cultural and institutional differences, and higher costs of overcoming political and commercial risks in a foreign country. These costs are higher in part because of numerous restrictions on cross-border business transactions that are imposed by national governments. Quotas are one form of restriction on business that include quotas on exports, imports, and foreign investments; regulation and licensing requirements and other barriers to entry by a new business; ceilings on interest rates and other price controls; mandatory credit allocations; and other restrictions on factor mobility. Tax-type restrictions include tariffs and other taxes on cross-border flows of products and funds, information costs of market and financial research and analysis, and transaction costs such as high brokerage fees and high costs of enforcing contracts internationally.

All of these various costs of going and operating overseas, including the costs of overcoming linguistic, cultural, political, institutional, and other barriers, can be considered to be the costs of operating at an economic distance. As may be logically expected, a firm will serve overseas markets that have a large profit potential but are at a low economic distance. Thus, U.K. and French multinationals tend to invest in former colonies (low economic distance), whereas U.S. multinationals tend to invest mostly in Western Europe and Latin America; and Japanese companies invest mostly in North America, Western Europe, and Asia for the same reasons.

Astute managers of MNCs know, though, that whenever they see restrictions on foreign direct investment, they also see the possibility of extraordinary profits for those who can overcome the restrictions. Thus, government and other restrictions on foreign direct investment and high profit potential for foreign direct investment usually can be seen as the two sides of the same coin. A major part of the economic distance, barriers to foreign direct investment, also correlates directly with the attractiveness of a particular instance of foreign direct investment.

The Benefits of Foreign Direct Investment

Among the suggested motives for foreign direct investment is the need to seek cheaper sources of factor inputs such as raw materials, labor, capital, technology, or a lower-cost tax and regulatory environment. Foreign direct investment also may be sought for economies of scale in production, marketing, financing, and research and development. Foreign direct investment also can allow a firm to profitably extend its expertise and corporate advantages in production, marketing, finance, technology, and management to other markets to generate extraordinary profits because prices can, in such cases, be based on marginal rather than full costs. Foreign direct investment can also enable the firm to achieve diversification of commercial, financial, and political risks and to achieve growth rates higher than those possible in its domestic markets. Generally, a firm considers foreign direct investment as a part of its overall business strategy, and it may be used to develop and strengthen the firm's competitive advantage. Such a strategy to use foreign direct investment may be either "offensive" or "defensive" in nature and may be an important expression of its "purposive" goal-directed drive to react to and modify its operating environment.[1]

A specific instance of foreign direct investment is generally a result of the unique interaction of firm characteristics and factors specific to that industry and country. As discussed above, a firm can serve foreign

---

[1]Further details of the "purposive" nature of FDI are provided in Raj Aggarwal, "Foreign Direct Investment: A Summary of Recent Research and a Unifying Paradigm," *Economic Affairs*, Vol. 22, Nos. 1–2 (January/February 1977): 31–45.

markets in a number of ways. Thus, for foreign direct investment to take place, the firm must obtain certain advantages by locating and owning a foreign operation. Generally, this means that the firm can make higher levels of profits by keeping its unique advantages internal instead of licensing or otherwise sharing it.

In addition to this internalization theory based on the need for an MNC to engage in foreign direct investment to maximize its profitability and growth by keeping its unique advantage internal, a number of other theories to explain foreign direct investment have been advanced. The classical theory says that international differences in interest rates and rates of return influence the global allocation of capital. Although useful, this theory does not provide answers to many details of the foreign direct investment phenomenon. Another theory suggests that foreign direct investment takes place so that investors can hold assets in preferred strong currencies and that companies from strong currency areas have a signoirage-related advantage in cost of funds allowing them a competitive advantage when engaging in foreign direct investment. Again, this theory explains only limited instances of foreign direct investment. Foreign direct investment is also seen as a means for a company to diversify its risks and as an outcome of organizational goals of growth or national goals of modern economic imperialism. Each of these theories explains only some instances of foreign direct investment and may be somewhat limited in explaining the full scope and range of FDI.

The International Product Life Cycle Theory

Having examined briefly some of the theories that explain why a firm may engage in FDI, the *international product life cycle theory* explains how a firm may evolve from a purely domestic firm into a multinational firm engaged in FDI. It should be noted, however, that this discussion is intended to serve only as an example, and it does not explain the evolution or development of all firms engaged in FDI.

The international version of the product life cycle has been advanced as one explanation of how firms expand and evolve to serve markets internationally. Although a number of versions of the international product life cycle have been discussed in the literature, the version discussed here assumes three categories of countries; the technologically advanced home country where the product is developed, followed by a group of countries that may be at the same or somewhat lower technological level, known for convenience here as the more developed countries (MDCs), and finally, a group of countries that are at a significantly lower level of technology and economic development classified here as the less developed countries (LDCs). Exhibit 9-1 depicts the process of how technology, production, and sales of a given

Phase 1: The product is invented or innovated. Domestic sales begin and domestic production rises to near full capacity. Production and sales are still only in one country.

Phase 2: Domestic sales grow at a declining rate and export sales to MDCs and LDCs begin. There is no overseas production yet.

Phase 3: Domestic sales begin to decline and production begins in MDCs. U.S. exports are now mainly to LDCs because MDC demand is being supplied from local production.

Phase 4: Domestic sales continue at a low level with no exports from domestic production. MDC and LDC markets now are supplied by MDC-based production.

Phase 5: Domestic market begins to face competition from MDC exports as MDC exports to LDCs begin to be displaced by LDC production.

Phase 6: Domestic and MDC production now displaced by LDC producers, which begin to supply most demand globally.

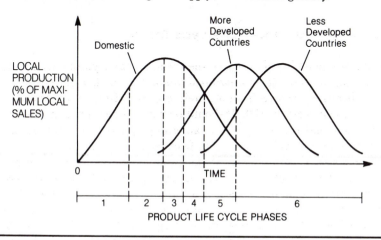

EXHIBIT 9-1 The International Product Life Cycle

215

product move across the three sets of countries and through the cycle of growth and decline in each area.

In the international product life cycle, the international involvement of the MNC is viewed as following sequential stages in the life cycle of the product or process it develops. Because of the restrictions in the flow of information across national boundaries and the evolution of demand for high-income consumer goods and labor-saving producer goods, innovation of new products is more likely to occur in well-developed, highly industrialized nations. These same innovations are more likely to be used in less developed nations later as they emerge and develop economies and consumer tastes similar to those of the highly developed nations in the years to come. Although new product innovation can and does take place in all countries, for the sake of convenience, we will hereafter consider only the case where the new product innovation takes place in the United States. But the analysis applies equally well to cases where new product innovation occurs in countries other than the United States.

This first phase of product development and domestic sales growth is critically important in the life of the product. It is during this stage that the product undergoes test marketing, product redesign and re-engineering, and production scale-up. Only if a product gains acceptance in the domestic market is there any need for discussion of the international aspects of the product life cycle theory. Generally, if a product does not gain domestic market acceptance, it probably will not be exported. If, however, the new product is accepted and during this phase domestic sales volume grows, the product reaches phase 3. During this phase, domestic sales continue to grow but probably at a decreasing rate, and exports begin to other more developed countries (MDCs) and, to a lesser extent, to less developed countries (LDCs).

Up to this point, all production is still in the United States. Export of the product begins for three basic reasons:

1. Because of the similarities between the markets in the MDCs and the United States, they evidence demand for the product.
2. The price for this product has decreased because of economies of scale as the supply increases.
3. The income level of the MDC may have increased.

During this phase, changes take place in the MDCs that in fact lead to the next phase. Because the expertise of MDC residents increases regarding this product, the probability of their being able to set up a manufacturing operation in their country increases. Other domestic firms have developed a similar or substitutable product that also is being sold in the United States and in the MDCs, and price competition results. Finally, the governments of the MDCs could have increased tariffs or set quotas to encourage the U.S. firm to invest in their country. Because of these and other reasons, the U.S. firm is likely to make the decision to invest in the MDC in the third phase of the life cycle of the product.

In the third phase of the cycle, when production has begun in a foreign market, U.S. exports to that market cease to grow as rapidly as before, and they may even decline. U.S. exports continue to go to markets where production has not begun. In the fourth phase of the cycle, U.S. exports to nonproducing countries begin to be displaced by exports from other nations. Markets overseas reach sufficient sizes that MDC manufacturers do not suffer from high costs associated with small scale: In fact, the MDC producing unit may be a subsidiary of a U.S. parent. Faced with lower labor costs but the same transportation and tariff charges, these firms take away markets in third world countries that were previously supplied from the United States. In the fifth phase, foreign production in some countries reaches sufficient scale that costs are low enough to overcome the transportation and tariff protection of the U.S. manufacturer. The United States now becomes a net importer of the product, and in the final phase the LDCs become exporters to both the MDCs and the United States.

Other Reasons for Foreign Direct Investment

As the various developing countries experience rapid economic growth and move toward increasing sophistication in the technology that they employ, the larger firms in these countries can be expected to experience the kinds of pressure to engage in foreign direct investment that the firms in the more mature economies once experienced. The early wave of multinationals from the largest and most technologically sophisticated countries can be expected to face competition and other challenges from newer multinationals based in the countries that have undergone recent economic and technological growth.

As can be seen from this analysis and as confirmed by various studies, the size of the firm and its market are important indicators of the propensity for foreign direct investment. Further, initial efforts at FDI designed to provide profitable growth opportunities are likely to focus on countries at the lowest economic distance from the home country.

FDI undertaken for other reasons, however—such as to obtain reliable low-cost access to factor inputs—may not follow this pattern and focuses directly on source countries for these inputs regardless of other factors such as economic distance. For example, it has been contended that in contrast to the pattern of U.S. FDI, the pattern of Japanese FDI reflects Japan's trade needs and therefore its need for reliable sources of raw materials and for export markets for its finished products.

As this review of the process of foreign direct investment indicates, a firm may have several reasons to engage in cross-border investments. Although the international product life cycle theory illustrates one way that a firm may evolve to become a multinational, it should be remembered that, as discussed above, there are many other ways by which a firm may become multinational.

ANALYSIS OF FOREIGN INVESTMENT CLIMATES

Before undertaking a specific foreign investment, a company generally analyzes the attractiveness of the overseas location for an investment. As in the case of a domestic investment, the firm must assess the nature of its competition and other business risks that it faces with the proposed investment. In doing so, the MNC must keep in mind the unique nature of the business practices in the foreign country. In addition, government laws and regulations governing private enterprise may be quite different in a foreign country. For example, a number of governments regulate prices charged for most goods even though produced by private businesses.

Although the firm may face some higher risks because it is a foreign entity, it may also have some technological or other advantage not enjoyed by local companies. In addition, in return for bringing in new technology, capital, or other skills, it is often possible to negotiate for government protection of the market against new competition at least for a few years after making an investment. On the other hand, the foreign company may face politically motivated risks of confiscation, expropriation, nationalization, or other restrictions on its operations, especially after the initial investment agreement expires. It is important that a company understand and analyze the driving forces causing these changes and their possible effect on the value of its operation in that country. In doing so, it generally has to analyze the local economic and political environment and the laws and regulations that apply to investments of the type being proposed.

A number of advisory services, large commercial banks, and government agencies provide generalized country analysis of the climate for foreign investment with some services even ranking the countries from best to worst. Although such generalized analysis may be a useful starting point, it should be noted that the business potential and political and commercial risks faced by a particular investment depend greatly on its specifics.

The Attitude of the Host Country

Most countries have an ambivalent attitude toward foreign investment. Host nations like the capital, technology, and other expertise that are contributed to its efforts for economic development by the foreign company. Plus, foreign investments supplement local investment capital for economic growth increasing employment and tax revenues. Foreign investment may also stimulate technological progress and provide access to global markets for the country's products.

On the other hand, most countries also recognize that foreign investments also can cause problems. It is alleged that foreign investors can dominate the local economy, monopolize scarce local resources, and exercise absentee management with little regard for the local effect of their decisions. There can be conflicts over other issues such as the sharing of the gains from foreign investment and the extent of corporate efforts to transfer technology and training to local entities and nationals.

In order to maximize benefits to the local economy and to minimize the costs, host governments provide a mixture of incentives and restrictions for foreign investors. Host governments provide a number of incentives such as tax holidays, exemptions from tariffs, direct financial assistance, remittance and repatriation guarantees, and, in some cases, even protection from competition in order to attract foreign investment. On the other hand, they also place restrictions on foreign investors. They may require certain specified minimum levels of local participation as equity owners, suppliers, and managers. They may close certain sectors of the economy and of the capital markets to foreign investors, place restrictions on remittances and imports, and require the MNC to gradually transfer its technological or other skills to its nationals and to generate certain minimum levels of exports. In addition to these and other restrictions on the operations of a foreign investor, a government may, in extreme cases, enforce a change in management control from the foreign investor to a local private or government entity.

Thus, a company should carefully analyze not only the operating environment within a country but also the probability and direction of changes in that environment for foreign investment. Because the sources of such changes in the environment for foreign direct investment are generally political changes in the host country, such analysis, called *political risk analysis*, is becoming increasingly popular among large MNCs.

Political Risk Analyses

Political risk exists to some extent in all countries, and it can manifest suddenly or be slow and creeping. It can be nondiscriminatory, and apply to all businesses, or it can be discriminatory and apply only to foreign-owned businesses. Analysis of historical data regarding expropriations of foreign businesses worldwide suggests that political risks faced by MNCs have been rising at least since the early 1960s. It seems that certain investments, such as natural resource-based investments are expropriated much more frequently than other types of foreign investments.

Political risk can vary greatly within a country depending on the home country of the investor, the industry and the region within the host country in which the investment is located, and the attitudes and behavior of the investor. The political risk faced by an investment also depends on the extent to which it contributes to the host country's needs, goals, and aspirations, its consistency with the local culture and ideology, the general political and economic stability of the host country, and the perceived role and value of the foreign investment and the foreign investor.

A number of quantitative and qualitative models for analyzing and forecasting the effect of political risk have been developed. These models have been successful in providing a systematic procedure for the analysis of political risk, but their success in forecasting unexpected political changes and events has been somewhat limited. Nevertheless, in order to assess the risks that it faces, an MNC requires an estimation of the likelihood, timing, and extent of possible politically related loss for each of its foreign investments.

In order to manage the effect of political risks, a company can follow one or more of a number of distinct policies. First, it could purchase insurance, if available, against such risks. Insurance against specific political risks is available from a number of sources including private insurance companies and home country government agencies such as the Agency for International Development (AID), the Overseas Private Investment Corporation (OPIC), and the Eximbank (for exports only) in the United States. Typically, the risks covered may include expropriation, inconvertibility, war, revolution, insurrection, and other political events. The cost of such insurance usually reflects the risk classifications of the host country and the industry and may, in many cases, be uneconomical. Thus, most MNCs generally depend on self-insurance and host country laws to recover political risk-related losses. Second, it could reduce the risk of its investment by the liberal use of local funds to finance the operation. It also could use the foreign operation as a cash cow, planning to divest it before political risks increase to unacceptable levels. However, such an action, if too obvious, may indeed invite intervention by the host government. Third, the company could try to be a good citizen and adapt to the national goals and requirements of the host country and develop local stakeholders. Fourth, it could raise the cost of expropriation for the host government by ensuring that only it can supply some critical marketing, managerial, production, technological, financial, or other input necessary for the continued success of the foreign investment. This strategy is easiest to follow if the investment is structured to operate with a number of different product and remittance flows between the foreign investment and parent operations in other countries. Of course, a company may follow a combination of two or more of the policies outlined here.

As the above discussion indicates, the analysis of the investment climate for a foreign investment is somewhat more complex than an analysis of the investment climate for a domestic investment. First, a foreign investment should be analyzed as a domestic investment in that foreign country, and second, this analysis must be supplemented by additional analysis to reflect the cross-border ownership of the investment.

INTERNATIONAL CAPITAL BUDGETING

Capital bugeting for international operations involves more extensive analysis than does capital budgeting for domestic operations. As in a domestic company, an MNC must develop estimates of the investment needed and the net cash flow generated by a proposed foreign capital investment. It also must assess the riskiness of these cash flows. Finally, it must then summarize the cash flow and risk analysis information into a measure of desirability for the project such as the net present value. The company then can compare the proposed investment with other possibilities and make a go or no-go decision.

Although this basic outline of the steps necessary to evaluate a specific long-term foreign investment is not much different from that followed for evaluating a domestic capital investment, the cross-border nature of the foreign investment may require the consideration of a number of additional factors such as the effect of currency and political risks on the project's value. The next section discusses some of the issues that may have to be considered in international capital budgeting.

The Parent Versus the Local Perspective

Should the proposed capital investment be evaluated from the viewpoint of the local firm or from the viewpoint of the parent? The objective of maximizing shareholder wealth would indicate that the parent company perspective should be used. However, the parent company may have supplied only part or none of the initial investment for the project. When using the parent company perspective, the project should be evaluated in terms of the parent's currency with the parent company's net initial investment and its net receipt of cash flows from the project discounted at a rate that is appropriate for the risks of the project cash flows and with the inflation rate of the parent's currency.

However, cash flows to the parent depend not just on the performance of the project but also on how the local cash flows are managed. For example, because of tax considerations it may not be optimal to remit all project cash flows to the parent, only then to have to send some or all of them back to be reinvested in the original foreign affiliate. In addition, value added by a project to a foreign affiliate will normally be reflected in the value of the parent company.

Thus, it may be better, even for shareholders' wealth maximization, to evaluate a foreign capital proposal from the perspective of its local affiliate using the total investment for the project and all of its cash flows discounted at a rate that reflects the local inflation rate and the riskiness of the project. In practice, most MNCs use at least the local perspective to evaluate a foreign project, and some MNCs supplement the local perspective with present value analysis from the parent's perspective to evaluate foreign affiliate capital proposals. In such a case, the foreign affiliate perspective is the primary basis for a go or no-go decision, while the parent perspective is used to ensure that the structure of the project investment and the disposition of the cash flows are consistent with corporate objectives.

It is important that cash flow projections be realistic and reflect local conditions regarding competition, inflation, price controls, and other government regulations. It is useful to identify and analyze the set of market imperfections that are giving rise to a positive net present value for a specific project and to assess how long such conditions are likely to exist. It is also important to assess the nature of political risks and determine an expected safe planning horizon during which these risks can be managed. An MNC also should be able to estimate the terminal value of the project at the end of such a planning horizon.

When taking the local currency perspective, the discount rate also should reflect a realistic assessment of the expected local inflation rate. This may be especially difficult given that capital markets in many foreign countries are often not free or efficient and interest rates do not reflect market expectations. Project cash flows should also reflect the advantages of using any subsidized financing that may have been used to finance the project.

When using the parent currency perspective, the discount rate should reflect the expected inflation rate in the parent currency, and foreign currency cash flows should be converted to parent currency cash flows using projected exchange rates. These projections often are based on the assumption that purchasing power parity will hold during the life of the project. In such a case, it may be possible to take initial-year cash flows and assume that increases because of local inflation will be offset exactly by declines in the exchange rate related to purchasing power parity. However, if significant deviations from purchasing power parity are expected, such a simplifying assumption would be inappropriate. In addition, high inflation rates may be accompanied by government price controls and a company may face a lag between allowed price increases and inflation, or it may be accompanied by other economic and even political instability. In such cases, simply assuming that purchasing power parity will hold may be insufficient, and additional analysis to reflect these factors should be undertaken.

International Tax Laws

An additional factor that adds to the complexity of international capital bugeting is the diversity in the international tax laws faced by an MNC. Should project cash flows be valued after all taxes—that is, after taxes paid at the foreign affiliate and at the parent company levels? The answer would seem to be yes, except that the timing and actual possibility of having to pay parent country income taxes depends on the remittance policy followed and the use of other tax-reducing mechanisms, such as the use of tax havens and transfer prices. Thus, the procedures and tax rates used to calculate after-tax cash flows would depend on the situation in a specific company.

Strategic Planning for Future Growth

Ideally, in an MNC, capital should be allocated to projects globally wherever it can earn the highest rate of return for the owners. In practice, this objective is difficult to achieve, especially because it is difficult to compare risks internationally on an objective, quantitative basis. Projects from different countries differ not only with regard to their business or commecial risks but also with regard to the degree of political risk they face. In addition, it is not easy to assess the systematic portion of the total risk of a foreign capital project and thus to develop the appropriate risk-adjusted discount rate that should be used to assess the project. Although a foreign project may seem to have higher overall risks than a domestic project, it also may offer greater opportunities for risk diversification.

As in the case of domestic operations, normal capital budgeting procedures are often inadequate in valuing projects in which a significant aspect is to position the firm for possible future expansion—that is, to generate a viable option for expansion that may or may not be exercised at some point in the future. Similarly, it is important that the MNC relate the funding of capital projects to its strategic plans for foreign operations.

Adjusting the Traditional Formulas

In view of these special characteristics of capital budgeting for international investments, traditional approaches to capital budgeting, such as the calculation of a net present value (NPV) using the corporate cost of capital, are often inadequate in a multinational setting. For example, the traditional approach assumes that financing and investment decisions can be separated and that the corporate capital structure represents the mix of financing appropriate for each project. Such an assumption is particularly unlikely to be appropriate in the case of capital projects in a multinational setting, especially in view of significant international variations in capital structure norms and the widespread use of subsidized project specific financing, loan guarantees, and insurance against political risks. In addition, political and currency risks may be special and unsystematic in nature for a capital budgeting proposal in a multinational firm, and project systematic risks may not reflect the systematic risk of the parent company. The *adjusted present value* (APV) approach has been widely suggested as being more appropriate for the capital bugeting process in a multinational corporation.

The APV approach differs from the traditional NPV approach because it uses an *all-equity* discount rate that reflects local inflation and interest rates and the systematic part of the business risk of a particular project. In addition, by using the value-additivity approach, the APV calculation adds the present value of after-tax amounts of any subsidies inherent in project-specific financing, as well as the present value of debt-related tax shields that reflect the capital structure appropriate for the particular project being evaluated, to the present value of the operating cash flows. Consequently, the APV approach encourages the decision maker to adjust project cash flows for specific project-related subsidies, and, in addition, project risks are accounted for by adjusting cash flows rather than by making adjustments to the discount rate. Thus, the APV approach allows the calculation of the project NPV to easily reflect the specific risks, capital structure, financing, and other conditions associated with a project in a given country.

As an example, consider the following formulation for the *adjusted net present value* (ANPV) of a project being considered by a foreign affiliate of an MNC:

$$\text{ANPV} = -I_o + \sum_{i=1}^{n} \frac{CF_i}{(1 + k_e)^i} + \sum_{i=1}^{n} \frac{T_i}{(1 + k_d)^i} +$$

$$\sum_{i=1}^{n} \frac{S_i}{(1 + k_d)^i} + \sum_{i=1}^{n} \frac{O_i}{(1 + k_e)^i} + \frac{TV_n}{(1 + k_e)^n}$$

where

I_o = the initial investment

k_e = the all-equity cost or discount rate reflecting the riskiness and diversification benefits of the project

k_d = the cost of debt

n = the number of periods in the investment horizon

CF_i = the after-tax net cash inflows for period i

T_i = the tax shield on debt service payments for period i reflecting the capital structure of the affiliate undertaking the project

S_i = the after-tax value of special financial or other subsidies associated with the project for the period i

O_i = the estimated value in period i of any options, such as the ability to enter a new business created by the project

TV_n = the estimated terminal value at the end of the investment horizon. This also could be the estimated present value of compensation received for an expected government take-over in period n.

The first term covers the initial investment. The second term reflects the present value of the net after-tax cash inflows that the project is expected to generate. These cash inflows are discounted at the all-equity cost that reflects the business risk associated with the project. The third term reflects the present value of the tax savings associated with use of debt in the capital structure. By explicitly accounting for the tax shields, it is possible to account for the unique capital structure being used by the affiliate that undertakes the project.

The fourth term reflects the present value of any financial or other subsidies that are often received by international projects from home, host, or other governments. The fifth term reflects the value of any options, such as the ability to enter a new business, whether exercised or not, generated by the project. These values may be zero or very small, at least for the first few years, and may often be difficult to estimate. Nevertheless, the APV approach at least provides an opportunity to value these options.

The last term reflects the estimated terminal value at the end of the investment horizon. Although there are many ways to estimate the terminal value, one approach commonly used is to set it equal to the present value of all future cash flows — that is, $CF \div (k - g)$, where CF are the annual cash flows after the investment horizon, k is the discount rate, and g is the expected growth rate for these cash flows.

Another approach that may be used in the case of projects in politically unstable environments is for the terminal value to reflect the expected present value of a possible future amount received as compensation for the government takeover of the project at the end of the estimated investment horizon. Other aspects of political risk also may be modeled as additional terms in the ANPV formulation.

As this example illustrates, the ANPV method allows for the explicit valuation of each cost and benefit associated with a project. The illustration used here included the use of an unusual financial structure, subsidized financing sources and other investment subsidies unique to the project, and the political risks of expropriation associated with the project. Additional aspects of the project, such as blockage of funds by host governments, may also be modeled as additional terms in the ANPV formulation.

An international capital budgeting decision is only as good as the analysis that precedes it. Because analysis in capital budgeting is based on estimates of projected cash flows and risks, and because these estimates contain a large element of judgment, good and reasonable capital budgeting decisions depend greatly on the level of business experience and knowledge that is brought to bear on the analysis.

CONCLUSIONS

There are many reasons for a firm to engage in foreign direct investment and a number of theories have been advanced to explain this phenomenon. FDI continues to grow in importance as it is undertaken by continually increasing numbers of firms from many countries. These growing numbers of firms engaged in FDI indicate that although the costs of doing business across national borders generally exceed the costs of doing business domestically, in many cases the benefits of engaging in FDI exceed those costs.

Among the benefits of FDI are the ability of a firm to take advantage of cheaper sources of factor inputs such as: labor; raw materials; capital; technology; better and more favorable business environments; and economies of scale in production, marketing, financing, or research and development. Among the costs of FDI are those of doing business in a foreign environment (such as language barriers and communications costs) and of overcoming regulations and barriers against crossborder investments. It should be noted, however, that such barriers very often create the conditions necessary for the extraordinary profits required to justify FDI.

The process through which the market for a particular product (or a firm in that market) becomes multinational is complex and may take many forms. The product life cycle theory describes one form that is fairly common. Throughout the process, a company must assess each potential opportunity for FDI, in terms of both the investment climate of that country and the present value of the cash flows associated with the project. Such a task is usually more complex than would be a similar assessment for a comparable domestic project. To accommodate this added complexity, firms often account explicitly for the various costs and benefits of cross-border investments by using the adjusted present value calculation.

The phenomenon of foreign direct investment is important and growing and it is one of the primary strategies for maintaining global competitiveness. Consequently, the analysis and assessment of opportunities for engaging in FDI is an important function in corporate finance and in corporate planning.

DISCUSSION QUESTIONS

1. What extra costs are incurred by businesses that serve international markets? What possible benefits are gained by serving international markets?

2. In what ways can a company serve foreign markets without undertaking foreign direct investment? What are the advantages and disadvantages of each approach?

3. How is capital budgeting for international projects different from capital budgeting for domestic projects? How can these differences be included in the process used for capital budgeting in a multinational company?

4. What economic factors influence the foreign direct investment process? Discuss how these factors may influence investments in the United States by Japanese automobile manufacturers.

5. According to the international product life cycle theory, what role will newly industrializing countries such as South Korea and Taiwan play in the U.S. market for consumer electronic products? For semiconductors?

6. The Agerson Industrial Group (AIG) is considering an investment in the country of Shangri-La. The initial investment in the project is expected to be 4 million nectars, and it is expected to generate 1 million nectars in net after-tax cash flows per year. The riskiness of the project is reflected by a

beta of 1.5; it has a risk-free rate of 8 percent; and an average market premium of 6 percent gives an all-equity discount rate of 17 percent for the project. This project is expected to have an investment horizon of six years, at which time it is expected to be sold to local investors for 4 million nectars.

The host government has offered subsidized debt financing of up to 2 million nectars at an annual interest rate of 7 percent, while the free-market rate for comparable debt financing is 9 percent. The after-tax value of additional subsidies associated with the project is estimated to be 500,000, 400,000, and 300,000 nectars for the first three years, respectively. The project will also create an option for AIG to enter a new business in its fourth and fifth years. These options are difficult to value but have been estimated to be worth 200,000 nectars after tax in each of these two years. The AIG local affiliate undertaking the project uses debt to finance 60 percent of its total assets and expects no change in its capital structure policy for this project. Interest costs are deductible (40-percent tax rate) according to Shangri-La tax laws.

a. Calculate the adjusted net present value of undertaking the project. Should the project be undertaken?

b. How does the ANPV change if the project faces expropriation with a probability of 30 percent at the end of six years? There is a 70-percent probability that the project can be sold to local investors for the estimated 4 million nectars. In case of expropriation, the host government is expected to pay AIG 3 million nectars after prolonged negotiations that end with the payment being received by AIG three years after the expropriation.

SUGGESTED READINGS

1. Aggarwal, Raj. "Managing for Economic Growth and Global Competition: Strategic Implications of the Life Cycle of Economies," in R. N. Farmer, (editor). *Advances in International Comparative Management*. Greenwich, Connecticut: JAI Press, 1986. Pp. 14–19.

2. Booth, Lawrence D. "Capital Budgeting Frameworks for the Multinational Corporation," *Journal of International Business Studies*, Vol. 13. No. 2 (Fall 1982). Pp. 114–123.

3. Calvet, A. L. "A Synthesis of Foreign Direct Investment Theories of the Multinational Firm," *Journal of International Business Studies*, Vol. 12, No. 1 (Spring/Summer, 1981). Pp. 43–59.

4. Caves, R. *Multinational Enterprise and Economic Analysis*. New York, New York: Cambridge University Press, 1982.

5. Dunning, John. "International Business in a Changing World Environment," *Banca Nazionale del Lavoro Quarterly*, No. 143 (December 1982). Pp. 351–374.

6. Kelly, Marie W. *Foreign Practices of U.S. Multinational Corporations.* Ann Arbor, Michigan: UMI Research Press, 1981.

7. Lessard, Donald R. "Evaluating Foreign Projects: An Adjusted Present Value Approach," in D. R. Lessard (editor). *International Financial Management: Theory and Application.* New York, New York: John Wiley & Sons, 1985. Pp. 570–584.

8. Shapiro, Alan C. "Capital Budgeting for the Multinational Corporation," *Financial Management*, Vol. 7, No. 1 (Spring 1978). Pp. 7–16.

9. Weekly, James K., and Raj Aggarwal. *International Business: Operating in the Global Economy.* Hinsdale, Illinois: Dryden Press, 1986.

Index